THIS IS NO PLACE FOR A WOMAN:

Nadine Gordimer, Buchi Emecheta, Nayantara Saghal, and the Politics of Gender

Joya Uraizee

Africa World Press, Inc.

P.O. Box 1892
Trenton, NJ 08607

P.O. Box 48
Asmara, ERITREA

Africa World Press, Inc.

P.O. Box 1892
Trenton, NJ 08607

P.O. Box 48
Asmara, ERITREA

Copyright: © 2000 Joya Uraizee
First Printing 2000

Cover Design: Jonathan Gullery

Library of Congress Cataloging-in-Publication data

Uraizee, Joya F. (Joya Farooq), 1961-
    This is no place for a woman: Nadine Gordimer, Nayantara Saghal, Buchi Emecheta, and the politics of gender / by Joya Uraizee
        p.   cm.
    Includes bibliographical references.
    ISBN 0-86543-766-1. --ISBN 0-86543-767-X
    1. African literature (English)--Women authors--History and criticism. 2. Feminism and literature--Africa--History--20th century. 3. Gordimer, Nadine--Political and social views. 4. Women and literature--South Africa--History--20th century. 5. Saghal, Nayantara, 1927- --Political and social views. 6. Women and literature--India--History--20th century. 7. Emecheta, Buchi--Political and social views. 8. Women and literature--Nigeria--History--20th century. 9. Decolonization in literature. 10. Sex role in literature. I. Title
PR9344.U7 1999
820. 9'9287'096--dc21   99-28635
                                                          CIP

To Aisha and Omar,
for making everything possible,
and
to Farooq,
for always being there

TABLE OF CONTENTS

ACKNOWLEDGMENTS

Rodopi publications (Amsterdam & Atlanta) is acknowledged for permission to reprint "Decolonizing the Mind: Paradigms for Self-Definition in Nayantara Sahgal's *Rich Like Us,"* which was published in its Critical Studies Series 7, *Writing the Nation: Self and Country in the Post-Colonial Imagination* ed. John C. Hawley, S.J., pages 161-175, and appears in this book as part of chapter three. *The Journal of the Midwest Modern Language Association* (Iowa City) is acknowledged for permission to reprint "Fragmented Borders and Female Boundary Markers in Buchi Emecheta's *Destination Biafra*," which was published in *The Journal of the Midwest Modern Language Association* volume 30 number 1-2 (Spring 1997), pages 16-28, and appears in this book as part of chapter five. Valentine Udoh James is acknowledged for permission to reprint "Buchi Emecheta and the Politics of Gender," which will be published in *Black Women Across Cultures* ed. Valentine Udoh James, International Scholars Publications (Lanham), and appears in this book as parts of chapters two, three, four, and five.

Acknowledgements are also due to Penguin Putnam (New York) for permission to use the quotations from Nadine Gordimer's *The Conservationist, Burger's Daughter,* and *July's People*; to Knopf (New York) for permission to use the quotations from Nadine Gordimer's *A Sport of Nature*; to W.W. Norton (New York), for permission to use the quotations from Nayantara Sahgal's *The Day in Shadow, Rich Like Us, Storm in Chandigarh,* and *This Time of Morning*; to George Braziller (New York) for permission to use the quotations from Buchi Emecheta's *The Bride Price, Double Yoke,* and *Second Class Citizen*; and to Heinemann Educational Publishers, a division of Reed Educational & Professional

Publishing Ltd.(Oxford) for permission for the non-exclusive use of the quotations from Buchi Emecheta's *Destination Biafra* (Allison & Busby) in the English language throughout the United States of America.

Sincere acknowledgments are offered to a number of mentors and friends who offered help and support. In particular, I would like to thank Margaret M. Rowe, Shaun F. D. Hughes, Aparajita Sagar, and Charles Ross, for their suggestions, advice, and support throughout the writing process. Thanks are also due to Georgia Johnston for her helpful advice and constant encouragement., and to Thomas Moisan and Raymond Benoit for their useful suggestions.

Finally, I would like to recognize my family for their patience and understanding, especially my husband, Farooq, and my children, Aisha and Omar, who put up with all my needs for time and space.

PREFACE

Literary representations of the postcolonial woman often take oblique or ironic forms and use multiple perspectives, such that the woman "speaks" from the "undersides" of texts, that are inscribed in ideological history. This book examines the writings of three postcolonial women writers who, despite having very different racial, class-based, national, and ideological backgrounds, nevertheless reveal striking similarities. South Africa's Nadine Gordimer, who was born in 1923, India's Nayantara Sahgal, who was born in 1927, and Nigeria's Buchi Emecheta, who was born in 1944, all show that the identity of the postcolonial woman is fluid and displaces itself in various positions on a constantly evolving continuum. In their writings, female identity is a product of the ideological history that surrounds it. Like many other postcolonial women writers, Gordimer, Sahgal, and Emecheta describe female subjectivity in terms of fragmentation, displacement, and marginality; indeed, they themselves are somewhat displaced from the mainstream cultures they are writing about, because of their own class-based, racial, or expatriate identites. However, despite being somewhat isolated themselves, all three writers frequently silence marginalized voices and issues even when ostensibly speaking on their behalf. For example, Gordimer is very concerned with race relations because apartheid, and her own racial background, has made her sensitive to the social and political implications of racial interaction. Yet, as many critics have pointed out, she has few black characters at the center of her novels. By contrast, Emecheta reveals a rather ambivalent attitude to race and ethnicity because of the prominence of her own ethnic group (the Ibo) in Nigeria, as well as the experience of racial discrimination in being black British. Like Gordimer, then, she deals with the implications of racism in the West while also describing forms of ethnic oppression in traditional Ibo society in Nigeria. Sahgal, however, elides the issue of race or ethnicity, despite being an upper-caste Hindu, and her novels imply that caste-based or racial discrimination in urban India is the result of either individual bias or is part of the baggage of Hinduism that needs to be thrown out. There is very little examination of caste as an ideological tool for bourgeois control of the economy and politics.

One feature that links Gordimer, Sahgal, and Emecheta, is the way they represent working-class voices. In general, they tend to present subaltern or peasant discourse as extremely marginalized and fragmented. Some of the fragmented voices in their novels belong to authority figures that are not all-powerful, women that are oppressed, and shadowy/silenced peasants that assert their presence through absence. In Gordimer's *The Conservationist*, for example, ancestral voices do not really have ancestral wisdom. So too, the spirit of religious tolerance in Sahgal's *The Day in Shadow* is really a Brahmanical notion of humanism. Similarly, the story-telling voices in Emecheta's *The Bride Price* are empowered more by the listeners' responses than by wisdom.

The figure of the alienated elite is another area which reveals similarities between the three novelists. In novels like Gordimer's *A Sport of Nature*, Sahgal's *Rich Like Us*, and Emecheta's *Second Class Citizen*, the upper-class woman is an isolated figure who is only partially integrated into society, and who assimilates through sex or social awareness or writing. Indeed, here the three novelists connect postcolonial feminine identity to formalized patriarchal oppression. Moreover, all three novelists link sexual oppression to male control over a woman's body but somewhat de-emphasize male domination of female labor and economic self-determination.

How postcolonial women imagine ideal nations or worlds is another area that links the three novelists. Ideal or alternate worlds appear as quests for alternative identities in Gordimer's *Burger's Daughter*, Sahgal's *This Time of Morning*, and Emecheta's *Double Yoke*. These quests are accompanied by visions and dreams in which alternative self-identities are conceptualized. Despite the presence of these visions in the narratives, however, the alternate worlds are largely unachievable. This is partly because the novelists tend to over-simplify the nature of the oppression facing postcolonial women.

Finally, the three novelists also examine the actual nature of the "new" world or society created by anti-imperial revolution. The new world is described as a realm of crisis in Gordimer's *July's People*, Sahgal's *Storm in Chandigarh*, and Emecheta's *Destination Biafra*. For Gordimer, the crisis only serves to highlight hidden social inequalities. In Sahgal's view, the crisis reveals how errors in judgment in the past can repeat themselves in the present. For Emecheta, the crisis is involves civil war and genocide. In all three cases, women become signposts of social upheaval. Ultimately, all the solutions offered, such as Hindu humanism or truth or willpower, fail to highlight the role of class in creating each crisis, since in each case, one particular class dominates society and assumes political leadership.

In conclusion, while all three novelists represent women as possible sites of change in the political status quo, their representation of race, class, and nation is contradictory and problematic. Although they create strong political narratives about upper class white or black women, they are not very effective in depicting lower class or racially marginalized characters. Moreover, they all seem to imply that postcolonial female discourse arises out of the contradictions and clashes within traditional patriarchy and Western capitalism. Thus, they represent the postcolonial woman as a voice that perpetually resists, within a discourse that is evolving and shifting, and whose power is both surrounded and limited by neo-colonial and patriarchal ideologies.

NADINE GORDIMER, NAYANTARA SAHGAL, BUCHI EMECHETA, AND THE POSTCOLONIAL CONDITION

Colonialism was one of the most profound historical encounters to affect more than half of the globe from the sixteenth century onwards. Beginning with the expansionist tendencies of Europe in the late sixteenth century, colonialism was a process of systematic political, economic, cultural, and religious brutalization, dominance, and exploitation, resulting in a complete disintegration of social, political, and economic superstructures in the colonized territories.[1] In political terms, colonialism meant direct control over a country, including the exploitation of its resources and labor, and a "systematic interference in the capacity of the appropriated culture…to organize its dispensations of power" (McClintock 1994:295). Colonialism was eventually countered with armed or ideological resistance by individual nations in Africa, Asia, and Latin

America.   While most of Latin America became politically independent early in the nineteenth century, many of the other nations had to wait until after World War II for flag independence. However, as many historians and literary theorists have pointed out, the centuries-long experience of colonization did not end with the transfer of political power; rather, it was perpetuated by the neo-colonial regimes that followed. In most parts of the colonized world decolonization was followed by the political domination of society by a "national bourgeoisie" that assumed leadership (Ahmad 1992:18) or by what Ngugi wa'Thiong'o calls a "comprador" bourgeoisie (Ngugi 1986:20). Both terms refer to a class of leaders empowered by—and often in a permanent alliance with—the former colonial power. These leaders were "conceived and born by colonialism" and their ideology and power as a group were not in any kind of major conflict with the "money-juggling classes [and]...Wall Street" (Ngugi 1993:64). The results of this were most often disastrous for the former colonies, especially since, as Frantz Fanon has indicated, the former colonized subject did not become a "master [but became]...a slave who has been allowed to assume the attitude of a master" (Fanon 1967:219). Since the neo-colonies of post-1960s Africa, for example, remained under the economic and political control of the West, (Ngugi 1986:4-5), the ruling bourgeoisie in those countries became the "neo-colonial slave drivers of their own peoples" (80).   In addition to this, imperialism itself continued to flourish, as Ahmad has shown, under the guise of aggressive capitalism, so that "all zones of capital," whether of the colonizer or of the former colonized, were brought into a "single, integrated market, entirely dominated by this supreme, imperialist power [the United States]" (Ahmad 1992:21).   This U.S. domination can, in fact, be called "imperialism-without-colonies," and it has taken distinct forms (military, political, economic and cultural), some of which were concealed and some, half concealed (McClintock 1994:295).[2] As a result of these new forms of colonialism, the newly-independent "national bourgeois states" were dominated and assimilated by Western capitalist hegemony, which at the same time isolated and disorganized "those poorer countries which had opted out of the system of national-bourgeois states in favour of a non-capitalist form of development" (Ahmad 1992:21).[3] This meant that the U.S. and the former European colonial powers became wealthier, while—with a few exceptions—their ex-colonies became poorer (McClintock 1994:300).

To take some specific examples, both India and Nigeria achieved political independence by the early 1960s and both states also experienced a transfer of power from a Western colonizer to a national bourgeoisie. They became neo-colonial states characterized by sharply divided social classes and enmeshed in a system of economic dependence and underdevelopment.[4] Political and intellectual power was wielded by a small upper class/caste, secure in all the privileges of inheritance and wealth, while the lower classes/castes remained in the same state of ignorance and poverty as they had always been. In literary terms, this led to a complex, hybrid culture—in the case of India, to what Ahmad calls an "unfinished bourgeois project: certain notions of canonicity in tandem with the bourgeois, upper-caste dominance of the nation-state; a notion of classicism part Brahmanical, part borrowed from Europe" (Ahmad 1992:15). In Nigeria, as in other parts of Africa, the comprador bourgeoisie established a culture in which language became the means of "spiritual subjugation" (Ngugi 1986:9),[5] because the language of the former colonial power became dominant in society and was the major means of control (Ngugi 1981:5).[6] In South Africa, however, the case was very different. Here, the colonial power, being what Ahmad and others have called a "settler" colonizer, had the ruling race in the minority until the 1990's.[7] In fact, it could have been called a "break-away settler colony" (McClintock 1994:5) or one which had broken off its original ties with the "Mother Country"

(Britain) and, in the process, made its own imperialist tendencies more "recalcitrant" (Ahmad 1992:31) and intractable. Therefore, until the 1991 ballot-box victory for the ANC, South Africa had not undergone decolonization (McClintock 1994:295), and even now the anti-colonial struggle is ongoing. Moreover, the role of socialist forces became more important in this context, because of the close alliance between the ANC and the South African Communist Party. This alliance was partly due to the popularity of the ANC among the large proletariat class, a popularity amounting to what Ahmad calls a "political hegemony among the majority of the population" (31).

Despite these differences in the colonial histories of South Africa, India, and Nigeria, there are some aspects of literary production that link all three cultures. Mainly, they are all affected by or complicit with the postcolonial condition. By "postcolonial" I mean an historical, psychological, economic, and political condition. In its historical sense, I would include what Bill Ashcroft and others have described as "all the culture affected by the imperial process from the moment of colonization to the present day" (Ashcroft et al. 1989:2). What makes writing essentially postcolonial, in their view, is the fact that it has arisen out of the experience of colonization and has asserted itself by emphasizing the conflict with and differences from the imperial power (2). As they point out, it is concerned mainly with defining the self and placing that self as precisely as possible (9), and this involves an examination of the political, imaginative, and social dominance imposed by the colonizer on the colonized (29), and by one colonized group on another colonized group (31). Such writing, therefore, "foregrounds a politics of opposition and struggle, and problematizes the key relationship between centre and periphery" (Mishra & Hodge 1994:276). However, in recent years, the literature of the former British colonies has created a kind of post-orientalism, or a radical kind of orientalism which suggests a close relationship between literature written in English and written and oral non-English discourses (279). In other words, it is a hybrid literature in which there are a multiplicity of centers and theories, so that an attempt to impose a comprehensive postcolonial literary theory is at once an over-simplification and a multi-disciplinary exercise (280).

In the psychological sense of postcolonialism I would include Ashis Nandy's idea of a "universalism" or state of mind that "takes into account the colonial experience, including the immense suffering colonialism brought, and builds out of it a maturer, more contemporary, more self-critical version of...traditions" (1983:75). In this sense, the colonial power becomes "a subculture meaningful in itself and important, though not all-important in the...[postcolonial] context" (76). This situation is also one of "cultural imposition" (Fanon 1967:85), so that even after independence is achieved, the colonized subject has not "become a master [but]...is a slave who has been allowed to assume the attitude of a master" (219). In the psychological sense, then, my definition of the postcolonial situation includes Fanon's concept of a society which has experienced racial and cultural oppression and which is still struggling to become free.

With regard to social and economic concerns, the term would include what Ngugi wa Thiong'o has called cultural imperialism or the domination of the language of the colonizer, which operates as a means of control (Ngugi 1981:5). It would also incorporate the dynamics of the means of cultural production in societies where the annual per capita income is between $150 and $300, where social security is non-existent (Mishra & Hodge 1994:285), where illiteracy rates are high, and where publication and allied costs keep book prices beyond the purchasing capacity of the working-class family. As far as politics are concerned, the term "postcolonial" would include issues related to marginalized, migrant, and culturally embattled cultures/groups (Suleri 1994:246-247), but this means more than a concern with just texts and discourses (Mishra & Hodge 1994:278), namely, radical deconstructions of alien sensibilities (281) as well as active participation in political processes and social change.

There is no single postcolonial condition, but rather many postcolonialisms. Besides the aspects mentioned above, these conditions could be interpreted very loosely as a very general sense of cultural oppression that is "always present" in "any literature of subjugation" (Mishra & Hodge 1994:284). It could also signify a very subversive mode of discourse, namely, "an always present 'underside' within colonization itself" (284) that threatens to disrupt the colonial power structure. It is this subversive colonialism or complicit postcolonialism that informs the writings of colonizing peoples who live among the colonized peoples and write in opposition to the colonial center. White South African writers like Nadine Gordimer or J. M. Coetzee are very relevant in this context. Overall, then, the postcolonial condition includes all the lingering legacies of the colonizer/colonized relationship, both positive and negative ones (Brydon 1987:4). Some negative legacies include economic and psychological dependency on the imperial power, cultural marginalization, and political tensions between imposed and experienced heritages (4). Some positive legacies include a welcoming of cross-cultural encounters (6), and a two-way traffic or cultural exchange (5) by subverting imperial perspectives to create new forms and ways of thinking (7). Brydon cites Bernard Smith's phrase, a "convergent culture" or a "culture of configurations" as a good description of the postcolonial situation (7), though, of course, it could also be a divergent culture or a culture in a state of crisis. Thus, the postcolonial condition is not a homogenous category across different postcolonial societies or even within a single one. It is more like a "typical configuration which is always in the process of change, never consistent with itself" (Mishra & Hodge 1994:289). Despite its time-based prefix, it should not be restricted to either the idea of linear progress or the concept of binary opposites (McClintock

1994:292). It refers to a multiplicity of powers and histories (302) which requires the engagement of a proliferation of theories and strategies (303).

In this context, Nadine Gordimer, Nayantara Sahgal, and Buchi Emecheta are particularly concerned with defining what it is that makes their nations postcolonial. They seem to endorse E. J. Hobsbawm's view that nations are actually "dual phenomena" or concepts that are "constructed essentially from above, but which cannot be understood unless also analyzed from below, that is, in terms of the assumptions, hopes, needs, longings, and interests of ordinary people" (1990:10). While the view from above is usually official government sponsored propaganda, the view from below is that of ordinary people and is therefore difficult to figure out because it constantly changes (11).[8] Their novels reveal that postcolonial nations have not two, but many different structures: the obvious and the official, several obscure and unofficial, and the "real" nation, if there is such a thing, seems to be located somewhere between these structures. Indeed, they seem to suggest that the nation is heteroglossic and multivocal, with structures of complicity and resistance contained within it.

Even Benedict Anderson's definition of the nation as an "imagined political community [which is]...both inherently limited and sovereign" (Anderson 1983:6) is somewhat univocal. Anderson argues that the nation is imagined because all the members within it will never really know each other (6); it is limited because it has finite boundaries (7); it is sovereign because it replaces the power of the divinely-ordained monarch (7); and it is a community because it evokes a deep sense of comradeship (7). However, while it is true that many nations are discursive constructs and do not have a pre-existing essence, nevertheless, they often cannot be reduced to products of the imagination. Also, some communities within the nation can experience a simultaneous sense of comradeship and estrangement.[9] Instead of such a definition, Gordimer and Emecheta in particular seem to argue, following a number of literary critics, that the postcolonial nation, as constructed by imperialism, is false and unnatural,[10] with imaginary claims to unity and collectivity, and corresponding to no real geographic space.[11]

Some of these situations can become clearer with specific examples. If we examine the writings of Gordimer, Sahgal, and Emecheta we find that issues of nation and class, besides those of race and gender, become particularly important. In their writings, moreover, the identity of the postcolonial woman is fluid and displaces itself in various positions on a constantly evolving continuum. For them, identity is both subject to and created by the ideological history that surrounds it. This history includes both presences and absences, such as their presentation of subaltern or peasant discourse as extremely marginalized, fragmented, and effaced and their representation of the domination of bourgeois ideology within the educated elites of their respective cultures. By ideology I mean an organized system of beliefs that operates in an individual, a text, or a society, through conscious or unconscious representation or figuration. It usually displays itself through notions of class relations, and this idea is echoed by Michel Pecheux and C. Fuchs (1982). They suggest that ideology is a set of formations which constitute a "complex ensemble of attitudes and representations that are neither `individual' nor `universal' but rather arise more or less directly from class positions in conflict with one another" (8). Louis Althusser points out that in any situation (except the scientific situation), ideology is always a unified and organized system of beliefs, and within it the meaning of a particular ideological concept emerges, through its relation to the ideological field (Althusser 1990:62). Since science is not particularly noted for its attention to its own presuppositions (Smith 1984:128), this exclusion of science from the field of ideology is problematic. However, Althusser also suggests that the way ideology actually operates in a society/text (he calls this the "motor principle") can only be figured out by examining what underlies ideology, that is, what he calls "actual history" (Althusser 1990:63). These ideas, then, suggest that ideology is a whole and cannot be broken up; it can only be evaluated by stepping outside it. This idea is also problematic, and what makes it even more so is the fact that, according to Althusser, ideology is "unconscious," that is, unaware of "the real problems it is a response (or non-response) to...[or of] its [own] theoretical presuppositions." As he goes on to suggest, the particular problematic within the ideology must be pulled out, as it were, from "the depths" within which it is buried (69).

In applying all this to the operation of ideology within Gordimer's, Sahgal's, and Emecheta's texts, then, I am dealing with gaps and absences, or a sense within the work of something below the surface, something that doesn't quite fit. As Pierre Macherey (1966) suggests, ideology is partly made up of those things that the text does not mention, that is, it operates silently, and its silences can be forced to speak (132). In fact, as Fredric Jameson (1981) points out, the act of writing (or painting or any "aesthetic act") is itself ideological (79). What this means is that not only does the writer/artist represent a particular (class-based) ideology (Macherey 1966:231), but that the product itself creates a reaction within the reader/viewer, a reaction that Althusser terms "ideological self-recognition" (156). This in turn implies that there will be confusion and contradiction in the way ideology operates, while the literary text seems to offer a symbolic or formal resolution of contradictions within itself.

However, as Steven B. Smith (1984) suggests, ideology can only be evaluated "functionally" or in terms of how it "respond[s] to certain basic human needs" (129). Hence, it is useful to keep in mind Raymond Geuss's description of the three ways in which ideology can be used, as described by Smith. The first is a "descriptive" use, which includes the beliefs, attitudes, and general concepts that a group adheres to. The second is the "pejorative" use in the Marxist sense of a "false consciousness" or delusion which needs to be changed. The third is the "positive" use, or ideologies which it is deemed necessary to consciously create and introduce to a group from the outside (129-130). In this context, Smith's own definition of ideology is fairly useful, since he describes it as "a well-organized system of beliefs which serves to reinforce or reproduce the existing set of social relations" and admonishes that, "rather than...explaining reality, ideology has to be treated as a part of that reality which is in need of explanation" (130). I will use this definition in my analysis of the workings of ideology in the writings of these three novelists.

Descriptive, pejorative, and positive forms of ideology are embedded in the writings of the three novelists and are revealed through "the unborn" or repressed (Lacan 1978:23) or unconscious levels of their texts. Jacques Lacan describes the unconscious as a realm which is made up of that which is refused by the conscious (43) or is "unrealized" (30) and, therefore, outside time and space (31). In the texts of our three novelists, however, the unconscious is more than an unrealized space; rather, it is a political space on what Jameson calls the "undersides" of texts which contains many contradictions, not all of which they are able to control (Jameson 1981:49). These contradictions are most obvious with regard to the representation of people and events in their narratives. Representation itself is problematic because it is "embedded first in the language and then in the culture, institutions, and political ambience of the representer" (Said 1978:272); hence, I will pay close attention to the absences in the narratives of all three novelists and try to represent their signficance. As Jameson suggests, absences in texts become visible only when we can set up the "series [of circumstances] that should have generated the missing term" (1981:137).

Thus, Gordimer, Sahgal, and Emecheta, despite writing

from very divergent political and social contexts, are connected in several significant ways. First, all three deal with questions of fragmentation, displacement, marginality, and dialogic discourse. They problematize the concept of the nation, and the clash between Western and non-Western cultures, though only Emecheta deals with issues of migrancy and immigration. Second, the sensibilities of all three writers seem to suffer from a sense of fracture or fission in that the limitations imposed on them by history and ideology prompt them to silence or displace certain marginalized voices and issues while claiming to speak on their behalf. For example, because of her white, English-speaking Jewish background, Gordimer's narrative focus is almost entirely on the limitations of white South Africans in dealing with the consequences of apartheid, and her depictions of black discourse are rather flat and unconvincing. Similarly, Sahgal's bourgeois and familial ties to India's "first family" in politics prevent her from adequately problematizing the caste and class basis of political oppression.   Finally, Emecheta's experiences with patriarchal oppression in Nigeria and economic self-sufficiency in England frequently blind her to sexual discrimination in England. Third, all three writers are somewhat displaced or isolated from the mainstream cultures they are writing about, either by virtue of class or race or by expatriation. Thus, all three provide unique versions of the politics of race, class, and gender in a postcolonial society and of the role of the postcolonial woman in shaping the political destiny of her culture.

Despite these similarities between the three writers, there are also several significant differences. Gordimer's chief preoccupation seems to be with race relations, Sahgal's with class conflicts, and Emecheta's with gender differences. In fact, all three are limited by their ideological and historical positions. Most obviously, their discourse is confined by their constant preoccupation with the ideology of the elite social class to which each of them belongs. For Gordimer, this is the white bourgeois class in South African society; for Sahgal, it is the Western-educated bourgeois class of urban India; and for Emecheta it is the Western-educated bourgeois class of urban Nigeria. Most of the voices that speak to us from their texts reflect the ideologies of this bourgeois class. As a result, they only partially critique the basis of that class's hegemony in their own particular society; nor do they seem aware of the hegemonic function of their own voices within that society/class. For Sahgal and Emecheta, the hegemony arises partly out of their acquisition of a reading public and a critical following in the West; for Gordimer, the dominance is largely a result of her being granted the Nobel Prize for literature despite the presence of many talented black South African creative writers.

Moreover, Gordimer believes that the task of the writer in South Africa is a very important one. The white writer, she believes, must "raise the consciousness of white people who...have not woken up. It is a responsibility at once minor, in comparison with that placed upon the black writer as composer of battle hymns, and yet forbidding, if one compares the honour and welcoming from blacks that await the black writer, and the branding as traitor,... that await[s] the white" (Gordimer 1985:145). Later, she declares that regardless of the writer's race, "the essential gesture" by which that writer "enters the brotherhood of man...is a revolutionary gesture" (147). She seems to have tried to follow her own dictum by being a "long-time supporter" of the ANC (although she didn't make her allegiance public until 1992) (Dreifus 1992:32); denouncing the government's censorship of PEN, the writers' organization; and helping to found the Congress of South African Writers, which is a mainly black writer's group (Prescott & Peyser 1991:40). She has also repeatedly claimed that whites must accept responsibility for all the injustice that is meted out to blacks because "we whites are solely responsible [for black deaths] whether we support white supremacy or, opposing, have failed to unseat it" (Gordimer

1976:3). Her books have been censored and banned by the South African government, and she has always firmly declined going abroad. When she won the Nobel Prize in Literature in 1991, she claimed it was her second great thrill in the past two years, the first being the release of Nelson Mandela from prison (Prescott & Peyser 1991:40).

Sahgal, however, claims that her only ideology is "that I do not believe in kings and queens and political dynasties" (Mohini 1990:65); she also argues that the writer's commitment is "to the writing of a story. He has no political commitment. It may get reflected but it is not a conscious effort" (67). If the political commitment is absent, then the writer writes because she wants to "make sense out of one's life, to understand it better...[it has] something to do with the urge to be free" (Sahgal 1972b:81). On the other hand, she argues that non-violence as a political strategy is both necessary and relevant to the Indian political scene (Mohini 1990:62). To be successful, the only thing it needs is "the right kind of leadership...change can be brought through the right use of vote" (68). Moreover, she views Gandhian politics as a perpetual presence in the Indian scene, claiming that it represents "the spirit of willing self-sacrifice and self-imposed discipline...[which is] the connecting thread through all her [i.e., India's] history, and the foundation of all her religions and philosophies" (Sahgal 1953:166).

Finally, Emecheta claims that to be an African woman writer is to be "determined. The first person you need to convince is yourself....Your truth may not be my truth. If I am speaking my own truth the way I see it, I must be prepared to defend it. That means having that belief in yourself and being prepared to write it as you see it" (James 1990:45). This personal truth seems to have something to do with a person's class or gender, or what she calls his/her "situation," but the main determining factor in being a successful writer, she says, is "the financial question." This is obviously a reference to whether a writer is self-sufficient or financially dependent (40). She points out that many African women writers are financially dependent on men, which hampers their creativity, but that despite it, the writing they produce shows how sympathetic they are to the female point of view (42). More importantly, she explains that many of the women of her own generation, whose social awareness she would like to raise, are illiterate and therefore would not be able to read her books. Even those who can read probably would not be able to, because most books sold in Nigeria are hardbacks which cost approximately $17 each—a "person's income for a whole month" (Topouzis 1990:69). Worse still, she suggests that the patriarchal situation in Nigeria has resulted in women who are "riddled with hypocrisy" so that they say what they don't feel and avoid laughing at anything too loudly (James 1990:38). When asked how women should deal with that patriarchal situation, she suggests that African women should "preserve what is good in traditional society and discard what is no longer relevant" (Topouzis 1990:69). By way of example, she mentions the traditional custom of the bride price as one that should be abandoned. However, she fails to mention any of the good customs that are to be retained.

Besides representing the domination of bourgeois ideology within the educated elite of their respective cultures, Gordimer, Sahgal, and Emecheta tend to present subaltern or peasant discourse as extremely marginalized, fragmented, and effaced. Moreover, their narrative representation of various class positions in society is invariably oppositional rather than dialogic. However, this constant opposition is rarely presented in the form of binaries; rather, the various voices and narratives continually "contaminate" each other to produce what looks suspiciously like master narratives. For Gordimer, a master narrative would be the inherent racism and deliberate collusion of white women in the perpetuation of apartheid. In fact, Robin Visel (1988) points out that Gordimer frequently castigates white women for their complicity in the perpetuation of apartheid (34). For Sahgal, a master narrative would be the social unrest and political decay that inevitably follow a conscious deviation from the tenets of non-violence and Hindu karma. Thus, Marcia Liu (1980) argues that Sahgal divides her fictional characters into aggressors and non-aggressors, or the active and the thoughtful, or those who are mainly concerned with making money and those who care about morality (52). In fact, all of Sahgal's novels contain protagonists who are non-violent and sensitive (the Gandhian politician) and antagonists who are brutal and aggressive (the violent politician) and her narratives are propelled forward by the clash between these two types. For Emecheta, a master narrative would be the social injustice and sexual inequality that result from a rigid adherence to the rituals of African patriarchy. Even then, her depiction of that patriarchy is not always accurate. Chimalum Nwankwo (1988), for example, finds what he calls her anti-male attitude rather bitter and distracting, besides which it trivializes other aspects of African soceity. He also suggests that the situation of the colonial/postcolonial Ibo female is not as grim and tragic as she makes it out to be, and that often other women were as responsible for the maintenance of the patriarchy as were men (40). Only Gordimer tends to critique the role of social systems like capitalism in perpetuating social injustice and inequality (as in *The Conservationist*); but then Gordimer's own politics are fluid because, as Dorothy Driver (1983) suggests, they have moved, over the course of her career, from "uneasy liberalism" to "a recognition of the marginality of liberalism" to a "revolutionary attitude" (30). Sahgal and Emecheta, however, prefer locating social ills within individuals and practices that have somehow deviated from or disregarded the capitalist system. In fact, in novels like *Second Class Citizen* and *In the Ditch*, Emecheta rather uncritically valorizes the competitive individualism that the capitalist system fosters. Thus, Lloyd W. Brown (1981) castigates her for her rather uncritical adoption of "Western modes of perceiving, and describing Africans." He cites her use of contrasts between the civilized West and the superstitious and crude world of Africa, and claims this shows an acceptance of old Eurocentric standards (37). In fact, Emecheta's early novels do tend to set up Africa and the West as binary opposites representing stagnation and dynamism. Only occasionally (as in *The Rape of Shavi* and *Destination Biafra*) does she describe the harmonious qualities within traditional African society. Finally, Sahgal rarely problematizes the impact of well ingrained and hierarchized social structures like the Indian caste system on the formation of a distinct urban political oligarchy in India.

Besides the issue of the representation of social or political systems, there is the question of what kind of consciousness appears in the writings of Gordimer, Sahgal, and Emecheta. On the one hand, all three writers are subject to some modern Western discourses that suggest that women are always confined or are passive. The psychoanalytic tradition, in particular, depicts the Western woman as "receptacle, womb, earth, factory, bank in which the seed capital grows" (Irigaray 1985:18). Luce Irigaray shows how patriarchal and psychoanalytic ideology constructs woman as lack (42) or as "indefinite, indefinable, non-sexed, unable to recognize herself" (Cixous 1981:46) and as being excluded from and deficient in male discourse (Irigaray 1985:49). The postcolonial woman, too, constitutes a gap or absence in hegemonic Western ideology and, like her Western counterpart, she is often represented in Western discourse as an "inter-dict" or object between signs, between meanings, without any signification herself (22). However, if Western woman is a void and unrepresentable (43), then how does one represent the postcolonial woman? Is she, like the Western woman, always doomed to be constituted in discourse as impediment, failure, lack, absence (Lacan 1977:25)? Just as Western woman is often made to seem a mirror of "specular duplication" who gives man back his own image while at the same time duplicating it (Irigaray 1985:56), is the postcolonial woman always a mimicker of the colonizer? Or is she destined to be an "endlessly circling speculum" with no closure and never reflected or represented (76)?

Postcolonial and literary critics have not really provided too many answers to these questions. For example, O. Mannoni regards the neo-colonial situation as a "Prospero-Caliban" relationship, or one in which the "paternal" colonizer's daughter has "suffered an [imaginary] rape at the hands of an inferior being [the colonized subject]" (Mannoni 1990:110). Indeed, the metaphor of rape/incest is often used in postcolonial literary contexts to signify the economic domination of the colonizer both before and after independence. However, while this metaphor can work as a signifier for economic and political exploitation, it tends to present the postcolonial woman as a victim.[12] Henry Louis Gates has pointed out that the postcolonial or black woman is often an ambivalent figure in literature because she uses the language of the colonizer in order to "posit a full and sufficient self," a language in which "blackness [or otherness] is a sign of absence" (Gates 1985:12). Also, Mishra and Hodge (1994) claim that the postcolonial woman is like a fragment or an oppositional system within the framework of colonization. They argue that women are "burdened by a twice-disabling discourse: the disabling master discourse of colonialism is then redirected against women in an exact duplication of the colonizer's own use of that discourse vis-a-vis the colonized in the first instance" (284).

Robert Young, describing Gayatri Spivak's preoccupation with the subaltern consciousness, suggests that she recommends an approach that would involve not retrieving the [female] subaltern consciousness, but reinscribing its subject position. This reinscription would involve showing how the subaltern consciousness subverts the dominant ideology (Young 1990:160). Thus, rather than speaking on or for the subaltern woman, the focus would be on the aporia or blind spot (164) or on how patriarchal ideologies construct false notions of the postcolonial woman (171). Chandra Talpade Mohanty (1994) echoes that idea when she points out that some Western feminist writings tend to "discursively colonize the material and historical heterogenous lives of women in the third world, thereby producing/representing a composite, singular `third-world woman'" (197). Whether we call this form of colonization essentialism or orientalism, "its imbrications of race and gender are accorded an iconicity that is altogether too good to be true" (Suleri 1994:46).

What is more apt in terms of my project is Anne McClintock's comments about the relevance of this discourse in the sphere of gross economic exploitation. Speaking generally of the former colonies, she asks: "in a world where women do two-thirds of the world's work, earn 10% of the world's income, and own less than 1% of the world's property, the promise of `postcolonialism' has been a history of hopes postponed" (McClintock 1994:298). The articulation of this history of female exploitation is an aspect that links the writings of Gordimer, Sahgal, and Emecheta, though Gordimer tends to focus more on black exploitation than on female exploitation. Nevertheless, as my subsequent chapters will show, although each writer's assessment of the politics of gender is different, they all problematize—in different ways—the role of the traditional patriarchy in the postcolonial world.

Patriarchy, as defined by Gerda Lerner (1986), is an institutionalized form of male dominance over women and children, both within the family and in society in general. It suggests that men hold the powerful positions in important social institutions, while women do not, although women are not entirely deprived of all economic, legal, and political rights. It takes various forms and modes in different societies and adapts itself in different periods of time (239). Emecheta consistently critiques the oppressive function of such a patriarchy as exists in postcolonial Nigeria; Sahgal examines specific patriarchal practices like divorce settlements that oppress women; while Gordimer in some of her short stories implies that Western and non-Western forms are equally oppressive.

Therefore, the interventions of Gordimer, Sahgal, and Emecheta are valuable primarily because they connect postcolonial feminine identity to the institutionalized nature of traditional, patriarchal oppression. While they all suggest that the dominance of patriarchal systems (Western, African, Indian) oppress and silence women of all classes and races, Emecheta and Sahgal tend to focus on individual males, like Francis or Som (who unfortunately degenerate into caricatures), as particularly brutal perpetrators of an oppressive system. Yet Lloyd W. Brown (1981) lauds the "fervor" and "rhetoric" of Emecheta's protest against sexual inequality, and calls her an effective "protest writer" because she blends impassioned protest with effective characterization (35). Moreover, all three novelists link sexual oppression to male control over a woman's body (such as Mehring's over Antonia), but de-emphasize male domination of female labor and economic self-determination. Only Emecheta—in her depiction of the commodification of Ibo women of all classes into producers of male children and bringers of large bride prices—suggests that patriarchal oppression is primarily economic.

Another way in which all three novelists deal with the issue of patriarchal oppression in their writings is their representation of aberrant behavior as a means of resistance to patriarchal domination. In Gordimer's narratives, this is sometimes represented as a strange desire on the part of white women to remain as close to the center of black suffering as possible (for example, Rosa Burger); while for Emecheta this is presented as a deliberate prostitution of mind and body in order to achieve sexual equality (for example, Nko). Most importantly, all three deal with rape as a metaphor for patriarchal and colonial domination.   Curiously, Gordimer and Sahgal represent rape metaphorically in their narratives, while Emecheta is more explicit.   Whatever their differences in representation, Emecheta and Sahgal both suggest that rape is the most explicit instance of male domination and brutalization of the land or the female body. However, Gordimer problematizes even that generalization in her depiction of white female voyeuristic fantasies about black male sexuality (see Maureen's interactions with July in *July's People*).

Although all three novelists focus strongly on the representation of male oppression, they do give the postcolonial female a voice.   Gordimer does so by focussing on the blind spots in male discourse (such as by showing us how Mehring speaks for Antonia or how Rosa's discourse evolves out of Lionel's). Sahgal's female voices, however, seem constantly displaced by male discourse (for example, Sonali and Rashmi rely entirely on male directives and commands).   Finally, Emecheta's female voices seem unable to speak except in total opposition to male discourse (as is the case with Nko and Adah).   Ultimately, though, all three novelists seem to imply that postcolonial female discourse arises out of the contradictions and clashes within traditional patriarchy and Western capitalism.

According to Sara Suleri (1994), two of feminism's most commonly articulated points are its marginality in male discourse and its "obsessive attention" to "the racial body" (247).   The racial body is a very important concern of Gordimer's, because apartheid has made her sensitive to the social and political implications of racial interaction.   Yet, as Abdul R. JanMohamed (1983) comments, the central space in Gordimer's fiction is rarely occupied by blacks, who "function primarily as catalytic agents in the moral and political development of her white protagonists" (147).   He suggests that the reason for this omission is that the political conditions of South Africa restrained Gordimer within her own world (149); while the reason Benita Parry (1978) suggests is that Gordimer could not break with the hegemonic

Western cultural consciousness (49). I would argue that the nature of the neo/postcolonial situation itself would make it very difficult for any novelist to break with Western cultural hegemony, both in her choice of language and of genre. Emecheta's awareness of the politics of race and ethnicity, however, result from being at once secure in the roots and prominence of her ethnic group (the Ibo in Nigeria) and marginalized in the hostility and discrimination practiced against her racial group (black Africans in Britain). Like Gordimer, then, she deals with the implications of white restrictions on black self-expression in Britain; but she also describes layers of social and ethnic oppression prevalent in traditional Ibo society in Nigeria (see, for example, her problematization of the treatment of *osu*s like Chike). Sahgal, however, almost completely ignores the issue of ethnicity, despite speaking from a position of ethnic privilege, preferring to deal with the implications of religious differences between people and its impact on politics. In fact, she also promotes a kind of enlightened casteism, as professed by Vishal Dubey in *Storm in Chandigarh*, for example.

The implications of these three approaches to race and ethnicity are very important. Gordimer, in her novels, seems to suggest that South African whites cannot escape the political and ideological implications of race (repression, guilt) and must constantly find ways to accept responsibility for black suffering (note, for example, the narrator's ambivalence or even censure toward Maureen's escape at the end of *July's People*). Emecheta, in her novels, seems to advocate a thorough Westernization of Nigerian patriarchy and in some places suggests that male oppression of female bodies and labor is more prevalent in black males than in whites (for example, see how the narrator of *Second Class Citizen* claims Francis' race makes him unable to change his oppressive and chauvinistic behavior towards Adah). Yet at the same time she repudiates white racism as she experiences it in Britain, especially if its perpetrators are lower-class whites. Only occasionally, as in *Destination Biafra*, does she critique Western nations directly. Finally, Sahgal's narratives suggest that discrimination based on caste or skin color in urban India either is the result of personal weakness or is part of the baggage of Hinduism that needs to be discarded. She fails to problematize the pervasive basis of that discrimination in political and public life. In *This Time of Morning* and *The Day in Shadow*, for example, she suggests that caste is a discriminatory and unjust feature in an otherwise pantheistic Hinduism and can be countered through a return to Gandhi's insistence on the importance of the individual. There is no sense, in any of her novels, of caste as an ideological tool for bourgeois control of the economy and politics.

Finally, all three novelists are not very effective at making the racial other speak in their narratives. Some of Gordimer's characters, like July or Jacobus, for example, seem able to use the white man's language against him quite effectively, but fail to formulate their own "metaphors for suffering." Conversely, several of Emecheta's characters, like Bill and Alan Grey, tend to be rather flat, just playing their role of white mentor or imperialist manipulator without gaining very distinctive modes of expression. Finally, the voice of the untouchable or *dalit* is absent in Sahgal, and his or her presence is represented only as a shadow (Simrit's servant) or a monstrosity (Rose's beggar) or a faceless mass (Inder's workers).

In conclusion, then, all three novelists tend to subsume social and economic categorizations under one dominant mode. For Gordimer race dictates political identity and behavior; for Sahgal class determines the appropriateness of political leadership; while for Emecheta gender power controls and dominates political action. What all this implies for the nature of postcolonial political fiction is that narrative voice and political identity are in a state of flux. Thus, the three novelists are articulate and expressive with regard to politics, class, and gender and, in examining them together, I will prove that the postcolonial woman is part of a plurality or continuum in which she moves in various positions, depending on what ideology is imposed on and by her. She is therefore represented as a figure that is being constantly displaced or a voice that perpetually resists within a discourse that is evolving and shifting. She is at once elite and powerless, at once subversive and exploitative. The focus of the following chapters is the gaps and absences within the writings of these three novelists that reveal their attempts to come to terms with the neo-colonial and patriarchal ideology that surrounds and limits them.

Notes

[1]Note that Gayatri C. Spivak, among others, cautions against using the label "third world" to designate all those territories colonized by European imperialists. As she points out, sociologists like Carl Pletsch and others have suggested that the term is "contaminated at birth by the new economic programs of neo-colonialism" and, at best, "gives a proper name to a generalized margin." She goes on to argue that the label is used by the center to denote not even a single race or social type, "but an economic principle of identification through separation" (Spivak 1993:55).

[2]As Ngugi has pointed out, there were a large number of Western-based or patriotically inspired military coups in Africa in the 1960's: in Zaire in 1960 and 1965, in Nigeria and Ghana in 1966, as well as in Sierra Leone, Sudan, Mali, Uganda. They often resulted in civil wars, as in Nigeria and Congo or monstrous dictatorships as in Uganda (1993:67). In the 1970s, as he points out, the U.S. overthrew the Allende regime in Chile and surrounded Africa with military bases (68-69).

[3]For example, the U.S. played an active role in ousting Lumumba and replacing him with Mobutu in what was known as Zaire (Ngugi 1993:66).

[4]For further reading on economic underdevelopment in Africa, see Walter Rodney's *How Europe Underdeveloped Africa,* revised edition (Washington D.C.: Howard University Press, 1982 [first published 1972]) as well as Bade Onimode's *Imperialism and Underdevelopment in Nigeria: The Dialectics of Mass Poverty* (London: Zed Press; Westport, Connecticut: Lawrence Hill, 1982).

[5]See also Chinweizu's discussion of the dominance of African literature by literature written in European languages. In the introduction to *Voices from Twentieth Century Africa: Griots and Towncriers* (1988), for example, he points out that Africa is unique in making its students of the humanities read "materials imported from alien conquerors" rather than "the classics of 5,000 years of African literature" (xxx). He also suggests that this practice has resulted in "European cultural chauvenism" or the "teaching of Western humanities as if they were the only and universal humanities" (xxxi).

[6]See also Ngugi's discussion of cultural imperialism in his *Moving the Centre* (1993). In it, he argues that because the comprador bourgeoisie had the same outlook as the former colonizer, "even after they [the comprador bourgeoisie] inherited the flag, their...attitudes toward their own history, toward their own languages...tended to be foreign." As a result, all the "economic, political and cultural" aspects of colonialism "remained intact" (85).

[7]Note that there are two types of Anglophone "settler" colony: that in which the settler became a majority at the expense of the indigenous populations (as in Australia, Canada, and New Zealand) and that in which settlement persisted as an activity of a minority disproportionately controlling land and economic wealth. In Kenya and Zimbabwe (Rhodesia) this minority was replaced only after a violent struggle.

[8]Benedict Anderson (1983) makes a similar argument when he describes two forms of nationalism that developed in the nineteenth and twentieth centuries: "official nationalism," and "popular nationalism." Official nationalism, he argues, developed in the late nineteenth-century and early twentieth-century and was characterized by a tendency on the part of European and Asian monarchs to "sidle toward a beckoning national identification"

(85). Thus, Czarist Russia and Victorian England developed nationalist agendas "*after* and *in reaction to*, the popular national movements proliferating in Europe since the 1820s" (86). All of them were "*responses* by power groups...threatened with exclusion from, or marginalization in, popular imagined communities [which]...concealed a discrepancy between nation and dynastic realm" (109-110). Popular nationalism, on the other hand, developed in the twentieth century mainly in the colonial territories of Asia and Africa, and as a response to global imperialism and industrial capitalism. Similar situations also occurred in Europe where "print-capitalism" helped create popular vernacular-based nationalisms (139).

[9]Note that other definitions of the nation are also somewhat univocal. For example, Hobsbawm (1990) has defined the nation as a social entity that is constantly changing, that belongs to a recent period of history, that corresponds to the modern nation-state, and that is artificial, socially engineered, and man-made (9-10). This definition fails to take into account that sometimes no real geographic space was necessary to imagine the nation. By contrast, Ali A. Mazrui (1972) argues that stable African nations can be built in five processes: "cultural normative fusion" or shared values and language; "economic interpenetration" or the active involvement of different subgroups within the country in the national economy; "social interaction" or the narrowing of the gaps between the elites and the masses, rich and poor; "conflict resolution" or the building up of institutions which throw up leaders and allow clashes to be peacefully resolved; and a "shared national experience" or a sort of historical awareness of a shared past which gives it a collective history (277-278). Mazrui insists that all five processes must interact with each other in order to create stable African nations. This definition disregards the fact that many postcolonial African nations have deep divisions based on ethnicity and religion and yet

still exist.

[10]They are false because the actual territories of most postcolonial nations were products of imperialism so that they were either drawn completely at random or to enclose a particular administrative zone (Hobsbawm 1990:137). Frequently, large postcolonial nations were created out of existing areas of colonial administration without any knowledge of the culture within them and without the consent of their people (171). These zones had a sort of artificial unity imposed on them which only sometimes produced a concrete sense of "nation-hood" (138). Also, many of the postcolonial nations combined what Anderson calls a "genuine, popular nationalist enthusiasm" with a systemic, even Machiavellian, instilling of nationalist ideology through the media (1983:114). This hybridity, combined with the fact that the national boundaries were arbitrary and class differences were great, means that the nations themselves were very artificial.

[11]Many literary critics would agree with this idea, adding that it is a discursive formation. Timothy Brennan (1988), for example, points out that a writer like Salman Rushdie shows that nations are imaginary by depicting how India has "(deluded) communal sharing of "nationality"" and how Pakistan has a "cohesion" based on "a military and juridical enforcement of community" (136). He would even go so far as to suggest that literary creations are "not only a part of the nation-forming process, but are its realization; that nations are mental projections...that nations are made out of citizen's councils and peasant armies physically enacting out the words of the national literatures that once imagined them" (137-138). Elsewhere, Brennan argues that "nations...are imaginary constructs that depend for their existence on an apparatus of cultural fictions in which imaginative literature plays a decisive role" (Ashcroft et al. 1995:173). He backs this up by stating that the novel was crucial

in "defining the nation as an "imagined community"" (172). Thus, one may conclude that both in terms of their modes of creation and their depiction in political and imaginative literature, nations and nationalisms are artificial and products of discourse on ethnic, religious, historical, cultural, and literary identity. For further discussion of this topic see Eric Hobsbawm and Terence Ranger's *The Invention of Tradition* (Cambridge, London & New York: Cambridge University Press, 1983), and Peter Worsely's *The Three Worlds: Culture and World Development* (Chicago & London: the University of Chicago Press, 1984).

[12] For example, Jenny Sharpe (1994) points out that the discourse of rape in E.M. Forster's *A Passage to India* "articulates the contradictions of gender and race within the *signifying system of colonialism* [and is therefore]...overdetermined by colonial relations of force and exploitation" (232). Referring to newspaper and other reports of the Indian Revolt of 1857 which contained ghastly but false and invented stories of rape and mutilation of British women by Indian soldiers, she suggests that such discourse shows "colonial power relations being written on the bodies of women....The response of [British] revenge for the dishonor of English women thus not only re-established a claim of lawful (sexual) ownership but also enforced violent strategies of counter-insurgency" (233). Her point is that the British imperialists repeatedly invented and used the idea of the violation of the pure English woman to justify their own excessive brutalization of colonial subjects. Thus, *A Passage to India* takes on, and struggles against, "a discourse of power capable of reducing anti-colonial struggle to the pathological lust of dark-skinned men for white women" (238).

"THEY WHO ARE BENEATH": SUBALTERN VOICES IN *THE CONSERVATIONIST*, *THE DAY IN SHADOW*, AND *THE BRIDE PRICE*

Class, according to Gayatri C. Spivak (1988b), is "not an inalienable description of a human reality. Class-consciousness on the *descriptive* level is itself a strategic and artificial rallying awareness which, on the *transformative* level, seeks to destroy the mechanics which come to construct the outlines of the very class of which a collective consciousness has been situationally developed" (14). In other words, the consciousness of one's class is a somewhat artificial awareness imposed from the outside and is more a product of the ideology of the perceiver than it is the awareness of a shared essence with other members of a particular group. An examination of subaltern consciousness, then, is not a discovery of "firm ground" or "some *thing* that can be disclosed" (10), but rather something that can "probably never be recovered" (12).[1] Spivak borrows the term "subaltern" from Antonio Gramsci, for whom the subaltern was the repressed peasant, and suggests that it is an intellectually and politically loaded term, functionally oppositional to "dominant" or "elite" (1). As regards the subaltern woman, Spivak suggests that she is a figure that moves from clan to clan as "daughter/sister and wife/mother [and who] syntaxes patriarchal continuity even as she is herself drained of proper identity" (31). [2] Such a woman is the object of oppression both in the Marxist sense of desire and power (Spivak 1988a:279) and in terms of race and class. As a result, she "disappears" into what Spivak calls "a violent aporia between subject and object status" (306). Spivak goes on to describe this "disappearance" explicitly in terms of subordination and silence, and she asks the question, "can the subaltern speak?" (283). She asks this specifically of the subaltern woman, and she points out that the situation of the female as opposed to the male is like that of the subaltern as opposed to the imperialist, because "the ideological construction of gender keeps the male dominant" (287). Since, she argues, the subaltern male belongs to the lowest stratum of society, he is, to some degree, inarticulate and silent (283). Therefore, if the subaltern male cannot "speak" in that he cannot express himself in terms that are understood by the imperialist, then the subaltern female is "even more deeply in shadow" (287) and mute. In addition, the very terms of her existence are dictated to her by the oppressor, and this implicates her in her own oppression. Hence, if the struggle of the colonial subjects is the struggle of a colonized people, the colonized woman becomes, in Sivanandan's words, "a colony of the colonized" (1982:76). One form of exploitation, therefore, works on another.

In the context of this silencing and exploitation, it seems very difficult to represent the repressed subaltern in a text. One way to do so would be through the gaps in dominant discourse, through overlay, and through constant displacement of hegemonizing voices. In this context, I will analyze three novels of the 1970s that are ambivalent in the way in which they deal with the figure of the subaltern. They are Nadine Gordimer's *The Conservationist* (1974), Nayantara Sahgal's *The Day in Shadow* (1972) and Buchi Emecheta's *The Bride Price* (1976), all of which deal with oppressed women, silenced subalterns, and authority figures that are not really all-knowing. *The Conservationist*, one of Gordimer's early works, is an ambivalent and counter-hegemonic text. The primary focus of the novel is the subjective consciousness of the white imperialist, Mehring, but his voice is constantly interrupted and threatened by the voice of his absent white mistress, Antonia, who seems to have become a victim of South African patriarchy. Her voice, again, is interrupted by that of Jacobus and the other black African laborers on Mehring's farm, who in turn are disturbed by the presence-in-absence of the body of the unknown faceless African man which slowly decomposes as the novel progresses. Behind him, in turn, are the voices of the dead ancestors, the Amatongo, who represent the Zulu myth of origins (Newman 1981:31). However, the Amatongo are finally revealed to be not ancestral voices, but voices presented through the orientalizing filter of a Christian missionary. Therefore, there is no sense of renewal or faith at the end of the novel.

The Day in Shadow, also an early novel, is an ambivalent text, though it is not consciously counter-hegemonic. Som, a rich industrialist, is the dominating force in the novel, the voice of literate authority and of economic power. Behind his voice is that of Raj, a middle class politician, who acts as Simrit's "redeemer" by "out-talking" Som and "rescuing" her from him, but who also ends up erasing her voice. Behind Raj's voice, again, is Simrit's, who paradoxically asserts her presence in the text through self-effacement. Behind Simrit, and even more effaced, are the voices of her children, who are pawns in her divorce settlement and do not really have clearly developed personalities. Deep in the shadows behind them are the voices of the true subalterns: the domestic servants, farmers, laborers, and prostitutes, who hover in the margins like dark shapes, never really emerging as actual presences. Finally, there is one more level of displacement in the text, that of "nature," both human and physical. This nature appears to be omnipresent and a source of both frustration and pleasure. As physical nature, it appears to be magnificent and beautiful, a presence which, once perceived, can prove a source of endless inspiration and renewal. As the archetypal "Hindu" nature/character, it appears to be unchanging and endless and, once "decoded," can provide the key to social change and counter-hegemony for the subaltern. All these different levels of displacement in the novel suggest that the characters are not just "flat" or "manichean" opposites like "cartoon baddies versus non-violent men of pure heart and good intent" (O'Faolain 1975/76:116). Rather, they are voices that constantly displace each other so that none of them can be clearly heard.

Buchi Emecheta's *The Bride Price*, also one of her earlier novels and set in colonial Nigeria in the 1950s, deals with issues of the subaltern, though in a rather different way. The narrative of the novel is dialogic, and many voices interact with each other. The voice of literate, patriarchal authority is that of Okonkwo[3] the village patriarch and Aku-nna's uncle, whose word is law, and who, with the help of his community, exerts a social and psychological hold over Aku-nna till her death. His voice is temporarily displaced by that of Chike, the village school teacher and son of slaves, who acts as Aku-nna's "redeemer" and helps her find temporary happiness and freedom. Ultimately, though, Chike is powerless to overcome the voice of authority that holds and paralyzes her. Aku-nna herself is a fragmented personality, and her voice is severely restricted. She seems to represent "tortured and dehumanized womanhood" (Emenyonu 1988:131) and speaks to us mainly through the voice of the third-person narrator. Deeper in the shadows behind Aku-nna are the voices of her mother, Ma Blackie, and her brother, Nna-nndo, who are also dominated and silenced. Behind them are the nameless village women who appear in the discourse at varying levels of exploitation, working hard, bowing to tradition, and speaking occasionally not as individuals but as a collective. Again, behind these voices is that of a third-person narrator who comments on the action at different stages and explains social and cultural customs and traditions to us. The final voice in the narrative is that of the oral storyteller who recounts stories about the ancestors or about members of the community as examples of wisdom or as warnings to would-be rebels. This story-telling voice has no ancestral or prophesying power and no ability to influence the action. As Cynthia Ward (1990) suggests, this multiplicity of voices in the narrative is true "orality," that is, "multiple, often contradictory stories, fictions, realities, meanings—none being allowed to have precedence over the others without being marked as overtly coercive" (87). Although Okonkwo's authoritative voice is often displaced, it is replaced by not one, but many "competing self-identities" (92).

The idea of voices in competition links all three novels. As Brian Macaskill has pointed out, Gordimer's text offers "a counter-hegemonic attack on the authoritarian word—an attack which involves more than the positing of an alternate mythology" (Macaskill 1950:166). However, I want to point out here that the counter-hegemony of the subaltern is somewhat of an abstraction and does not really alter the repressed position of the subaltern, because the subaltern is always dominated and can only speak obliquely. As Raymond Williams has suggested, a

hegemonizing voice never "just passively exist[s] as a form of dominance. It is continually to be renewed, recreated, defended, and modified. It is also continually resisted, limited, altered, challenged by pressures not all its own" (Williams 1977:112). The space for subaltern resistance lies, therefore, in the gaps and incompleteness of the dominant discourse. Thus, I would argue that all three texts are able, through their multiple subaltern voices, to exert a counter-hegemony on the imperialist discourse of the main texts. Moreover, each text's narrative style, while being "self-consciously counter-hegemonic" (Macaskill 1950:156), disrupts or interrupts the hegemonic discourse of the colonizer and is able to achieve counter-hegemony in the sense of making the discourse dialogic. Indeed, subaltern voices often are, in the words of Cynthia Ward (1990), irreconcilable and competing, being both oral and literate (96). I would argue, then, that the subaltern can speak but is often unheard, because the intervention of alternative voices and ideologies silences him/her. At best, he/she is represented as an absence.

If the subaltern is absent from these texts—or, rather, is effaced—the figure of the aggressor/imperialist is present and highlighted. Gordimer, for example, centered the narrative of *The Conservationist* around Mehring's voice, and this is very significant because it seems to be her way of showing up the prejudices and hypocrisies of the white ruling class. The novel is a masterful revelation of the social, political, and cultural bases of the ideology underlying apartheid. Because Gordimer is at odds with the politically elite whites in South Africa, she uses irony and indirection and a fractured narrative style to show up their evils. As she herself once said, "if you write honestly about life in South Africa, apartheid damns itself" (Schwartz 1977:81). Brian Macaskill has argued that "Gordimer's text offers a dialogic interruption of text and subtext," mainly through her use of quotations from Zulu myth, and this "not only challenges Mehring, but also calls into doubt the entire process of conservation itself" (Macaskill 1950:166), as well as the process of "print-capitalism"[4] and therefore Gordimer's own text. (Of course, the myths themselves are accessible to Gordimer only through print capitalism.)

Mehring's ideology is the central focus of the novel. His consciousness filters through most of the action and his opinions color our perspective of Antonia, Jacobus, the other black laborers, and the dead man. His is the voice of literate patriarchal authority which erases almost all other viewpoints. He buys a farm with the notion that he is conserving nature and becoming more humane himself. In fact, he completely dehumanizes blacks and women or anyone who holds a deviant viewpoint. Since his voice dominates, most of the major events in the novel are narrated in such a way as to "privilege" his consciousness (Macaskill 1950:157). This means that the narration objectifies women, regards black people as animals, views the land as if it is a sex object, and justifies Mehring's actions on the grounds that they are sincerely done for overall well-being. Mehring is not really a farmer. He belongs to the former business class which, because it did not have to contend with organized labor unions, exerted what Paul Rich calls a "far more visible hegemony [over black labor] than its counterparts in North America or Western Europe" (Rich 1982:61). Having bought a farm (and the black laborers working on it) as a whim and made it a "going concern," Mehring feels a sense of "superiority" (Gordimer 1974:208), a sense that he alone can appreciate nature (205). Despite the poverty and exploitation that exists on his farm (the laborers live in "boxes" with one door, one window, and one chimney), and the violence and crime in the black township nearby, he reassures himself that his farm is serene and pristine (199). Of course, he avoids direct contact with the problems of farming, absenting himself during a fire and a flood, and to reassure himself that he is a good farmer despite his frequent absences, he carries on an interior monologue addressed mainly to his absent mistress, Antonia. Macaskill (1950) calls this a "drama of memory whereby Mehring reconstructs as a textual presence his now physically absent mistress" (161). Through memory, he tries to justify his ideology on the basis that he is producing the means that everyone else is living off of. For example, he points out sarcastically that attractive middle class white women like

Antonia and the young "boys" she associates with aren't really capable of initiating calls for racial justice and equality, since they use the system to their own advantage whenever they need to (Gordimer 1974:79).

As for women, he sees them as nothing more than objects to be devoured, with body parts like "stupid chunks of meat...wanting to be stroked" (Gordimer 1974:127). Antonia's intellect irritates him; he uses her unceremonious flight from South Africa as a means to belittle it (107). However, his own assurance is short-lived because he uses his visits to the farm as an escape, as a means of getting a false sense of security, away from other white people and their problems. He tries and fails to suppress his deep-rooted fears of isolation or of being buried alive. When his leg gets caught in mud, he panics and thinks of it as a "soft, cold black hand" (228) that pulls at him. As Judie Newman suggests, the black man is an "image of his [Mehring's] subconscious" and is associated with "the melting surface beneath him" (Newman 1981:40). Being buried by blackness, being deserted, dying without white people noticing: these are the fears that occupy his mind constantly.

The last part of the novel charts Mehring's progressive paranoia about being buried alive and about losing his money. The constant interruptions by the imagined voice of Antonia, together with the strange reappearances of the body of the unknown dead man heighten his fears. As he tells himself at one point, "they [black people] have been there [on the farm] all the time and they will continue to be there. They have nothing and they have nothing to lose" (Gordimer 1974:260). Thus, when he is found flirting with a colored girl (who he thinks is white) by a thug-like policeman, his impulse is to run away. Even then, his last thoughts are about his property and power. His death (imaginary or real) highlights his obsessions with possessions and power as well as his compulsive fears of being abandoned. His body remains forgotten and unburied, dispossessed by that of the unknown black man who finally gets a decent burial.

Mehring's white mistress, Antonia, is an alienated individual who seems to be, as Abdul R. JanMohamed (1983) suggests, "at home neither in the fascism of South Africa nor in the self-indulgent liberalism of Europe" (118). Hers is a repressed voice not in the sense of race and class—for she is an upper-class, white woman—but in the sense of gender domination. She is dominated socially, politically, and sexually; depicted by the various narrative voices in the text as static and silent, and her sexuality is closely linked to her repression. As Mehring presents her, she is, in many ways, just as responsible for the racist situation in South Africa as is Mehring (Visel 1988:34). In fact, she seems to dabble with blacks and politics just for a thrill. According to Mehring's account of her, she concerns herself with black working-class labor without really understanding its misery and diverts herself sexually by sleeping with white capitalists despite abhorring their politics.

However, as readers and critics, we know her only as Mehring remembers her, through conversations that are partly real and partly imaginary. This presentation of her actually defines Mehring's preoccupations more clearly than hers, and it also prevents her character from being integrated (Macaskill 1950:162). She hardly says much herself and is frequently described by Mehring as someone who thinks she's smart (Gordimer 1974:42), but who is actually nothing more than a "bitch" (43). Mehring's constant complaint is that she talks down to him and shows off how clever she is (174), rather than being docile and submissive. He dismisses her opinions about his colonizing tendencies as so much nonsense and reminisces that when she was arrested for anti-government activities she looked very frightened (71). Indeed, all her political activities seem to him to arise more from arrogance than from genuine convictions, which is why he thinks her liberalism is a sham. For example, he thinks she wants to change South African society only in ways that suit her lifestyle, not radically (79). Only one of his recollections of her seems to have anything forceful about it, namely, the occasion when he remembers she had lectured him about responsibility. She accused him of focussing only on "development" and refusing to acknowledge his own racist politics (82). This one eruption by Antonia does seem to shake up his complacency somewhat. In fact, his irritation with her is a sign of his uneasiness.

Mehring also dehumanizes her constantly, comparing her hair to cow's tails (Gordimer 1974:175), her swinging breasts to "weights in a sling" (177), and their bodies separating after sex to the pulling apart of two parts of a ripe fruit (176). Of her brain he remarks that it is opaque and as easily visible as "the innards in the bodies of those pale ghekos that ran on the ceilings in Central Africa" (178). Of course, Antonia is by no means the only woman in the novel to be dehumanized by him; as he tells her at one point having sex with a woman he's paid money to get gives him an added thrill (77-78). Here, sexual and colonial exploitation are linked, so that "sexual guilt functions as a surrogate for colonial guilts" (Newman 1981:36). However, Mehring seems to project some of the guilt on to Antonia, too, since he believes she sleeps with him because it gives her a perverse thrill. In his monologue he asks her, "Isn't it your perversion to dirty yourself with what you call a tycoon?" (Gordimer 1974:151). Yet, he flatters himself, she also secretly admires him (77). In the absence of any response to his accusation, we are left with the impression that in fact she sleeps with him as a diversion because she despises, but is amused by, his politics, and because she seems to be somewhat voyeuristic.

To what extent, then, does Antonia speak in the novel? One could argue that she doesn't speak at all, since all her conversations take place within Mehring's mind, and some are clearly fabrications. Moreover, she is never represented outside his consciousness, and speaks only through his ideological bias.

Frequently, she merges, in his memory, with his other women or with his son or with his black laborers. At such times, she becomes his enemy—or his opposite. He imagines that when he confronts her (and her friends) as adversaries, they won't have any accusations to throw in his face, indeed, they will remain completely silent (Gordimer 1974:79-80). At the end, when she has to flee the country, he accuses her of betrayal, of always promising what she can't give (136). In his mind, he fabricates a final phone call from her, in which she becomes "flesh...at either end of the line...a live wire clutched to the ear...at whose touch each nipple breaks out of its little worn brown parcel of slack skin" (223). Overall, she appears to be objectified, static, predictable, and silenced.

Antonia's abilities to speak are complicated further by the interruptions from the other subalterns in the novel, namely, the black African voices, which fall into four groups. They are the voice of male authority embodied by Jacobus; the voices of dependents, represented by Phineas's wife; the voices of inner subjectivity, revealed by the corpse of the unknown man; and the voices of oral authority, reiterated by the quotations from the buried ancestors. All these voices are presented obliquely, as interruptions to Mehring's monologue addressed to Antonia, and they also constantly erase each other.

Jacobus, the foreman, speaks to us through the filter of a third-person narrator who seems to be less detached than Mehring and does not seem to block his consciousness as effectively as Mehring does Antonia's. Yet Mehring's ideology frequently intrudes. Jacobus is in the ambiguous position of being both exploited laborer and exploiter of his own people. On the one hand, he is colonized by the imperialist, who regards him as little better than an animal; and on the other, he makes the rules to which his own people must submit. As the narrator tells us, he was half on the side of authority and half the protector of his people against that authority (Gordimer 1974:33); at once "responsible" for his people and a sycophant to authority (12); both all-knowing (57) and animalistic, his walk being "loping" and wolflike, his teeth dirty, and his face, black and impassive (206). He is in control of the white man's language (64), has the power to intercede with him for jobs, and is the boss when the white man is away (37). Surrogate colonizer himself, he decides when and where the others come and go and effectively silences opposition: "Nobody said anything. Jacobus was speaking and he must be heard through" (67). He speaks for them, not with them, and tells their stories of survival and trouble. Just as Mehring regards him as a faithful but dumb animal who isn't clever enough to deceive him (145), so too Jacobus regards the other Africans as cattle: he frequently keeps an eye on them just as he would if he were showing a white farmer some prime cows on a farm (144-145).

The "cows" themselves speak occasionally through the mediation of the third-person narrator. The men—Izak, Phineas, Solomon, Witbooi, and Dorcas's husband—appear in the text as subhuman and are usually identified by their appendages. Thus, Solomon is recognizable by his scar which becomes "a thick pair of puckered lips sewn together right across the forehead" (Gordimer 1974:96); Izak is identifiable by his "black and white checked cap" (67); a nameless man seeking employment becomes a "head" that "has a mothy dimness, half-effacing itself into the perimeter of the firelight" (67); while Dorcas's husband feels "tethered to the weight of the boots in which he had worked in blood all day at the abattoir" (125). When Dorcas's husband finds the words to protest his dehumanization, he is silenced by the arguments of his friend, William, who asks him sarcastically what he will revolt with even if he succeeds in getting rid of Mehring. He points out that he certainly won't inherit his farm, and will, indeed, be homeless and on the run (125). In general, these laborers are exploited, dehumanized, and silenced, with no means to change their situation. They earn a meager salary from their work on the land, are susceptible to crime and violence from the black township nearby, and are in constant danger of losing their jobs if old or disabled. They own no property, not even cattle (even a dead ox would have cost six months' worth of Solomon's salary). They are also out of touch with their own traditions, so that when Solomon is beaten up by the henchmen of his creditor, the others believe that the dead man's spirit attacked him. Indeed, the corpse frightens all of them, and they believe it has evil powers. Frequently, Solomon thinks of himself as the corpse, because he had almost died after being beaten up and can remember only the dark, extremities of existence (167). Darkness, fear, and superstition, the narrator tells us, fill up their minds and, since we never hear their thoughts, that is the impression we are left with. We could therefore conclude that Gordimer herself is unable to present their thoughts adequately and that she, too, is not free from racial stereotypes.

Besides the men, there are the women who seem to be even deeper in the darkness. They are described as bits of humanity—bodies, arms and legs—who move like animals. Phineas's wife seems to have some powers of prophecy, but even that is debased—she appears to the others like a public nuisance. Her initiation ceremony as "witch doctor" lacks a spiritual dimension, since the point of interest is the meat from the goat (to be eaten) and not the powers of prophecy she possesses (Macaskill 1950:164). Her dreams take frightening form as she sees herself as snake and lizard and she almost dies when she tries to perform a ritual dance, her body sweating profusely, and her energy ebbing quickly (Gordimer 1974:166). Although she is represented as one who is close to her ancestors, we never hear her speak to them. As for the other women, they don't speak at all, they "neither greet nor expect to be greeted, they do not see themselves at all" (145). Above all, they suffer in silence, working in extreme temperature conditions, and seeming like nothing more than bits of "newspaper" flung against the walls

(249).   In the deeper shadows behind the women are the children, who are blown about the streets like bits of refuse. Mehring sees them as "paraffin tins with legs" whose parents don't care about them (44).   Overall, the black Africans in the text are bodies without minds, passive and subhuman.   Whether they are represented in Mehring's discourse or in the third-person narrative, they are used and abused to perpetuate apartheid: he makes them build a fence around his farm to prevent other black people from entering it (35).   Gordimer seems to be suggesting here that blacks under apartheid are silent, shadowy figures with some potential to articulate their condition but without the power to change it.   This is a troubling representation of black subaltern consciousness.

Besides these subaltern voices from the living, there are other displaced voices from the dead, one being that of the dead man who manages to interrupt and disrupt the imperialist's discourse.   On his first appearance in Mehring's third pasture, the dead man asserts his presence by disturbing Mehring's complacency.   He intrudes into Mehring's thoughts as he lies under the ground; he disappears in fire and reappears in water; and he slowly decomposes till he becomes unrecognizable as human.   Finally, he remains not so much a bodily presence as a smell of "rot" (Gordimer 1974:245), a "stink to high heaven" (246) that embodies the decay and corruption in the social hierarchy.   The dead man, then, suggests the inevitability of a return to origins; that is, the idea that black people will claim, even in death, the land that is rightfully theirs: "they [the farm laborers] had put him [the dead man] away to rest, at last; he had come back.   He took possession of this earth, theirs; one of them" (267).   On this note the narrative ends, and all the problems of exploitation and silencing that it has depicted up to this point are left unresolved.   However, since the narrative progresses through a dialogic discourse, that is, through a series of voices appearing behind other   voices and through constant interruptions and displacements, such an ending is not entirely inappropriate and, in fact, achieves a kind of balance. By the end of the novel, the narrative has become a kind of "intertext" which not only projects Mehring's thoughts, but also speaks in his absence (Macaskill 1950:158). One instance of this speaking-in-the-imperialist's-absence is the narration of the lifestyle of the Indian shopkeepers, where the narrative begins and ends with descriptions of hierarchies: the Indians below the whites and below them the blacks. Another instance is the description of the experiences of the black farm children when they go to the township nearby. The narrative voice describes how they feel awestruck when they see finely dressed black men, black women with straight hair, and black boys gambling and throwing knives at each other (Gordimer 1974:86).

More importantly, however, the narrative balance at the novel's end is achieved through the use of one final voice that speaks throughout the dialogic discourse. This voice is that of the Amatongo or buried ancestors, which appears before each major episode in the main narrative in the form of italicized quotations, separate from the main text. As Macaskill points out, these quotations, which are from Zulu mythology, are not part of the main story nor do they serve as epigraphs to it (159), and the story they tell is that of Zulu culture (Newman 1981:32). Of course, they tell of a culture as filtered through the eyes of the missionary Canon Henry Callaway whose (unfinished) exposition of the Amazulu was published in 1868-70 and was the source for volume 6 of Frazer's *The Golden Bough,* on the Scapegoat. Therefore, instead of being the "voice" of the subaltern it is, in fact, a file from "The Imperial Archive."[5] This filtered Zulu culture is at first described as one of farming and praying and bringing up children. This first set of quotations precedes the sections of the main text that deal with the farm and the life of the laborers, including the problems associated with drought. The next set of quotations describes dreams, prophecies, and disappointments, and this comes just before the episodes in the main text that led to the strange attack on Solomon at night. Later, the quotations describe the Amatongo as ancestors beneath the earth, and this occurs soon after the strange reappearance of the dead man on Mehring's farm. Again, the quotations describe the ancestors themselves, pointing out that they have strange powers, including the bringing of rain. This precedes the description of the flood in the main text, a flood that dislodges the dead man again. Finally, the last set of quotations suggest that destiny and the black race will prevail so that when one black man dies, others, with other names, will take his place: "When he died, there arose others, who were called by other names" (Gordimer 1974:247). These quotations, or this voice, then, suggest that the persecuted, the dead, and the buried will eventually prevail and will always exert their presence, even when effaced.

However, this ancestral voice does not really exert a counter-hegemony over the dominant discourse, since, as Macaskill has argued, the Zulu myth itself is displaced, as it appears in the text in the form of "transliterated quotations" which are "wrenched out of context" by the Christian missionary, Callaway, in whose book they appear (Macaskill 1950:160). Thus, although this voice does interrupt the hegemony of imperialist discourse, it is "already contaminated" by Callaway's Calvinism and therefore is not really the "primal voice" of the subaltern at all (161). Rather, it is an abstracted voice, that speaks for the Zulus through the filter of a Western missionary: "The Amatongo, they who are beneath. Some natives say so called, because they have been buried beneath the earth. But we cannot avoid believing that we have an intimation of an old faith in a Hades or Tartarus, which has become lost and is no longer understood" (Gordimer 1974:163). However, the fundamental questions it raises about inheritance and presence lead us to assume that the implication at the end of the main narrative is correct; that is, that black man, the original, primal presence in

Africa, will ultimately assert his presence and prevail. Yet, this will not happen through a simple process of substituting one ideology with the other, since, as the quotations show, each is deeply influenced and contaminated by the other. Thus, the sense of balance at the end of the narrative seems to be achieved as a blending of voices, in which each voice influences and is influenced by the other. Finally, then, Gordimer's narrative suggests that the subaltern can only be made to speak through a process of constant displacement, with various levels of hegemony and counter-hegemony taking place at once. Ultimately, though, the hierarchies will always exist, even if in a state of flux, and this will always prevent the subaltern from being heard. More importantly, the hierarchies suggest that Gordimer herself will never be able to "give" the subaltern a voice, and the only power that she sees the African primal presence having is his refusal to stay buried. Thus, the dead man and the farm laborers seem like voiceless bodies because they are knowable only through Mehring's representation of them. So too, Antonia is objectified and her voice is filtered through Mehring's consciousness. Similarly, the black women are silent figures on the margins of Mehring's consciousness. Finally, the ancestors are really voices represented in an imperial archive. Thus, all four groups—black men, white women, black women, and ancient ancestors—seem less than human and powerless because they are given no narrative space outside imperial consciousness. There is no sense of empowerment at the end, then. Mehring-Antonia-Jacobus-black laborers-dead man-ancestors-Christian missionaries-Gordimer: one is always displacing or speaking for the other. Gordimer's use of a narrative style that involves constant interruption (Macaskill 1950:175), constant displacement, and constant fusion means that there can be no monolithic imperialist and no monolithic subaltern—each partakes of some of the qualities of the other.

Like Gordimer's narrative of constant displacement,

Sahgal's *The Day in Shadow* also uses a narrative pattern of constant displacement to depict the oppression and silencing of marginalized voices in Indian society. The chief object of concern is the subjective consciousness of the protagonist, Simrit, who is oppressed by her husband, Som, sexually, psychologically, and economically. As a result, she shuttles between, in Spivak's words, "subject and object status" (Spivak 1988a:306) as she is objectified and dominated by both Som and Raj. In her writings Sahgal seems to have been very interested in Simrit's kind of oppression and has voiced her dissent against the ideology of the patriarchy on many occasions. As she stated in an essay:

> even in a free country like ours where women are equal citizens, a woman can be criminally exploited without its creating a ripple....If at a divorce he [a man] inflicts a financial settlement on her [his wife] that enslaves her with taxes...no one will take any notice because this is a kind of beating where blood and bruises don't show. But in addition, and this is the crux of the matter—nobody bothers about it even when they do. (Arora 1991:97)

Despite these righteous sentiments, Sahgal is severely limited in her social criticism because her elite status keeps her removed from the daily contact with economic hardship and exploitation. The main hardship that she faced in her personal life was the trauma of divorce, which was a very unusual situation for an Indian woman, and which she successfully exposes in the novel. Simrit's emotional and financial agonies resulting from her divorce from Som, are, in fact, the central focus of the novel, and despite all the economic privileges she has, she is oppressed in the sense that she remains in social and psychological bondage to Som. As Jasbir Jain has suggested, freedom for Sahgal's characters is meant to be not just economic or social, but also emotional and physical (Jain 1978a:45). Jain points out that almost every central woman character in Sahgal's novels "moves toward an awareness of her emotional needs and reflects the writer's own life and sensibility" through uncertainty, bewilderment, suffering and self-questioning (Jain 1978b:61-65). Simrit does seem to go through this process of suffering and self-questioning, but she fails to "liberate" herself in any true sense of the word.

Although Som's presence dominates the discourse, it is really an indirect domination because we never hear his thoughts or see him in isolation—his voice is only heard through his interactions with others and through the impact he has on them. Most often, we hear him speak through Simrit's memories and through the third-person narrative voice. So his position is a reversal of Antonia's in *The Conservationist,* although he is more powerful than her. Overall, though, as his son Brij suggests, the impact he has on people is similar to that of intense heat: that is, he makes people "shrink and shrivel" (Sahgal 1972a:68) or produces in them "sharp and nagging pains" (71).

Som is presented in the text as not being very good with words, yet he nevertheless manages to silence most deviant viewpoints. Shyam Asnani believes that Som's voice is "too educated and formal for the brutal nature he is meant to personify [namely]...an unpleasant, old-style Englishman; a hard-drinking, swearing, bullying, country-squire type—a paper Heathcliff, so to say" (Asnani 1973:68). In my view, Som's voice is all external, and the reason we never hear his inner thoughts is because he doesn't have too many. As Simrit realizes, behind his exterior harshness there is actually nothing, because he is a man with a hard exterior but no moral core (Sahgal 1972a:79). He has no softness within that she can hold on to, because he has no other side. This harshness is also shown by his anger, which is most often directed toward Simrit. Indeed, it is in anger and in a spirit of vengeance that he draws up the terms of the divorce settlement (Consent Decree) and forces her to sign it.

Som's blatant manipulation of the divorce into a financial trap for Simrit is his way of avenging himself for her "walk out."

In fact, as Raj suggests, the terms of the settlement actually become a part of Som's psyche itself, and therefore resembled the kind of total destruction that must have happened after the bomb was dropped on Hiroshima (Sahgal 1972a:138). Raj's mentor, Ram Krishan, also sees the terms this way, calling them "needless destruction" (178-9).

Destructiveness and cruelty characterize Som throughout the novel. After the divorce, when Simrit tries to persuade him to change the Consent Terms, she realizes with a shock that he will not, simply because he has no pity or concern for her or for anyone else. Moreover, he abruptly takes custody of Brij and seems completely without guilt or remorse. From Raj's point of view, his cruelty translates as "atrocious bad manners—no consideration for the other person" (Sahgal 1972a:226). While that statement is as much a reflection of Raj's bourgeois sensibility as it is an indictment of Som, he (Som) does seem obsessed by "affluent arrogance, sensuality and utter lack of refinement...success and money at any cost are his goals in life" (Rao 1976:59). Overall, I believe his obsession with destruction and materialism is what distinguishes Som the most.

Som is also sexually aggressive and exploitative, regarding Simrit not as a partner, but as an object to be dominated. According to Simrit, most often he excludes her mentally while he flirts with her (Sahgal 1972a:27), so that when they have sex she feels imprisoned "within the act" (25). He seems unable to regard love-making as anything other than "just sex," and cannot relate it to the moods and emotions of everyday life. Hence, as Simrit slowly becomes more and more passive and remote from the sex act, Som becomes more and more abusive. In one scene, when Simrit realizes that his unscrupulously materialistic lifestyle is the cause of her acute unhappiness and the deadening of her sex drive, Som is annoyed. As the narrative voice tells us, he takes her sexual withdrawal personally and treats it as an assault on his manhood (90). As a result, he gives her an ultimatum: sex with him or an end to their relationship (97). The narrator tells us he feels no remorse in rejecting Simrit, pointing out that if sufficiently provoked, a man is entirely justified in even murdering his wife. "Either a woman wants you or she doesn't," he tells her, suggesting that if she doesn't, "the law" doesn't matter (28).

The very fact that we never hear Som's own voice or inner thoughts suggests that his speaking power is not absolute. Not only do we hear him only through the mediation of Simrit or Brij or the narrator, but his discourse is also undermined by the presence of Raj, who, without ever meeting him, "overcomes" him. Raj helps Simrit free herself from Som's stranglehold, but simultaneously obliterates her presence almost as effectively as does Som. Rather than speaking to her, he speaks for her. Unlike the case with Som, though, we do hear Raj's inner thoughts which are presented to us through the narrator or Simrit. And wise thoughts are, to Raj, almost as important as good actions because he believes that all Indians who are free thinkers should exercise their judgments for the wellbeing of society (Sahgal 1972a:106).

By profession a politician, Raj is a good talker, with genuine sympathy for the oppressed; he has socialist leanings; he believes and acts on his convictions and he is a born leader. He is presented in the narrative as a man who "looks like Mr. Right—albeit slightly Left—an idealistic politician...who seeks to integrate Hinduism with social progress" (Levin 1972:40). However, his attitude toward Simrit is rather ambivalent because, on the one hand, he wants her to be a complete individual and not a sex object, but on the other hand he orders her around and speaks for her, not to her. The ambivalence is caught in his stimulation of her inner, creative voice, and his stifling of her individuality.

As a statesman his ability to think originally and speak effectively is what distinguishes him the most from the other politicians. Even outside Parliament, he has the power to attract people by his discourse, and Simrit is no exception. As she recalls, when she heard him speak the first time, he had not spoken very loudly or for very long, but she felt he had expanded her knowledge greatly (Sahgal 1972a:18). What it reveals about himself is that he is an "impassioned" socialist in search of an Indian definition of socialism (18), and that he has the power to enable Simrit to "talk easily" (20) with him on a variety of topics. At any rate, he asks questions that interest her enough to think carefully about her replies, and she is attracted by his discourse. What attracts her in particular is his originality and his ability to flaunt this originality. She finds that he was slightly proud of his ideas in the same way as other men were proud of their clothes (100). Unfortunately, though, this brilliance has the power both to attract and to subdue, so that rather than producing a dialogue, he produces a monologue.

Unlike Som, however, Raj's ideas are usually motivated by ideals and beliefs that are not overtly materialistic. First, he has a positive attitude about life and people and is able to transmit that attitude to others. The narrator tells us that he "radiates" a sense of happiness and joy to Simrit during one of his early meetings with her, a sense that, she believes, surrounds her completely (Sahgal 1972a:7). On another occasion, when Simrit is carrying on a monologue inside her own head while listening to Raj, she finds that he has the power to almost literally give her a new life. As she realizes, his ideas could free her because she'd been like an old wooden statue in a Hindu temple who had now come to life (11). Second, Raj is not fatalistic and realizes that one doesn't have to accept one's lot in life unquestioningly (145). His involvement in Simrit's tax problem is a result, he claims, of "pure" conviction (that the taxes are grossly unfair), and not personal feelings. He believes that becoming extremely anguished over something outside oneself is the only way to mature (41). However, as the ending of the novel makes clear, his involvement in Simrit's problems is just as much a result of sexual attraction as it is outrage against injustice.

Simrit, too, seems to think that Raj's strength is his involvement in social welfare, but she views it as a means not of personal growth, but of public recognition. In one scene, she muses to herself that Raj was going to make it big in the political arena because he was a born leader and educator (Sahgal 1972a:236). This seems to suggest a dominating rather than supporting role in her life. And indeed, he does dominate her, giving her orders, scolding and trying to jolt her into activity. Although he claims that what he wants is not "Simrit for himself" but "Simrit for herself" (167), yet he finds it necessary to dictate to her the ways and means of doing that. At social gatherings, for example, he talks for her, "covering her silence" with the sound of his own voice (7). However, more disturbing than his casual drowning out of her voice is his control over her actions at the end of the novel, such as the way he casually announces to Ram Krishan that they are going to get married (231). This announcement alarms Simrit because she is not ready for marriage and does not expect Raj to force her to make a choice so soon. In this episode, as well as in others, Raj silences her individuality as effectively as does Som. In fact, as Arora suggests, Raj appears to be the "angelic" protector, but "somewhere deep down, the patriarchal attitudes are embedded in...[him] too" (Arora 1991:96). The redeemer, then, helps but also silences Simrit.

Simrit's voice is therefore effaced in the text. She seems to assert her presence only through indirection, such as when she watches herself in a mirror and sees herself acting the part of perfect hostess for her husband's guests, with a completely blank expression on her face (Sahgal 1972a:86). Through most of the action she is either being abused by Som or is suffering from guilt at having left him, and this prompts Margaret E. Derrett (1973) to call her a "passive pawn in a game, seeking escape from even *that* limited share of reality. She is not even nostalgic for a structured past, but an escapist" (727). Derrett also claims that Simrit's dilemma is "largely self engineered" (278) and that "she seems to suffer from prolonged emotional shock" (278). I would argue that she is primarily a fragmented personality who is silenced, static, and sexually abused.

Simrit is a fragmented personality in that she feels lost, without bearings, emotionally torn to pieces and isolated. The narrator tells us, she is a cultured brahmin married to a callous businessman, by her own choice, and this is a significant point because it reveals the narrator's, and perhaps even Sahgal's, caste-bias. The narrator describes the differences in outlook that the two castes give them, suggesting that it prompts Simrit into hiding or protecting her own personality traits. As Som's wife, she has no real sense of purpose beyond being a good hostess and mother, and she frequently sees herself as abandoned (Sahgal 1972a:6). To others like Raj and Ram Krishan, she appears to be a person with no forceful traits, passively waiting for something (174). More importantly, she is fragmented because after the divorce she feels as if she'd been cut to pieces and left out in the cold (16). Often, this feeling of not being completely whole recurs in her dreams, where she finds out that her body was full of broken bones and nerves (51). Like a victim who feels guilty for having pain inflicted upon her, she waits, both in sleep and when awake, for "the pain to catch up with her" (52). The cause of all this fragmentation is, of course, Som, who, she believes, is so obsessed with materialism that he does not even recognize how rotten he has become. Som's single-minded pursuit of wealth and "self-advancement" (89) withers Simrit's will to live creatively and actively. Although she does appear to be creative and active at the end of the novel, due to Raj's ministrations, this is illusory because she is unable to find her own voice.

Both Raj and Som frequently exclude Simrit from their discourse. So she muses to herself, "Som's world had been commerce, never shared with her at all. And here was politics, utterly confusing" (Sahgal 1972a:12). This exclusion by both men is deliberate and not just a result of indifference, and Simrit herself seems unwilling to take any initiative to include herself despite male opposition. The end result is that she never achieves a sense of direction, even when she moves out of Som's house. Instead, she withdraws into herself and isolates herself from the outside world completely by giving herself up to sorrow and negativity (76). This negativity takes the place of human contact, and although she claims that it provides her with a source of "contentment" (76), yet it is essentially a negation of communication. This lack of communication and resulting fragmentation leads, as the narrator tells us, to a nervous breakdown, which Som is unable to understand. We see Simrit's agony through Som's perspective, as he complains to his friends that he cannot understand why she is so unhappy and confesses that she strikes him as a highly-strung child who needs pacifying,, someone to be pitied and comforted (78).

Besides being fragmented, Simrit is also static and objectified, passive and unassertive. Whether she is described by Som, Raj, or the narrative voice, the overwhelming impression of her is that of an unquestioning dumb animal, and she herself acknowledges that she'd been treated all the while like a well-trained domestic pet who obeyed orders and was therefore well fed (Sahgal 1972a:57). After her divorce she becomes less a domestic animal and more a prey for parasites because the burden of taxes would "feed" off of her (59). Even Raj objectifies her because he treats her as if she were a "sapling, something separate to be planted and watered" (139). Overall, then, despite her intelligence, she becomes, in the discourse, the stereotypical "Hindu woman" who has no rights except those that men give her voluntarily (168). Even the fact that she is a creative writer with the ability to describe external nature minutely doesn't alter the fact that she speaks to us only through the viewpoints of others.

In fact, we never find out what she writes about, except that it has something to do with nature. She remains, in the discourse, as a "shadow" (136), stuck in time, unable to remove herself from the past nor do anything positive in the present (139). Her only accomplishment is that she does free herself from Som's psychological domination in that she partially overcomes her feelings of self-pity, guilt, and fear (181).

Related to her condition of being fragmented and objectified is the fact that she is always silenced in the discourse. Quiet by nature, she dislikes "talking about things that mattered deeply" (Sahgal 1972a:6). Som encourages her silence by excluding her completely from his world, making it obvious that he wants her only for sex and that he wants his business transactions to be a secret even from his closest friends (46). Most often, though, he just doesn't care enough to talk to her about anything, so that Simrit realizes that she urgently needed someone she could talk to about books and ideas (93). The implication is, of course, that even if she were to talk freely, neither Som nor Raj would listen to her; moreover, she is so conditioned to waiting for their approval that she seems unable to initiate talk on her own. In fact, at social gatherings Raj speaks for her; and when they are together by themselves, he talks and she listens: "you came into my garden that day to hear me *talk*" he tells her, and she replies, "I used to get quite desperate for it" (159). Clearly then, although Raj doesn't shut her out like Som does, he doesn't help much in creating dialogue. Even when he asks her soul-searching questions, he doesn't wait very long to get answers. Most damaging of all, he assumes that her attitudes are like his. Toward the end of the novel when he suddenly decides that they are going to get married, Simrit wonders what he's getting at, since he hasn't discussed it with her (231). She remembers that they had decided that all important decisions would be made of her choice and at her leisure (232). Raj tries to justify his domination on the grounds that he needed a witness for his announcement, and because it is hard to get a Hindu to verbalize a commitment, but that is unconvincing. Being able to speak, then, becomes a necessary condition to set Simrit free. As Rao (1976) suggests, "communication, discussion and dialogue...are all celebrated in her [Sahgal's] work as the necessary accessories to freedom in action" (70).

Finally, Simrit is frequently unaware of the extent to which men sexually abuse her. To Raj her ignorance stems from her being a typically passive and docile Hindu woman, who cannot do things for herself even though she is educated (Sahgal 1972a:37). Raj's comment here seems to stereotype Hindus and/or Hindu women and he seems very much a member of the Westernized "comprador bourgeoisie" compared to, say, Ram Krishan. Som does not stereotype her, but he treats her like a body, often squeezing and caressing her body parts at the same time as he shuts her out of his conversation. Rather than being tender towards her, he thinks of her as a tasty "peach" (27), so that when he kisses her in the presence of his friend, she feels a sense of fear (84). Sex, for her, includes tenderness and humor (90), but for him, becomes a means to exert his will. As a result, when she begins to physically recoil from him he tells her that they should end the relationship (98). The implication, of course, is that she should produce sex on demand, and if she doesn't, she should be dismissed.

With Raj, she experiences a more communicative sexual relationship, but for all his attempts to let her develop her own personality, he leads and she follows. Because she is attracted by his mind and his body, she is able to achieve a combination of love and friendship (Sahgal 1972a:182), which, as both she and Ram Krishan believe, is the strongest bond possible between people. Despite this, she seems unable to develop an independent personality, believing instead, that they must have been lovers in a previous life since they are able to get so intimate so quickly (206). At best, it is a relationship that involves a sort of partnership in which sex becomes an emotional as well as physical act, not just a power game (207). Overall, then, in recognizing Simrit's individuality and in helping her overcome her fear and numbness, Raj is a positive influence in Simrit's life; but in organizing her life according to his desires and in speaking for her, he is a destructive influence on her, a milder version of Som. Sahgal does not seem to recognize the destructiveness of Raj's influence, or that of other "benevolent" males like him. The destructiveness of the benevolent male, including his suppression of female self-expression and his concept of leadership from above, are not problematized in Sahgal's narrative. As such, Simrit remains silenced and somewhat fragmented even at the end of the novel.

Behind Simrit there are her four children; their voices also interrupt, but are silenced by the male-dominated discourse. They are so severely repressed that they only assert their presence through absence. Curiously, though, their interactions mirror those of the adults, so that the boy, Brij, is more vocal and aggressive, while the girl, Jaya, is quiet and undemanding. As for the two younger girls, they are only objects of pity with no faces, no personalities, and no names.

Brij is, in many ways, a clone of his father, liking power, affluence, and violence and overcoming the pain of being at once favored and neglected. He loves the opulence and control in his father's office, thinking it "beautiful" (Sahgal 1972a:67). Money and authority, he believes, provide security because they protect one against disruption and pain (68). In his father's office, in fact, he ceases to be an individual, and becomes a miniature Som, feeling confident and successful (68). Also, he tries to be aggressive like his father, whom he sees as a successful destroyer of enemies (69). He, too, believes in battering people physically and mentally, telling Simrit that he does a good job of thrashing people he doesn't like. Like his father, too, he ignores the emotional trauma associated with this reliance on power and violence and finds ways to stop up his emotional hurts (71). The pains are also due to the fact that as the only son he is favored and given twice the inheritance of his three sisters combined, yet he is also neglected when his father has no time for him. Som's secretary comments about this situation accurately when she complains that rich people believe they've taken good care of their children if they gave them generous amounts of money after they died (214).

Jaya is more unassuming, but also seems to possess more of Som's qualities than Simrit's.   She likes money and possessions, Simrit tells us, and reads glossy magazines full of glamorous advertisements (Sahgal 1972a:65). As for the other two girls, they do not even appear as complete individuals, being referred to as "the children" (62) or "the litter" (157) because Simrit believes that they are still part of herself (62). Silenced by Simrit as well as by the men, they are silent spectators in the adult discourse.

Behind the children, again, are the voices of the servants and laborers and prostitutes who neither speak nor participate in the action and only make their presences felt through effacement and contrast. They lurk in the shadows, spoken to and viewed by the characters and the narrative voice as little better than animals. These shadowy shapes in the margins of the discourse constantly undermine the ideas of material and social progress espoused by Som and Raj.   Indeed, these creatures are not silent merely because they speak indirectly and suggestively, but also because none of the others can really understand and appreciate the horror of their lives.

Simrit, for example, sees her domestic servant as a "dark shape" which does not even reflect clearly in a mirror, being neither in motion nor immobile, and even when she realizes he is a human being, she thinks of him as a "dark moth" which is drawn close to them every time food needs to be served (Sahgal 1972a:86). And she is unable to hear them speak, she can only imagine how it must be like to be a poor, abandoned child, with little food and no place to call home (87). Raj, too, realizes they are voiceless but is also unable to make them speak, philosophizing that the average Indian tended not to act very aggressively to make changes to his/her life. He thinks that if the average passive Indian didn't do something soon, brutal and more aggressive Indians would do something violent, very suddenly (43). His own inability to "wake them up" lies partly in the fact that he sees social progress as an expansion in Delhi's upper middle class' buying power, so that he rejoices when locally grown mushrooms and cheeses become hot commodity items (43).

As for Som, he doesn't even regard the servants and laborers as human, condemning the Partition of India for the losses his family sustained in jewelry and carpets, and completely ignoring the human tragedy of the refugees outside, who have lost everything and whose future looks hopeless (Sahgal 1972a:24). And then there are politicians like Sumer Singh who view them as animals to be beaten. He tells a prostitute that even in the next century the average Indian farmer would still be completely servile and childlike in terms of getting his basic necessities, seeming no better than cattle (100). This is the perspective of an upper class politician who has never experienced hardship nor had to struggle to make ends meet. Of course, he realizes they have their value, too; thus, when he wants to use one of them for sex, he chooses one (Pixie) who has only a body and no mind or voice, and who appears and disappears instantly, as if by magic (111). However, when Pixie tries to use her mind and questions his political decisions, he is annoyed; and when she becomes an unwilling sex partner, he strips her of her livelihood (her job and house) and puts her on the streets.

The only way the Indian subaltern seems to have any impact on the discourse at all is through the creation of atmosphere, that is, by threatening to disrupt the status quo, or, what Raj describes as a vague sense of uneasiness.   This translates as the threat of strikes and mutinies, resulting in "terror and a rigid system" (Sahgal 1972a:230). The pressure that the subaltern exerts on the patriarchal discourse of the main text, then, is a dark sense of unease that threatens the neo-colonizer's voice indirectly.   This presence-in-absence is never really explored or revealed, and is even less effective at "speaking" than the body of the dead man in *The Conservationist.*   Finally, there is one further level of displacement in the text, namely, the interruption of nature. First, there is geographic nature, which is presented as a kind of ideal, a renewal, but is also so romanticized that the renewal seems empty. For one thing, Simrit is the only character who can sense its presence, but when she tries to articulate this, she makes it appear almost too good to be true— ancient mountains, "ecstatic" rivers, immense oceans and diverse plains (Sahgal 1972a:35-36). Sahgal herself does not seem to be as critical of this romanticism as we, the readers, are. Simrit, for example, summarizes it as an "inheritance" which has no beginning and no end, and is capable of renewing itself constantly (36). She is filled with a desire to put words to this inheritance, because it gives her a sense of calm, of freedom, that makes her absurdly happy. This elemental presence provides a means for her to forget her problems, but because she divorces the land from the people on it and because she is unable really to make it speak or be relevant to everyday living, she fails to make it anything but a presence in the background, a shadow.

The same is true of religious nature. In the text, archetypal Hindu nature is presented as that which exists before and after everything else and which provides the solution to all the political, social, and personal problems. It is a "blend of Nature and human situation" (Rao 1976:67), being partly the Hindu character and partly the amoral state of political life in Delhi. It is therefore a presence that is not really understood and must be "made to speak," as it were, in order to have an impact. In particular, it must be shown with all its hypocrisies and idiosyncracies, yet clearly no one, not even Sahgal, is able to do that.   As Sahgal said in a radio talk, the religious/political atmosphere of the novel took on a life of its own, independent of her agency: "While I was writing *The Day in Shadow* the whole political atmosphere of the book became so strong and overwhelming, it almost became another character, with a life of its own" (Sahgal 1974:41-44).

Raj, the Christian, regards the Hindu nature as almost indecipherable, because it is static and unchanging, and all experiences ultimately link back to two thousand years of civilization (Sahgal 1972a:103).   Here, Raj appears not just a member of a minority religion but a spokesman for the comprador bourgeoisie, which tends to stereotype the "other" in terms such as these.   To Raj, the Hindu religion appears endless, with thousands of "crevices" and "folds," which confound philosophers because rather than leading up to a concrete belief system, it leads to pluralism or the "endless spongelike capacity to absorb" (13). This view is strengthened by the many examples in the text of socially-sanctioned religious hypocrisies, such as the removal of liquor from parties in which the tee-totaling Minister of State for Petroleum is expected, or the use of Gandhian icons by politicians who have long since abandoned non violence and non-materialistic ideals as their political slogans (Rao 1976:56).

On the other hand, Ram Krishan views Hindu/Indian nature as eminently decipherable, because the religion is dynamic and creative.   He admits that since the Hindu approach involves existence and acceptance, it is in danger of stagnating, especially since it posits that God, with His complete vision, regards the universe as good, so all evil, including poverty and disease, are illusionary.   Yet, like any other religion, the primary focus is on "devotion to the good" (Sahgal 1972a:201), and that "awareness of good" is pervasive in Hindu society (201), but has as yet not produced results.   The problem, then, according to Ram Krishan, is how to make this belief in goodness produce concrete results.

One way he suggests this be done is to make evil or wrong matter enough that Indians will want to fight it; that is, use the basic ingredients of Hinduism to resist evil so that Hinduism will provide the "stamina" or "sticking point" (234). And the best way, according to him, to do that is not through reading and practicing religious books and rituals, but through "character and example" (235).

 While Raj is correct on a day-to-day, mundane level, Ram Krishan is correct on an abstract or philosophical level. The essential solution, then, that the text seems to espouse, or rather the essential balance that will bring about the "new order," is to make religious philosophy work on a more mundane, day-to-day level. However, the constant displacement in the discourse of the text does not lead to this kind of workaday philosophy because the neo-colonizing and silencing forces represented by Som and Raj are not effectively countered. The novel also makes it clear that India is no longer "the land of Faith" which contains all "contradictions tenderly, peacefully" (Sahgal 1972a:196). In this regard, closing the novel on the level of Hindu philosophy is overly simplistic and ineffective, because what is left after all the series of displacements is a vaguely defined spirit of religious tolerance or social integrity. That is, the implication is that no matter what sexual and economic injustices exist in Indian society today, they will sometime in the future be countered by character and religion. Rather than integrating the personal with the political, as Rao suggests (1976:64), this ending fails to make any of the subalterns speak. Simrit can only make herself heard partially, while the servants and laborers cannot be heard at all. Yet they all cast an uncanny shadow on the narrative. The final voice of authority and renewal is therefore a vacuum, with no substance at all.

 Like Sahgal's notion of Hindu-ness and Gordimer's motif of the dead African who refuses to stay buried, Emecheta's *The Bride Price* falls back on a concept of orality that is valuable chiefly in the "discussion it [a story] generates after it is told" (Ward 1990:88). More importantly, the value of this orality in the context of Emecheta's theme is that it reveals how effectively traditional superstitions and taboos have replaced traditional wisdoms and how they enforce their pressures on individuals by psychological and emotional torture.

The primary focus of *The Bride Price* is the social and economic bases of patriarchal exploitation in the town of Ibuza in the 1950s. Overall, the novel highlights some important aspects of life in the '50s: education, gender relations, rural and urban problems (Taiwo 1984:106). One aspect that gets particular attention is the relationship between "communal will and Aku-nna's own strength of will" (Brown 1981:49), as well as specific customs that cause problems for women (Ward 1990:93). More importantly, the novel's narrative also shows how "women's and men's perceptions of these customs are continually changing, depending on the speaker's age, roles, audience, and subject" (93). In this context, it is important to remember the interactive nature of the narrative because it highlights the idea that "just as an oral language cannot be separated from its speakers, in Ibuza, status, value, and self cannot be separated or alienated from the context that gives them significance: other people" (94).

Okonkwo, Aku-nna's uncle and step-father, speaks in the narrative with the weight of traditional male authority. This voice expects obedience from others, especially women, and erases deviant viewpoints by coercion. In the narrative, this power to assert his will is emphasized to the exclusion of everything else so that some critics have described him, along with other patriarchs in her other novels, as "one-sided and flat" (Uyoh 1981: 34) or as "villains, at best caricatures" (Emenyonu 1988:131). Okonkwo's almost caricaturish authoritarian role is commented on by the third person narrator in a scene in which Okonkwo and Aku-nna face off after a visit from her beloved Chike. The narrator claims that Okonkwo's voice is that of legal authority whose power is linked to the weight of tradition, a power from which Aku-nna can never free herself (Emecheta 1976:116). Indeed, the novel as a whole shows how traditional customs are used as "institutionalized forms of male oppression" (Frank 1982:483), and here Okonkwo acts as the spokesman of that oppression. The one-sidedness of his authoritarian voice is also apparent in the fact that he never participates in the discourse except as spokesman for tradition. In general, his is a voice that is loud and decisive, that wields the force of traditional law behind him, that commands obedience, that bends local rituals and beliefs to suit his own purposes, and that silences opposition.

At several stages in the narrative, Okonkwo loudly reminds his family that his word is law. For example, he points out that Ezekiel, his younger brother, must obey his commands if he decides that it is time that Ma Blackie (Ezekiel's wife) must leave the village and return to the city (Emecheta 1976:49). At other times, he enforces his will more subtly. For example, when Ma Blackie, now married to him, becomes pregnant with his child, he knows she will do whatever he commands, without him having to enforce any rules (115). At the same time, he expects quick and unwavering obedience and is also firm in his belief that the traditional customs are the best. Thus he orders Ma Blackie to cure her supposed infertility by purifying herself in the Oboshi river, and later marries her so that her daughter's bride price could come to him (72). Personally, he wants to use the money to get himself a title ("Eze") and become a respected elder.

Okonkwo is also a dangerous man when angered. He uses traditional practices like "black magic" to wreak vengeance on Aku-nna when she prevents him from collecting her bride price by marrying Chike. First, he divorces Ma Blackie publicly (Emecheta 1976:155), and then he uses a doll made to look like Aku-nna to torture her. The impact of all this is, of course, more psychological than real, but Okonkwo claims that he is able to call Aku-nna back to Ibuza through the wind. In fact, psychologically, this is very effective, because Aku-nna seems to "hear" his voice and succumbs to fear. Curiously, the religious forces he uses are presented as an exclusively male prerogative, and Emecheta seems to exclude women from having any power in religion. Overall, then, Okonkwo is the stereotypical African patriarch: oppressive, authoritarian, selfish, and cruel, who speaks with the weight of tradition and custom, and commands obedience.

Chike Ofulue is Aku-nna's "redeemer," but unlike Raj in *The Day in Shadow* his strength lies not in his ability to talk but in his ability to understand and remain silent. He is respectful and understanding, loves Aku-nna for herself, and wants to make her happy, but like Raj he is an outcast who ultimately fails to "rescue" her from the power of the patriarchy. Although he is able to reduce Okonkwo's powers by freeing Aku-nna temporarily, his voice is displaced by the power of traditional authority because he is the son of slaves.[6]

Chike's ability to respect and understand other viewpoints is reflected in his actions as well as his speech. Aku-nna articulates this ability when she points out that she loves him for his kindness, his understanding nature, and his respect for other people (Emecheta 1976:149). Katherine Frank suggests that the reason Chike is is so sensitive to the oppression of women is because he experiences the same oppression himself as the son of slaves (Frank 1982:485). Lloyd W. Brown echoes the same idea in suggesting that when Aku-nna marries Chike, "Emecheta's narrative analogy between women and slaves is underscored by the sexual union: both groups are denied full equality with the males of 'free' families and both are subjected to restrictive taboos" (Brown 1981:52). More importantly, as the narrator tells us, his voice itself is melodious and calm (Emecheta 1976:67). In fact, it is a generally good humored voice, but one that can also become soft and sad: "low, sad voice...[and] eyes which mirror[ed] all the worries in his mind" (111). Finally, his voice disappears altogether for large sections of the action, because Chike himself is silent by nature (105).

Despite Chike's love of silence, he is able to articulate his love for Aku-nna and, strangely, he falls in love with her at first because of her helplessness. He realizes he pities her because she is "so dependent, so unsure of herself, so afraid of her own people" (Emecheta 1976:80). Reciprocally, she likes his ability to make her feel "treasured and loved" through his actions rather than in words (82). Clearly, silence is very effective at expressing their love, especially since they cannot openly verbalize it because of the taboos that forbid it. Therefore, Chike relies on actions to speak his love, so that the gentleness can show through: "He touched her breasts, the way a suitor might, not the way the rough boys squeezed them just for fun" (97). Throughout, his actions and speech reveal that he regards her as chaste and unsullied (104). Silence is also the chosen medium for expressing their fears about social acceptance of their love, so that when they both realize it will be hard to come by, he sits "mutely" and she stops asking questions (108).

On the few occasions when Chike does use his voice, it is usually in argument with someone else regarding Aku-nna, such as when he tells his father to "keep his money" because he will not go to the university to study unless Aku-nna is with him (Emecheta 1976:105). At most other times, however, he relies on actions rather than verbal arguments, such as when he punches Okoboshi in the face for hurting Aku-nna, and when he rescues Aku-nna after she has been kidnapped. When he rescues her, he literally seems to bring her "back to life" from death (145). And after their marriage, he relies on love-making rather than words to express their love, and he teaches her how to participate in the love-making so that they both can get pleasure from it (154).

Despite all his strengths and convictions, however, Chike ultimately fails to rescue Aku-nna from the stranglehold of superstition, mainly because he himself is an outcast from Ibuza society. Referred to in the text most often as "not one of us" (Emecheta 1976:70) and the "son of slaves" (79), he is subjected to prejudice and sexual segregation. All this is due to what the narrator presents as an arbitrary twist of fate; that is, a princess's (his grandmother's) capture and subsequent relegation to slavery, resulting in all her descendants becoming known as slaves. Currently a highly educated and cultured family of teachers, doctors, and lawyers, they are   nevertheless still ostracized as *oshu* or sons of slaves. This fact of slave descent prevents Chike and Aku-nna from getting social approval, and even when Chike disregards the disapproval and marries her anyway, the prejudice ultimately catches up with him. Aku-nna, he realizes, is plagued by feelings of guilt and depression, to which she finally succumbs. Clearly, the son of a slave—for all his money and education, his sincerity and integrity—is no match for the voice of authority.

Aku-nna is a subaltern not because of her social class, but because of her gender.   She is static and homogenized, silenced and sexually violated.   Her marriage against social customs brings, on herself and her family, social disgrace, exile, and death.   In much of the narrative she stands bewildered, in Taiwo's words, at a "cultural crossroads" (Taiwo 1984:107), enslaved by traditional rules and taboos (Frank 1982:483). Under male scrutiny, she appears insecure and silent, her main distinguishing feature being, according to the narrator, "gentle helplessness" and silence (Emecheta 1976:119).   Hers is a fragmented personality and the first view of her in the text is that of someone who is lost. In Lagos, the one person who seems to understand her is her father, but when he dies, she is left "frightened" and "hypnotized" (12), grief stricken and disoriented. These fears arise because without a man, a family is thought to be lost.   As the third-person narrator explains, a family without a father ceases to be a family (28). Part of Aku-nna's feelings of being lost arises from the fact that she is very insecure through most of the novel. Thus, when she moves back to Ibuza from

Lagos, she and her brother become even more confused (82). In fact, Aku-nna never properly adjusts to all the social rituals and taboos of Ibuza, becoming confused and unhappy, or, in Chike's words, "afraid of her own people" (82). The only person she can depend on is Chike, and she ends up leaning on him so much that when he considers leaving Ibuza without her, she feels devastated: "if he left, left her here alone in this town, she would be heartbroken. She would be lost, like the ants without their tracks" (91).

Another distinguishing feature is her loneliness. In one scene, she breaks down in school, sits under a tree, and reflects on her lonely life. She counts off all the people she needs who are not there for her, including her father, mother, and brother, and concludes that she has no one to go to for help (Emecheta 1976:89). Like Simrit, she seems unable to communicate, so that she thinks that even if she had their attention she would not be able to explain any clear reasons to them as to why she feels so unhappy. Chike provides solace and companionship both before and after she marries him, and her feelings of loneliness do subside then. However, even after her marriage, she remains insecure and is troubled by feelings of guilt and depression. Rather than making the most of her companionship and prosperity, she becomes afraid and begins to hear voices. The voices she hears are those of her own people, condemning her for her unpaid bride price, and this alarms her so much that she is afraid to be by herself after a while. She keeps hearing a voice that repeatedly commands her to return to her own people (163). Only Chike and his father are able to rationalize that the voices are not real, but are actually psychological pressures imposed on her by the weight of custom. But the fact that social custom has such a hold over her suggests that she has been indoctrinated into believing and fearing taboos and warnings. Fear, then, is the key to the power of these customs, the narrator suggests, and "that was the intention behind all the taboos and customs. Anyone who contravened them was better dead" (141). These powerful voices seem to "suck her blood" till she dies in labor due to weakness induced by anemia. As Brown suggests, she literally "dies of the fear that the curse will be effective, and on this basis her death flows from the novel's central thesis: that fate or destiny in its most significant sense is not based on the mysterious predispositions of inscrutable supernatural forces, but on the function of social institutions and the shaping patterns of cultural traditions" (49).

Besides being fragmented, Aku-nna is also listless and without a sense of purpose. Just as Simrit realizes she is valued by her husband only for sex, so too, Aku-nna realizes that the only reason she is tolerated by her community is because of her bride price. Both situations are, in fact, very similar.

From her childhood, Aku-nna is physically weak and frail. Made to feel insignificant because of her gender and her small build, she is frequently scolded by her mother for being unable to decide whether she was going to die or remain alive (Emecheta 1976:9). Even when she is an adult, her listlessness is mystifying to her relatives, so that again, they conclude that she must be an *ogbanje* (79). "Sickly," "fragile," and "delicate" are the words used most often to describe her. Frequently, too, she is commodified into an object for sale, since society in general values her solely for the money she will bring them with through her bride price. As Katherine Frank argues, in the novel, women are seen mainly as "marketable commodities" (Frank 1982:484).[7] First her father and then her uncle want her bride price money, while her cousins complain that educating her is a waste of money.

Part of the reason why Aku-nna is so passive in the face of all this oppression is because she is silenced and unable to articulate the terms of her oppression. Like Antonia, she speaks only through absence because she is quiet by nature and because her inner voice (or *chi*) needs a respondent in order to be able to communicate (Ward 1990:88). Even when she is happy she seldom talks, a condition which to her relatives seems unnatural and eerie, but which the narrator explains was a result of her desire to "listen to [her]...heart" (Emecheta 1976:105). However, the reasons for her silence seem more developed in the narrative than Simrit's are in hers. In the scene of her father's death, for example, after having been encouraged to express her grief loudly and somewhat artificially, she promptly loses her voice. The effort at self-expression seems to overwhelm her and, without a voice, her real sorrow remains within her, oppressing her with its weight (37). One could conclude that her abilities to articulate her status as subaltern are limited. Even questioning it seems difficult, given the discouragement she experiences about asking too many questions. Faced with no outlet to vent her anxieties, she retreats into submissiveness that translates as a preference for death over retaliation against abuse. What makes Aku-nna's silence even more significant is the fact that her inner voice, *chi* is also stifled and oppressed. At the end of the novel, her inner voice is completely erased by Okonkwo's accusing her of betrayal.

Finally, Aku-nna seems to be in perpetual physical violation. Although she is not actually raped, her body is violated and abused by men in other ways. As an adolescent, she fears sexual violation and prefers death to sexualcontact with strange men. She reacts to the onset of menstruation with fear and disgust, not just because of the pain and messiness, but also because of her fear of being forced into sex because she is now fully mature and can be married off to any man, even against her will (Emecheta 1976:92). To her, puberty and sexual awareness means a change in lifestyle and attitude, and this makes her afraid. The fact that Okoboshi, whom she hates, has the power to rape her when he kidnaps her horrifies her so much that she hopes to die. In fact, the rape does take place verbally, if not physically, when it is articulated by Okoboshi's family. They warn her that if she resists Okoboshi's sexual   advances, drunk male family members would enter the room and pull her legs apart so that Okoboshi can have sex with her. They add that the men would not be reprimanded, either (135). Notably, this statement also shows how much she has been 1982:484). Later, she is uncomfortable with even Chike's love-making, and trembles in fear the first time (Emecheta 1976:153). When she becomes pregnant, her body is unable to cope.   In a somewhat melodramatic death-bed scene she tells Chike to rejoice in their daughter and then dies in a fit of trembling (167).

Overall, then, Aku-nna experiences the worst kinds of physical violation: exile, ill health, and death. She is defeated by a patriarchal society that consistently subdues her by fragmenting her personality, silencing her inner voice, and forcing her into sexual violation. Even after her death, her community exercises over her a "psychological hold" (Emecheta 1976:168) which influences opinion against her. As Frank suggests, her death is "appropriated by the very power she sought to overcome, and is perverted into a threatening exemplary tale to coerce and intimidate women into obedience to traditional society and the men who rule it" (Frank 1982:486).

Behind Aku-nna's voice there are the voices of her mother and brother, which are also partially erased and unable to make themselves heard. Ma Blackie is little more than a pawn in patriarchal power politics and is always subject to male authority. She has no inner voice with which to contravene its laws and is subservient to the whims of her two husbands. She is passive, compliant, dominated, and silenced. She rarely disobeys male authority unless an emergency requires it. So when she hears that Ezekiel, her first husband, is ill, she decides for once to contradict her brother-in-law Okonkwo's wishes, and leaves Ibuza. Later, when she is "inherited" by that same brother-in- law, and becomes his fourth wife, she has even less authority. Although she is somewhat independent financially, she has no will or time of her own. She would acquiesce to Okonkwo rather than upset him (Emecheta 1976:111), and is therefore "passive" (116) to his commands. Even when Aku-nna is kidnapped, she is not permitted to make any decisions regarding her future. Most damaging of all, she uses Chike as a "tool" or a convenient support to get them through a troubling time in their lives (122), and then rejects him when Okonkwo disapproves. Overall, in her desire for acceptance and recognition by patriarchal authorities, in her worries about breaking customs and taboos, and in her emotional dependence on Okonkwo: she is oppressed, inarticulate, and complicitous in her own and her daughter's oppression. She is complicitous because, as a victim heself, she has somehow internalized and then perpetuated the oppression she experienced.

Nna-nndo's is also a marginalized voice, although he does have the potential to speak with the voice of authority later in life. In the narrative, his voice is muted because he is frightened by his father's death and becomes disoriented during the abrupt transition to Ibuza. Nevertheless, he is somewhat privileged because his gender exempts him from certain abuses and he is spoiled and lazy. He is also intolerant of Aku-nna's sickliness and echoes his mother's words when she keeps falling sick, saying cruelly that she seems unable to make up her mind about whether she is alive or dead (Emecheta 1976:95). Yet he stands up for her when she is shunned by the community, and he is able to distinguish the truth from the lies. When she is kidnapped, he "speaks back" to her kidnappers and warns them of dire consequences. He also supports her when she is dying but is unable to do more than cry. Basically, he is powerless to effect any change.

The real subalterns in the novel are the poor village women who are economically exploited and socially abused. They don't speak much and hover in the margins of the discourse. Although they have a lot of potential as a voice of the collectivity or orality, they are not developed much as speakers. They are described as working hard all day carrying heavy baskets on their heads, or selling their wares in the markets, yet they also have the ability to offer words of sympathy to other unfortunate women when needed. They are all fairly young, and those among them that are not very healthy suffer a lot. The narrator tells us in passing that in Ibuza, many teenaged girls died during labor and their deaths were very painful (Emecheta 1976:79). Those among them who commit terrible sins are thrown into the "bad bush" (128) and excluded from the "quality of ease" that comes with communal living. These poor women don't voice any opinions and are silent reminders of what can happen to girls like Aku-nna.

At a further level of displacement there is a another voice, namely, a third-person narrator who tries to explain all the cultural customs and taboos of the community, but ends up erasing its own authority. This voice interrupts the narrative very frequently to explain actions or events, and the degree of explanation suggests that the listeners must know nothing about Ibuza culture. In this context, it is useful to remember what Emecheta herself has frequently stated, that is, that she writes both for a Western and an African audience (Emenyonu 1988:131). Examples of cultural explanations abound in the narrative. The voice comments and explains Ibuza social interactions, Ibuza family responsibilities, eating habits, mourning and death ceremonies, and marriage and fertility rituals. These descriptions are significant because they appear in the text at the same time as Aku-Nna herself becomes aware of them, through a series of dramatic episodes (Brown 1981:50). For example, she knows nothing about death until her father dies, and then her experience of the death ceremonies makes her realize that death is not only inevitable but that it can result in the dead man's widow and children being transferred to the brother. Similarly, the beginning of her menstrual cycle marks the onset of her physical maturity as a woman as well as her first taste of unhappiness with the significance of that maturity in her culture.

More importantly, though, this narrative voice seems to be entrusted with the ideal of the community and, in this regard, at first appears to function rather like the ancestors in *The Conservationist*. Also, this voice explains another area of Aku-nna's ignorance: the impact of group psychology. As the voice suggests, Aku-nna didn't know that the people of Ibuza have what is known as "the group mind" in that they all think and do things in exactly the same way, and don't ever consider changing them (Emecheta 1976:16). By contrast, the narrator implies, its own voice is knowledgeable about both Ibuza customs and Western psychology. Ernest Emenyonu would go so far as to call this voice one that indulges in "anthropological discussions" (1988:132), and this idea is corroborated by the next comment, which describes how mixed-up Ibo culture can become when it is slightly removed from Ibuza: it becomes a mixture of traditional African and European traditions so much so that sometimes people would be confused about where exactly their loyalties lay (Emecheta 1976:29). This is the first indication that the narrator is not the final authority on this culture, because the original records lie in oral tradition. Oral records, we are told, indicate that the Ibuza people had originally migrated there from Isu, a town in the east. The narrator also suggests that the evidence for this lies in the similarities in the traditions and customs of the two towns. Again, this claim is used to suggest that Ibuza culture itself is fairly new, and that its people are all immigrants (107). This phenomenon is then compared to that of the "very civilized peoples of America, Britain and Russia" (107). This last statement has little irony, and is clearly being used to suggest that the narrative voice is well-informed about both Western psychology and history as well as Ibuza history and culture. Moreover, it suggests a rather uncritical depiction of the West as being the true seat of civilization, a depiction that frequently recurs in Emecheta's fiction and, to a lesser extent, in Sahgal's and Gordimer's.

Other customs the narrative voice speaks authoritatively about deal with sexual double standards and exploitation. In an aside on Chike, the voice informs us that in Ibuza it was common to find men who raped adolescents but later married unsullied virgins (Emecheta 1976:84). To illustrate this point, the narrator again assumes the guise of psychologist/anthropologist, and shows us how Aku-nna is ostracized for supposedly not being a virgin: "Anyone who contravened them [taboos and customs] was better dead. If you tried to hang on to life, you would gradually be helped towards death by psychological pressures. And when you were dead, people would ask: Did we not say so? Nobody goes against the laws of the land and survives" (141). The idea is that patriarchal authority, tradition, and superstition are really nothing more than "psychological pressures," that is, not repositories of ancient wisdom, but mind controlling devices. There is also a hint here that once this idea of mind control has been deciphered by the object of control, the psychological impact will be much less.

The narrative voice, then, is not really an authoritative voice at all, but rather a psychologizing voice of explanation. Behind it lies the final authority in the narrative—the power of the oral storyteller. Storytelling voices intrude in the discourse at various points in the form of songs and stories about the Ibuza ancestors. Each story, however, emphasizes the artistry of the storyteller rather than the wisdom of the ancestors. The passionate cries, sad songs and lyrical poems (Emecheta 1976:23) of the storytellers reveal only how the ancestors themselves, who were forest people, must have sang and danced (24). Even when a particular family's ancestry is being described, its exploits are literally silenced by the emotions of the chroniclers. Thus, when Ezekiel's lineage is described, the story tellers groan with sorrow and their listeners cry and their hearts beat loudly (29). The final reference to storytelling voices chronicling the ancestors occurs in a strange way at the end of the novel. This interjection suggests that, ultimately, it is the oral storytelling voice that will prevail: "Every girl born in Ibuza after Aku-nna's death was told her story to reinforce the old taboos of the land....It was a psychological hold over every young girl that would continue to exist, even in the face of every modernization, until the present day. Why this is so is, as the saying goes, anybody's guess" (168). Here the narrative voice and the discourse stop, leaving a void by the profession of ignorance and resignation. The suggestion is that after all the levels of displacement in the narrative, the last word goes to the oral storyteller whose art depends on interactive feedback from his/her listeners. This storyteller at the novel's end is a voice speaking for Okonkwo and tradition, and against Aku-nna and individualism. Curiously, though, it also makes Aku-nna into a kind of ancestor, that is, an ancestor who set a bad example. Finally, then narrative power lies with that storyteller who can effectively frighten all prospective listeners into awe and obedience. All other voices must concede defeat.

This ending leaves us feeling dissatisfied because, as Emenyonu points out, it describes all the problems of "African womanhood...while firmly withholding a balm for its gaping sores" (1988:135). However, perhaps Emecheta is suggesting that the power to articulate the subaltern's condition lies not in written, but in oral discourse. As Ward has pointed out with regard to *The Joys of Motherhood,* the kinds of voices Emecheta's narrative uses are the "multivocal voices of oral subjectivity, represented by Emecheta's *chi,* and the univocal, literate voice of authority. All the voices are necessary and true. They can only be reconciled, unified, made into some meaningful, written whole, at the cost of the voice of the *chi,* which protests its significance in a small voice" (Ward 1990:96). I would conclude by suggesting that Emecheta's *chi* cannot speak in the discourse. Instead, we have a series of voices: Okonkwo—Chike—Aku-nna—Ma Blackie and Nna-nndo—village women—third person narrator—oral storyteller—Emecheta and the listeners; one voice is constantly displacing and being displaced by the other.

Thus, all three novels deal with the constant displacement of voices in textual discourse, so that the voice of the patriarch/imperialist is constantly threatened, but never loses its ability to oppress and silence the marginalized and subaltern voices. All three narratives interweave the various voices in such a way that we are led to expect a single powerful voice of authority to dominate/reveal itself at the end, but in each case that final revelation suggests an absence.   Gordimer uses Zulu ancestors, Sahgal invokes goegraphic/religious nature and Emecheta defers to an oral storyteller, but none of these have the power or ability to enforce their wisdom on others.   This final negation of authority lies in part in the fact that Gordimer, Sahgal, and Emecheta, due to the restictions of race, class, or gender, seem unable to sufficiently problematize the nature of that authority.

Notes

[1]Spivak elaborates this argument that the subaltern consciousness cannot be fully recovered by explaining that since its interpreters are always subject to the ideology of the elite, it is always "askew from its received signifiers...it is effaced even as it is disclosed...it is irreducably discursive" (1988b:11). Moreover, its consciousness operates within a "network" of "strands" including politics, ideology, history and others (13). She therefore suggests that the task of the Subaltern Studies group is really informed by a sense of "historical" failure because it documents the failure of elitist historiography to reflect the subaltern consciousness while at the same time being aware that its own project also controls the subaltern by seeking to "know" him (9).

[2]Again, Spivak (1988b) critiques the Subaltern Studies group for not sufficiently problematizing the position of subaltern female. She points out that the exploitation of sexual difference was very important in various insurgency movements (27). For her discussion of this issue, see pages 26 through 32 of her article.

[3]Note that this name is an echo of the central character of Chinua Achebe's *Things Fall Apart,* and therefore seems to signal a move on Emecheta's part to rewrite Ibo women back into a reconstructed Ibo history that Achebe, in fact, wrote them out of. However, Aku-nna's inability to cope with the restrictions Okonkwo places on her suggests that the two histories are not very different.

[4]I have taken the term "print-capitalism" from Benedict Anderson (1983) who argues that in eighteenth- and nineteenth-century Europe, access to printing presses and their commercial use to disseminate information helped create popular vernacular-

based nationalisms (139).

[5]See   Thomas   Richards'   *The   Imperial   Archive:
Knowledge and the Fantasy of Empire* (London & New York:
Verso, 1993).

[6]The Ibo concept of slave is fairly complex. The *osu* or
oshu were, according to Robert M. Wren (1980), the lowest of
the three ranks of Ibo society. Above them were the slaves and
the freeborn. An *osu* could not rise into the other ranks and,
together with his descendents, was doomed to his social stigma
forever. The other ranks could, however, fall into the rank of
osus. Despite their lowly status, *osus* could farm, raise families,
and collect titles. Many of them were sent to school and to the
church for education and careers (40).

[7]With regard to the use of women as commodities, see
Gayle Rubin's "The Traffic in Women" (1975), which traces the
ways in which political and psychoanalytical philosophers have
traced/perpetuated the exploitation of women. Discussing Marx,
Lacan, Freud, and others, Rubin points out that women have been
commodified as a reserve labor force for capitalism (160), are
part of the process of reproduction of labor (162), as a basic form
of gift exchange (173), among others.

MUTATION OR CHOICE? MODES OF ELITISM IN *A SPORT OF NATURE, RICH LIKE US,* AND *SECOND CLASS CITIZEN*

S ome postcolonial novels are centered around the figure of an elite woman, that is, a protagonist who is educated, insightful, articulate, and creative and who belongs to the socially or economically dominant class of a particular society. According to *The Oxford English Dictionary,* an elite is "the choice part or flower" of society, which could be a particular body or class of persons. It also means that which is chosen or elected to office (142). Both meanings are relevant to my focus in this chapter, namely, the ways in which postcolonial elite women, experiencing isolation from a traditional patriarchal society, choose different modes of assimilating with that patriarchal society. Some women exploit their sexuality, others try social interaction, and some utilize their writing skills.

The three women I will discuss in this chapter all belong

to the economically or socially dominant class of their society, so that they have the means to express themselves. In Nadine Gordimer's *A Sport of Nature* (1987), Nayantara Sahgal's *Rich Like Us* (1985), and Buchi Emecheta's *Second Class Citizen* (1974), the protagonists Hillela, Sonali, and Adah are elites who are isolated from their own communities, but find acceptance in others. In all three novels, the socially advantaged heroines develop their own self-expression, thereby alienating them from the social group that otherwise shapes their identities. They are isolated because they are outsiders within their own communities, but they gain acceptance within others through sexuality or social awareness or creative writing. However, that acceptance is only partial. *A Sport of Nature* is one of Gordimer's later novels, and its protagonist is Hillela, a white, liberal, upper-class woman who is socially marginalized in white South African society under apartheid, but who gains partial acceptance in the upper-class black community. *Rich Like Us,* one of Sahgal's most recent novels, has an upper-class female protagonist, Sonali, who is estranged from the urban, bureaucratic society of Delhi, but who eventually finds a place in it with the help of a foreigner. Adah, the upper-class Ibo protagonist of *Second Class Citizen,* is socially isolated in both Nigerian and English society, but later finds a place for herself in England through her ability to write fiction. Hillela uses sex as a means of political involvement; Sonali tries to be more socially interactive; while Adah communicates through writing and religion. Finally, although the novels depict the "coming to consciousness" of their protagonists, this depiction is very convoluted. Specific incidents are narrated in detail, others are glossed over very quickly, both of which suggest that the main foci of the novels are not Hillela or Sonali or Adah, but neo-colonial patriarchal oppression, in which even elite women remain outside the socio-political power structure. At the end of the novels, neither Hillela's nor Sonali's nor Adah's political and social problems are solved, and their attempts at assimilation are only partially successful. In conclusion, I would suggest that despite being elites, Hillela, Sonali, and Adah are only partially able to overcome the patriarchal, neo-colonial condition that defines them.

In *A Sport of Nature,* Hillela is an exiled elite. While her race gives her a great deal of political and economic power in society, she disregards it and remains alienated from white society. In order to survive, she becomes ruthless in her relations with people, adapts to diverse situations, and relies on her instincts. More importantly, in order to be accepted in black society, she exploits her sexuality.

Hillela is portrayed in the narrative as a strange sort of elite, or a kind of freak, or "spontaneous mutation" that does not fit into any accepted mold. As Kenneth Parker suggests, her status as "variation" confers not typicality but marginality (Parker 1989:220). Frequently, she assumes different roles: "somewhere along the journey the girl shed one name and emerged under the other" (Gordimer 1987:1). Through the course of the novel she changes more than a name: she moves among different schools, households, and countries. In each case, her movement is heralded by some kind of unorthodox behavior: flirting with a "colored" boy, incest, adultery, and marrying across the color bar. Rather than submit to racial restrictions, she tries to "'give up being white' and seek out levers of power wherever they may present themselves" (Peck 1988:80). At her Aunt Pauline's house, she makes her own rules of behavior, so that Pauline says "She's a-moral. I mean in the sense of the morality of this country" (Gordimer 1987:45). She seems to reject the codes and norms of society with ease, associating with whomever she pleases and not thinking in terms of white or black: "categories were never relevant to her ordering of life" (112). Thus, she decides that the best thing to do after Pauline finds the "two in his [her cousin Sasha's] bed" (93) is to move out to another place. The freedom provides her a casual contact with politics and subversion through her lover, Andrew Rey. The fact that she is unaware that he is actually an agent for the secret police reflects her ignorance of political realities as well as her rootlessness.

Later in the novel, Hillela tries to assimilate with black Africans by becoming Mrs. Whaila Kgomani and a tangible presence among the exiles in West Africa. Yet she still remains strangely aloof. The narrator tells us she remains a figure of the present and seems to provide Whaila with a sense of self (Gordimer 1987:188-189). She herself does seem to find a sense of direction at this point, and she plays the part of "wife of revolutionary." However, her interest in politics at this stage is hardly revolutionary because it is more a concern for Whaila the man than a belief in a cause. For Whaila's sake, all else becomes secondary, but Whaila himself feels her lack of identification with "her own people" despite the fact that due to her marriage, to her, the race and class struggle was already "one world; what could be" (215).

After Whaila's assassination, she plays the role of isolated elite, educating herself in the ways of revolution and teaching herself the art of diplomacy while trying to meet people's needs (Gordimer 1987:83). As Peck suggests, however, her contribution to the cause during her stay in Eastern Europe consists of little more than typing and translating (Peck 1988:83), and then she disappears again into what the narrator tells us is "known about the mission, in that country, at that time. No history of her really can be personal history, then; its ends were all apparently outside herself" (Gordimer 1987:233). Surfacing again as a diplomat to Africa from the United States, she becomes a professional bureaucrat (249).

As diplomat, she shows her aggressive ability to survive and make an impact by arguing in support of her most controversial claims and by breaking down all opposition in a systematic way. However, as Peck points out, she gets sidetracked by a preoccupation with the suffering caused by the wars, in particular, starvation (Gordimer 1987:278).   In her personal affairs, though, she is as ruthless as ever, telling one lover, "I've been with Reuel, on and off, when I was in Africa. I don't think you'd be able to—well, to manage with that" (273). Why, we may ask, is she so attracted to Reuel? For one thing, he is a highly articulate intellectual black man and is also a militant revolutionary in the struggle for South African independence. More importantly, though, perhaps she likes him because he teaches her that soup powder "won't stop the wars, and the wars make the refugees....That's the important thing, to be the side that gets the guns" (277). This part of Hillela's political development is a process of "moving on" into the circles of power. As General Reuel's unofficial envoy and mistress, and later, his wife, she is the one who is able to see the flag unfurled in the newly independent South Africa, "Whaila's country" (354).   Clearly, Hillela tries to gain acceptance into the black world through a form of sexual politics.   Dorothy Driver indicates that for Gordimer's female protagonists, sex is a form of communication (Driver 1983:35) and a means of social mobility (36). So too, Kenneth Parker argues that Gordimer's message in the novel is that the "only way that white South African women can influence change is through their sexuality" (Parker 1989:218).   In fact, Hillela uses sex in the following ways in the novel: to create casual pleasure as an adolescent; to further her ambitions to "get on" when she is independent; to cross the color bar in adulthood; and, finally, to gain power and to "get on" in her post-widowhood phase.   Through the narrator, Gordimer seems to ironically suggest that, rather than politics, sexuality is a woman's—and particularly Hillela's—major area: "Hillela's field was, surely, men" (Gordimer 1987:290).

Sex for casual pleasure or sexual freedom, as it is described in the first part of the novel, is Hillela's "road to revolution" (Visel 1988:39). In this stage, her sexuality is just a "source of pleasure and of the truth" (Peck 1988:87). To her first two lovers, Sasha and Andrew Rey, she offers a means of relief. Andrew, for example, would use sex with her to feel in control and important, two things he couldn't feel in his own work (Gordimer 1987:114). Thus, while black activists are tortured all around her, she lies in the "alternating current of the man's [Andrew's] frustration and resolve, the thrilling tension into which, in his command of her body, he converted the dreadful happenings around her" (117). Sex as an escape from political realities, then, marks her early attempts to escape white society, and the same is true of her affair with Emile Mezieres, the French Ambassador. Even when she marries Whaila, she is still the same person to her earlier acquaintances: "Hillela's a natural mistress, not a wife" (183).

Sex and love with Whaila is what draws her into the political struggle. As Peck (1988) suggests, she moves from love for him to love for his people to love for the cause (81). With him, she is able to visualize a time when love between black and white can be natural. She is able to conceive of a natural physical attraction because of the way the laws in South Africa defined race on the basis of facial features and skin color (Gordimer 1987:184). Whaila finds that her sexual energy is transmuted into a "zest that kept her working all day...she could be felt...willing the direction of a discussion, seeing, moves ahead, what would put Whaila at a disadvantage" (188-189). Whaila seems to achieve an almost mythic stature to Hillela, which has something that is not just sexual attraction (208). Even a decision to discuss covert guerilla action is described in terms of a clasp of the hand. After Whaila's assassination, she dedicates herself to the cause, and here sex is associated with power: power to get weapons from Europe, humanitarian aid from the U.S., and levers of power from Africa (Peck 1988:83). Only when she meets Reuel does she feel that he offers her "desire" and that "only a man could comfort for the loss of a man, only the smell of a man could make it impossible to disbelieve that a man actually came to an end on a kitchen floor" (Gordimer 1987:278).

Her relationship with Reuel is strange because she claims to be involved in his political affairs, but she becomes his mistress, with uncertain political alliances. The narrator tells us that her relationship with the ANC is never made clear, beyond the fact that she's Whaila's widow. Altogether, then, when she returns to South Africa at the end of the novel, she commits her "one and only political action," namely, using her knowledge of key politicians and organization members in shaping a negotiated settlement (Parker 1989:217). Whether she is really politically active or not, she is clearly important both as a diplomat and as a sexual partner to the General and is his match in both (Gordimer 1987:347). Moreover, I feel that although her methods are unorthodox, she is the only white person in the novel who does make any kind of contact at all. Also, it must be remembered that when her baby is born, Hillela delights in the fact that she is able to reproduce not herself, but blackness (202).

So what kind of elite does Hillela prove herself to be? She is clearly no Rosa Burger. Nor is she like the black elites Whaila and Reuel. Whaila is presented to us as a dedicated revolutionary, an intellectul, and a martyr. Reuel is, in turn, a successful general, Hillela's political tutor, a resolute fighter, a powerful President, and a dictator. Hillela is also unlike the other black leaders like Nelson Mandela, who is silenced in the narrative. The narrator tells us in passing that he was sentenced to life in prison for treason and his speech in court went unheard (Gordimer 1987:68). Finally, Hillela cannot really be compared to any elite black women because there are no such women at the center of the narrative. Indeed, she seems largely unaware of political realities, so that the narrator can tell us at one point that "that year when Hillela was living in the city with some man was the same year when torture began to be used by the police" on mostly black suspects (117). Hillela seems quite ignorant of black misery, whether inflicted on elites or subalterns.

Her main interactions with black Africans is through sexuality, and even the narrator does not seem to approve very much of her method of connecting to people. The narrator's disapproval shows through on many occasions, such as when he/she implies that Hillela wanted to marry Brad only so as to become an American citizen (Gordimer 1987:287) and this disapproval increases in intensity as the novel progresses (Peck 1988:88). One reason for this censure, according to Peck, is because Gordimer finds Hillela's method of successfully surviving in South Africa "distasteful" (89) because, although it might be "efficacious," it "may not preserve human values" (87). However, I think Gordimer uses this narrative style because she wants us to see that her main object of concern is not Hillela's development as an elite character, but the impact of apartheid on South African society. That is, Gordimer's aim is to show that apartheid brings not just misery and devastation for black Africans, but also isolation and exclusion for elite white Africans. The isolation that Gordimer hints at is suggested by the fact that although sexuality and power are linked throughout the novel, but the power itself is very limited. Hillela cannot communicate effectively—she has no narrative power—hence, her achievements are always undercut by irony and sarcasm. This could lead us to conclude that Gordimer's main point is that for an elite white woman in post-revolution South Africa, there are only a few possible choices left.

And what are some of the choices open to Hillela? As an elite, her first choice could be that of oppression, that is, reinforcing white patriarchal rule, as her Aunt Olga seems to do: to Olga, black Africans are servants to be appeased by high salaries and refrigerators. There is also the option of sympathy and appeasement, so that black Africans may be pacified into living with the system. This seems to be her Aunt Pauline's option as she works for black education and uplift, but does not approve of black power. Hillela chooses to involve herself with black revolution through sexuality, an attempt to "give up" her whiteness and her guilt, which is as ruthless and limited, in its own way, as the other two.   As the narrator tells us, her "privileged class" and her race limits her from seeing that, often, there is "the necessity to deal in death, no way out of it, meeting death with death, not flowers and memorials" (Gordimer 1987:237).   Clearly, Hillela avoids choosing another unstated and implicit option, one of accepting responsibility for—and actively agitating to end—black misery with black rule.   Ending black misery is implicit in Hillela's activities, but black majority rule is not always what she achieves.   In several comments, the narrator suggests that Hillela's zeal is perhaps somewhat misplaced: her "real family" is not her "rainbow" family with Whaila, but the family that suffers from malnutrition, starvation, lack of sanitation, disease, and death (260).   As the narrative voice suggests, Hillela tends to dictate to blacks, instead of listening to them.   Indeed, even the ANC had always reacted to moves made by whites rather than vice versa (332).   The implication here is that now the whites should be the listeners and responders, and that Gordimer herself should present white characters who respond to black forces rather than initiate actions on their behalf. All these comments suggest that there are large areas of understanding and awareness that are still lacking in Hillela and are necessary if she is to become the "new" white South African woman.

At the end of the novel, then, although the revolution is presented as successful, the socio-psychological problems of apartheid are not resolved.   On the social level, neither the problems of intolerance and exploitation nor the silencing and marginalization of black Africans are solved: they still exist.   On the personal level, neither Hillela nor any of the other whites enter the "center" of power; they only come near it through sexuality. There is no suggestion in the novel that Hillela is able to communicate without her body or to any blacks other than those in the elite.   Her center is, as the narrator tells us, in the "non-matrilineal" unit of the President's home, which she has "invented" (Gordimer 1987:322).   Thus, although the novel closes on a moment of hope and triumph, yet this does not bring with it a revolutionary change of heart.   Hillela gains power, but the type of power she chooses is very limited.   Moreover, she is never in control of her own discourse: she cannot communicate with all of black Africa nor with us.   Thus, she is unable to escape the colonial ideology that surrounds her.

Like Hillela, Sonali in *Rich Like Us* (1986), one of Sahgal's later novels, is also an isolated elite, who tries to assimilate with her society, but the method she chooses is different.   Primarily, Sonali is isolated politically and socially, though not economically.   She illustrates the idea that Marcia Liu (1980) suggests is typical of Sahgal's novels, namely, that, despite being educated elites, many of Sahgal's protagonists are outsiders, who are either cut off from or absent in the surrounding community (46).   Thus, although Sonali is at the "center" of political administration, yet she is also an outsider in the corridors of power.   She moves in a man's world and appropriates "male" values, but is accepted in neither the women's nor the men's worlds.   She tries to assimilate by making social contacts with friends and those in need.   Rose, the other main character in the novel, is marginalized politically and socially, but is ultimately destroyed by the political system.   As a displaced Englishwoman, she is an elite who tries to appropriate the ways of the Hindu wife, but fails in the attempt.   Both Sonali and Rose try to become insiders by displacing others, but they ultimately remain on the outside of all the social groups in the novel.

As Neena Arora (1989) points out, Sonali is presented as an elite senior civil servant in the novel, but one who is anguished by the systematic erosion of democratic ideals during the State of Emergency in India (131).   Her isolation is presented in terms of both a personal crisis (losing her job, coming to terms with political realities, learning to stand up for what is right) as well as a contrast to the struggles of the past freedom fighters. The entire political drama of the Emergency is thus seen from her point of view; and while she is idealistic and brave, she is also, as Jain (1989) points out, naive and politically ignorant (145). Only when she is pushed out of her privileged position does she begin to understand the extent of political corruption around her and the implications of her own complicitous silence. She realizes that she doesn't fit in the system and that she has to face up to the consequences of that fact.

While working as senior civil servant, Sonali goes to great lengths to explain why she feels politically isolated. She explains that politicians and bureaucrats were now interchangeable (Sahgal 1986:24). This mixing is reflected in the fact that she is humiliated in her job (and therefore resigns) for not granting the appropriate political favors to "Madam's" (Mrs. Gandhi's) hanger-on, Dev. Yet, even when she has a chance to change the situation, she remains blind to the problems and injustices that surround her. She tells herself, by way of consolation that bureaucrats like herself knew all about Mrs. Gandhi's political machinations but kept silent to avoid trouble. She sees this as an example of political "blindness" (25). What she does realize, though, is that, as Jain points out, her administrative training has not prepared her for the new situation (Jain 1989:44). Unlike her colleague and former fiancé, Ravi, she has no survival skills to deal with the situation. So she retreats rather than face the status quo.

In addition, Sonali is unable to deal adequately with the men in her world. She realizes that the difference between her struggle and that of men like Ravi is that they "had never fought a battle for freedom, never been patted down firmly when [their]...sap was rising...never had a sari throttling [their]...legs" (Sahgal 1986:101). Thus, after she resigns her job, she isolates herself from men socially and retreats to her own room instead.

There, she tries to think things out for herself, emerging occasionally to consult her friend, Rose. The only interaction she has with the male world at this point is her request to Ravi to help Rose from being cheated out of her (Rose's) money by Dev. And even though she has to overcome her pride to ask Ravi, she romanticizes his eagerness to comply with her request. She sees her request to him as his one chance of escaping from the morass of political corruption that he has sunk into. He had, she muses, the appearance of someone who was learning to walk all over again (204). Ironically, it is never clear that she herself learns to "walk again." Despite her improved relations with Ravi at the end of the novel, most of her initiative for action comes from Marcella, a friend, who offers her a job. In fact, although she remains hopeful about her future, she is clearly unable to take that first step alone: "Until she [Marcella] said it I hadn't realized the Emergency could ever be over, or that my future hadn't come to an end on a steamy day in July this year" (233).

Rose's alienation is of a slightly different type. As a foreigner who is outspoken to the point of rudeness, she is the intruder who is resented and then partially accepted by Indian society. Surprisingly, she integrates with the neo-colonial society a little more effectively than Sonali is able to. As Jain points out, Rose didn't always belong to the elite class, but she is able to overcome both the political and social disadvantages of that. Conscious of her individuality, she compels others to recognize it (Jain 1989:44) and is able to overcome the loud hostility of an indignant community that ostracizes her, namely, that of her husband's first wife, Mona, and her father-in-law. Yet she finds that it is the "undeclared hostility around her now" that is "harder to understand" (Sahgal 1986:53). This hostility comes from a corrupt younger generation, quick to succumb to the amoral atmosphere of neo-colonial, emergency rule. Her adopted son, Dev, and his henchmen, play up to the political power-mongers for all they are worth, and find Rose's morals a problem and a liability. Thus, Rose finds out, late in the novel, that Dev has been building a factory against the government's rules, supposedly to manufacture a drink and make car parts (219). When she protests against this, Dev is so enraged he threatens to kill her (14). In this war of morals Rose finds herself always at a loss (58). Like Sonali, she feels cut off from the surrounding environment, especially when she realizes that ultimately she would become "less than mist, there wouldn't be a trace left of her dreams or her nightmares, no one to regret her going, not a tear to mark her passage" (64).

Like Sonali, too, Rose dreams of an ideal world— "Cythera,[1] her exile, her home" (Sahgal 1986:67)—in which she is freed of all problems and is alone with her husband, Ram. Curiously, when Ram has affairs with other women, Rose mirrors Mona, her rival in that like Mona she, too, cries silently and with the utmost sorrow (94). At one stage, she takes on Ram's business acumen, restocking his shop's shelves with his father's help and even sends Ram to other cities for cloth while she looks after the shop (107). Above all, it is her bluntness in speech that both endears her to Sonali and isolates her from the rest of society, because the truths hit home too closely (22). At the end of the novel, Dev makes good his threat and gets his henchmen to murder her because he fears she will upset all his plans. When she hears about it, Sonali compares her death to those of women who are burnt alive through *sati* and, indeed, they are all marginalized in a society without a means of appropriating power to themselves. On the other hand, Sonali's comparison is largely romantic in the sense that Rose has some degree of control over her situation, while the other women are mostly helpless victims. By comparing Rose with these women, then, both Sonali and Sahgal seem to blur the distinctions between elite and subaltern victims of brutality.

In *Rich Like Us,* sex and physical relations are also connected to politics, since one form that political activity takes in this novel is physical involvement between men and women. According to Liu, while Sahgal does articulate the need for women to become equal partners with men, she constantly portrays women whose characters are entirely formed by men (52). Jain echoes this comment when she indicates that Sahgal's women characters are often seen merely as sex objects by her male characters (Jain 1978b:45), and that only a few of her women characters seek freedom outside the confines of marriage (48). Conversely, she points out that sexual activity reflects freedom and individualism for the women characters and that sex is usually dealt with in terms of the degree of emotional involvement that goes along with it (Jain 1978a:46). Thus, in *Rich Like Us,* political sterility or non-involvement is shown in terms of sexual sterility or deformity, particularly in the case of the women. Also, the results of political oppression are often shown in terms of sexual/physical victimization. In the case of Sonali, her social isolation, mentioned above, together with her lack of physical/sexual relationships with people, reflects her political isolation. There almost seems to be the implication that political commitment is like a physical encounter. Sonali's lack of physical contact mirrors her political sterility.

One example of this is her attitude towards her career. Her choice of a career is always presented in terms of an alternative to marriage and children. When she acts as narrator of the text, she takes pains to dissociate herself from the other women she knows. Remembering the marriages she had seen in her childhood, she resolves never to marry, for the brides seemed to her like prisoners, with their clothes like tents, their jewelry like chains, and their postures, submissive (Sahgal 1986:48). To escape marriage and entrapment, she takes to "frantic competition, to stardom in my studies...everything afterwards" (51). Her awakening from political stupor and indeed her whole political career, is also presented in terms of a tussle with Ravi, because while he was more concerned with finding a way to use

Marxist principles to bring about a better society for all, she was interested in its implications for her own personal affairs (99). Their friendship is both intellectual and physical and, ironically, they break off their engagement because they cannot agree on "step three and step four of the Marxist process" (180).

Later, it is their difference in ideology that separates them.   Ravi plays along with the powers-that-be, while she disengages herself from the corruption till it is almost too late. Significantly, the one selfless act that Ravi does (namely, speaking up for Rose against Dev), puts him out of favor and they both realize, almost simultaneously, that "things [politics] have slipped out of control.   There are no rules and regulations any more" (229).   However, there is an element of hope in that at one point they are able to resurrect for a short time their old, ideal friendship, one that is meaningful and in which affection is not a mistake.   At the same time, they also realize that there is a way out of the morass.   As Jain suggests, Sonali realizes that she must not only fight "the myths which persist about a glorious past" but also maintain a constant vigilance to retain her idealism and ethics (Jain 1989:147).

In a similar fashion, Rose's involvement in her life with Ram also leads to a greater political awareness on her part.   Ram explains to her the full implications of World War II, and she herself notices how the Quit India Movement fosters a sense of fraternity between Hindus and Muslims, and upper- and lower-caste Hindus.   During the Partition of India, she is more affected than Ram is by the "ragged, bloodstained knots and bundles that turned out at close range to be people, sights to make her heart leap into her throat and stop there" (Sahgal 1986:144).   Also, her obstinacy in staying on as Ram's second wife, against all odds, makes it impossible for her to give up and leave in times of trouble, and the memory of the sordid working-class life her parents had led in England reinforces her resolve (56).   Even Ram's affair with Marcella doesn't deter her; instead, she asks herself if she could have stopped it (176). Her repeated statement, "I could never bear to lose Ram" (192) also reflects the intensity of her commitment to India. However, in old age she realizes that "she hadn't even conceived, which might have made things easier, made her, however resentfully, acceptable, since a woman is a vehicle for the next generation" (63). Ironically, Dev, whom she adopts at Mona's request, proves this point by murdering her. Thus, Sonali and Rose remain outsiders at the end of the novel. At first, they both seem to have the ability to displace those less powerful than themselves: thus, to Rose, Mona appears as a "phantom presence" (Sahgal 1986:92) rather than a flesh-and-blood woman, while to Sonali, her sister Kiran is mindless and effete, rather than her father's other daughter. It is only when they both face the pain of displacement at a personal level that they integrate better with society. Rose, then, becomes Mona's friend, and takes on the responsibility for her son; while Sonali is able to enjoy brief moments of communion with Ravi and her mother. But these are small, isolated incidents, and at the end of the novel both women are still isolated: the assimilation is only partial.

So what are the choices facing Sonali and Rose if they want to assimilate fully? Their choices seem largely dependent on the state of political crisis described in the narrative, which is the fact of Emergency rule. What is the role of women during this Emergency rule? At first glance, it seems ambivalent, in that women are both inside and outside the socio-political infrastructure. On the one hand, there is "madam" herself, who is often described as the "many-armed goddess" (Sahgal 1986:152) or seductive dancing girl (154). In describing "Madam" as the goddess and the dancer, Sahgal mixes up political and sexual discourse. She goes on to suggest that this political and sexual power source has the ability to throw powerful opponents like J.P. and intellectuals like K.L. into jail at the slightest pretext, and have them beaten up like common "bicycle thieves" and "commies." The nature of her dictatorship is suggested in a general way by repeated references to the arbitrary functioning of supreme power. Not only are sudden arrests and continual censorship of news common, but even people's personal habits and private relationships are threatened. All this is achieved because "madam" has made the Constitution of India "null and void" and is thus able to rewrite history (157). There is also the clique of upper class, mindless sycophants, in the faithful service of "madam." One scene, in which vasectomizing the lower classes is discussed, is a case in point. Complacent, mindless, privileged women, out to impress the matriarch, tell one another they need to take their cues from the government and rigorously enforce vasectomies as a preferred method of birth control among their domestic servants (78). This "businesslike programme" results in the macabre rounding up of available bodies, even disabled ones; thus Rose's daughter-in-law, Nishi, "pounces" on a disabled beggar and begins a fight with him to force him to the vasectomy clinic (81).

On the other hand, there are the outcasts or outsiders, who make up most of the other women in the novel, and who are, by and large, powerless. Besides Sonali and Rose, there are the women, mentioned earlier, who step out of the pages of Sonali's great-grandfather's memoirs, who are the victims of institutionalized *sati*. The fact that the digression on *sati* is so long is, I think, significant. In the first place, it reinforces the rhetoric of neo-colonial authoritarianism, in which the subaltern is presented as "degenerate" and one who must be "protected" from barbaric customs by the "moral" colonizer (Chakravarti 1989:35). And in the second place, it suggests that the matriarchal dictatorship, besides being authoritarian, is also the means of patriarchal or male oppression (that is, it is actually patriarchal rule). Under such circumstances, it should come as no surprise that women are still burned alive by their own relatives and are often forced to choose to die. For example, one mother Sonali reads about makes a deal with her brother such that she would agree to commit *sati* in exchange for her brother sponsoring her son's education in a good university (Sahgal 1986:135). The gruesome stories narrated or reported in the digression on *sati* all seem to reiterate the fact that beneath the so-called progress in the neo-colonial society, there will always be "the subterranean layers of ourselves we cannot escape" (135). Significantly, Sonali ends this digression by reflecting on the situation as an outsider, that is, she thinks, at the end, not of the plight of the women, but of the heroism of the boy who tried to save one of them (136). In fact, the *satis* in the novel are examples of the marginalized and exploited women that the emergency has brought, and of a society in which political and sexual power relations have gone sour. The emergency is also characterized by "tanks...and beggars," by "tear-gas and...empresses" (150). But what is most significant of all is the frightening realization that Sonali has at the end of the novel, that for the non-elites life in the neo-colonial state is always life in an "emergency" (227).

The ending of the novel, then, is important, and no analysis can afford to ignore it. In the first place, the power structures that come into play on a social and personal level are ambivalent. On the social level, neither the problems of the emergency nor social evils like *sati* and bride-burning are resolved; they still exist. On the personal level, neither Sonali nor Rose are drawn into the center of the power structure: Rose is murdered by her son and Sonali is "bought off" by the remnants of colonialism, and cuts herself off from personal and political problems at home. Thus, although the novel does, in a sense, open up the past to "imaginative revision" (Slemon 1988:165), yet this leads to no change of heart or of politics. Both Sonali and Rose are unable to free themselves from the neo-colonial ideology that defines them.

Like Sonali, Adah, the protagonist of *Second Class Citizen,* one of Emecheta's early novels, is an intellectual who exhibits typically middle-class attitudes about wealth and status in post-independence Nigeria, especially the necessity of going to the U.K. and becoming a "family of Ibo elites" (Emecheta 1974:25) on their return. Yet she remains an elite only after a tremendous struggle which involves alienation and a withdrawal from family/communal relations. At the end of her struggles she emerges a battered and miserable survivor. Katherine Frank (1982) calls her a "liberated, self-sufficient heroine" (478), but I would argue that her liberation is more symbolic than real. In fact, Frank regards Adah's feminist aspirations and her African aspirations as mutually opposed throughout the novel, so that in order to maintain a free existence she has to continue to live in the West (492). This is an over-simplified approach to Adah's struggle, since, as Ketu Katrak has shown, both capitalism (i.e., Western culture) and patriarchy (i.e., African culture) oppress women equally (Katrak 1987:160) to create an "analytic dualism" (Barrett 1980:23), or they oppress women by working in tandem, as Sangari and Vaid (1990) have shown. According to them, both tradition and modernity in India have been "carriers of patriarchal ideologies...[and are] colonial constructs" (1990:17). The same argument could be applied to Nigeria, where, as Katrak suggests, "capitalism and patriarchy have joined hands to control women" (Katrak 1987:160), with the result that postcolonial Ibo women became dominated by men economically, politically, and socially. Whatever few political rights women were given under African patriarchy were taken away by capitalism/colonialism so that "postcolonial Capitalist society in Nigeria landed Igbo [sic] women with different forms of oppression [without changing]...any of the institutions" of oppression already in place (163). This, then, is the kind of oppression Adah struggles against in the novel, and which she finds particularly difficult to overcome.

Adah is an elite because she reflects the values and biases of the Western-educated, affluent class in Nigeria. Moreover, in her presentation of Adah's biases, Emecheta reveals her own class prejudices because she never criticizes or problematizes the basis of Adah's assumptions. For example, Emecheta describes how Adah resents the blurring of class distinctions that takes place among the Nigerians in London and strives to maintain her elite status. She prides herself on her educated background and her well-paying job (which pays more than that of anyone else in her family) and is horrified at the prospect of having to fraternize with Nigerian servants in London. Calling them illiterates, she hates being told to be happy with factory work, having to use free/second-class hospitals for her children, and making them wear used and dirty clothes. Overall, she believes she is as good as if not equal to white people, and rejects the idea that black people are inferior. While these are valid sentiments, they also partly disclose, as Sougou suggests, Adah's own prejudices and middle class assumptions.

One of the chief kinds of oppression that Adah experiences is alienation resulting from mental and physical abuse, acute loneliness, and misery. It is an exile imposed on her both by her family/community and by Western society. As a child, Adah is neglected and unloved because she is not a boy, and in adolescence she endures hard labor and daily chores because she does not have a father. She soon realizes she is valued for purely capitalist reasons, namely, her bride price money and her ability to work hard and that she is "controlled and owned" by males who appreciate only her ability to produce other males and make money. Katrak (1987) calls this biological and economic control (163). Control is maintained by frequent beatings, both at school and at home, with which she copes by excelling at studies and hardening her heart. On one occasion, rather than mutely submitting, she refuses to break down even after being caned for a long time all over her body (Emecheta 1974:22). Even in adulthood the beating does not stop, as her husband, Francis, beats her frequently, even when she is convalescing after a stay in the hospital: "she was dizzy with pain and her head throbbed" (147). In each case, she survives by using her will power and ingenuity and by becoming more shrewd and cynical, but she cannot escape being objectified by a man who regards all women as commodities that are "bought and paid for and must remain like that, silent obedient slaves" (156).

As a result of all this abuse, Adah remains lonely and isolated, unable to completely articulate her oppression. For example, even though she knows that she is valued only as a commodity in her community, she still feels an intense loneliness when she leaves her homeland "only she and Boy [her brother] remained of that life which she had known. It was never going to be the same again" (Emecheta 1974:34). Yet this life she had known was almost exclusively one of isolation because she was orphaned young, and was later forced to marry a selfish man in order to continue with her studies without being labeled a prostitute (122). Later, this yearning loneliness is worsened by the deliberate and cruel abuse she is subjected to from Francis. Because he values her only for her salary, he does not even bother to express any humane feelings for her, and accuses her of failing as a wife and mother when she stops working due to ill health. His sadistic oppression is based on capitalist and patriarchal principles by which he, being a man, had the right to control every aspect of her life (28). Instead of marriage and sex being a process of learning and a means of communication, they become the source of her physical and sexual exploitation. As Frank (1982) has pointed out, the real "second class citizenship [she experiences]...derives far more from Adah's anatomy than from the colour of her skin" (492). To be more precise, "the economic oppression of woman-as-slave [is] represented by Emecheta literally, in the institution of slavery, and metaphorically, in the institution of marriage—the woman in both cases is owned, body and soul" (Katrak 1987:165).

Aside from the personal degradation she suffers, her

marriage also makes her acquire a distaste and fear of sex, partly due to her own ignorance of it, but mainly due to the repeated pregnancies Francis forces on her.   In fact, for her, sex and marriage become an endless grind of hard work, continuous cycles of pregnancy and sickness, and physical and mental abuse. Indeed, the only way she can communicate with Francis is through providing him with sex and money, and so she soon learns to manipulate him with these.   She begins to deny him sex until he agrees to take some responsibility for their housing, and she also withholds money until he begins to contribute some, too. Finally, she gives up on marriage as a means of communication when she realizes that Francis only values her because her money pays for his education.   She feels betrayed and lost, and to hide these feelings, she projects a cold exterior to the world (126).   All this oppression leaves such an impression on her that even when she finally chooses to leave Francis she is overcome not by relief but by loneliness: "she cried then.   She was lonely again, just as when Pa died and Ma married again and she had to live in a relative's house" (147).   All she has with her in her new-found freedom at the end are her children and her job (171) together with a painful conscience.   As Frank suggests, she cannot "shrug off years of conditioning that have inculcated wifely subservience to one's husband" (Frank 1982:493).   In fact, Adah's freedom is rather like a reliving of the nightmare she had during her stay in hospital, in which she kept running round and round in circles (Emecheta 1974:107).   The final vestiges of her self-esteem disappear when she is completely disowned by the very husband she worked as a slave for, and her economic independence is undercut by the fact that she has no child support or monetary help from him.   He even goes to the extent of disowning his children in court to avoid paying child support (174).   As a woman, wife, and mother this is the cruelest form of exile, and Adah is left trying to cope with it.   This ending to the novel shows Emecheta's dual concern with the biological and economic control over women within patriarchal and capitalist postcolonial Nigeria, and how one form of control often reinforced the other (Katrak 1987:159).

Despite the ominous ending to the narrative, Adah retains her independence from Francis primarily because she is able to overcome all the obstacles facing her. Even if her freedom is rather hollow, she is able to achieve it. She does this by using a number of different ways to articulate the oppression she faces, the implication being that articulation is the first step toward achieving freedom. Since she faces a dual oppression and is uncommunicative by nature, she initially has very few means to articulate her misery. Rather than communicating through sex, like Hillela, she chooses religion, education, children, and writing. For Adah, the Christian religion is both a constant form of self-expression and a source of confusion. Soon after her marriage to Francis, she becomes confused by the various religious practices of her new family, and doesn't know how to reconcile them. Frequently, she feels like a "guilty person with a nasty conscience" (Emecheta 1974:30) and so she resorts to a more personalized god. This god, who is more like her *chi,* sometimes supports her silently and at other times tells her what to do. She calls this god or voice of conscience the "Presence," and it is at once her unconscious and her conscience, her dreams and her desires, her memories and the source of her faith. When she thinks back to her earliest memories, for example, she cannot recall a lot of important details like her age, but she can recall a "Presence" that gave her a sense of purpose (7). At other times, it is a source of inspiration to her, a sense inside her that goads her to work hard and achieve good results. In one scene, it tells her that she would later excel in her studies at a very good school (20). Soon the Presence becomes a friend or companion to her.

The fact that the Presence is more like the force of her own will power or self-esteem is revealed when she confesses that after her first real hardships in England, the Presence temporarily deserts her. However, before she decides to stop supporting Francis and live only for her babies and herself, she senses the Presence again, and this time it clearly seems to be her inner will power or *chi*. It becomes a presence to talk to and be reassured by (Emecheta 1974:150). Emecheta's recourse to the *chi* here is her way of using "good" African tradition. She shows how this personal voice or consciousness within Adah enables her to find some means to cope with her oppression. However, despite all its power, the "Presence" is fairly limited because Adah gains a deeper sense of self-esteem from her Canadian friend Bill, who encourages her to write. The fact that Adah needs encouragement from Bill despite the support of the "Presence" suggests that a Western white male redeemer is a critical need for an oppressed African woman. Thus, she is able to articulate her oppression chiefly through knowledge and insights gained during the course of her education.

Schooling and education are some of the main excitements that sustain Adah from childhood onwards because of the glamor, the discipline, the organization, or "the cleanliness, the orderliness and the brightness" (Emecheta 1974:17). While Western education is shown, in the novel as a whole, to be "the key to success in the changing Africa of the late forties and early fifties" (Sougou 1990:511), yet the idea of a girl being educated is a novel one in Adah's community. Thus, Adah's decision to study means she has to defy tradition and strive for excellence. Studies become both a substitute for her absent home/family and a means for her to survive as an independent woman. When faced with a lack of funds for school, she resolves the problem temporarily by winning a scholarship. After five years, though, she tries another solution which she thinks is permanent, namely, a marriage which would give her the social status she needed to continue her studies in Lagos (Emecheta 1974:23). This is a "marriage of convenience" which is highly untraditional since "the dowry is not given by the husband" (Sougou 1990:512). More importantly, this solution turns out to be the worst of all, since Francis becomes a burden and an oppressor and Adah's ability to communicate her desires through her education comes to an end soon after her marriage.   So she chooses another means of articulating herself: her babies.

Adah is able to articulate some of her affections and desires quite well through her children.   First of all, she owes part of her elite status to them, since her ability to produce a lot in a short period of time is very highly regarded in her community. Despite the fact that she becomes pregnant five times in five years, with at least three being more-or-less against her will, she regards her children as people she can love and rely on.   She says on many occasions that she "lived in her children" (Emecheta 1974:58), and vows that her sons would learn to respect women for who they are and not for their money, and her daughters would be taught to do the same for men (121-122). Unfortunately, though, her children are too young to participate much in the narrative, so the communication she plans does not actually take place.

However, Adah finds another method to articulate her agony, namely, writing, and she "discovers" this very late in the novel.   Writing ultimately becomes the most effective way for her to articulate the roots of her misery; she connects this with the reading and learning she had begun before her marriage.   In fact, writing, for her, is a form of self-education or what Frank (1982) calls "the second phase of her move towards freedom" (493). With Bill's prompting and encouragement, she begins reading about American writers like James Baldwin and European political philosphers like Marx.   What her readings give her is a sense of self-dignity and self-esteem which enables her to begin writing.   She is able to write an entire novel in a matter of months and enjoy doing so; and although she thinks her treatment of the subject matter is over-romanticized, it does give her a sense of release: "It mattered little to her whether it was published or not, all that mattered was that she had written a book" (Emecheta 1974:64). Later, when Bill tells her the story is good enough to be published, she realizes that she had written it out of a compulsive urge to articulate herself: "The words, simple, not sophisticated at all, kept pouring from her mind. She had written it, as if it were someone talking, talking fast, who would never stop" (165). Most important of all, writing gives her a sense of control over her own life because to write about an experience is to get some power over it, or to completely transform it (Frank 1982:494). Thus, writing gives her a sense of balance or contentment. After talking to Bill about her book, she tells him that she felt like she was creating another baby. This baby, her "brainchild," then enables her to "do her own phrases her own way. Adah's phrases, that's what they were going to be" (Emecheta 1974:166).

Unfortunately, as with all Adah's other methods of communication, this one too, is almost destroyed by Francis. First, he calls her book "rubbish" and tells her that "she would never be a writer because she was black and because she was a woman" (Emecheta 1974:168). This criticism almost destroys her new-found self-esteem. Then, he sadistically burns her manuscript when he perceives it as a threat, and this act finally destroys whatever feelings she had left for him. She walks out on him soon after, so, indirectly, her writing is successful in maintaining her self-identity, because it gives her the resolve to free herself of him. However, its actual impact remains a thing of the future, since her present remains, even at the end of the narrative, full of misery and abandonment, and she is still not in complete control of her destiny. The ambiguousness of the ending of the narrative suggests that perhaps sometime in the future, when she is able to free herself completely from abuse, she will take up writing again: "It was like Fate intervening. It was like a story one might read in a true story magazine. This old friend of Adah's paid for the taxi that took her home from Camden Town because he thought she was still with her husband" (175). We are left with the impression that Adah is poised on the brink of overcoming her exploitation and becoming more self-assured, but that she hasn't quite made it yet. She is not quite the "triumphant spirit" Nwankwo claims (1988:37), but has the potential to triumph.

However, Adah's experience of racism and sexism is not the only concern of the novel, which also shows how a patriarchal culture, when brought into contact with a capitalist culture, often renews its power to oppress the elite woman. The novel is also very much concerned with the ways in which racial, sexual, and class-based oppression are inextricably linked within a culture, so that one kind of oppression often leads to another. For example, the narrator tells us that living in a "white" society somehow brings out all the worst aspects of Nigerian class and race prejudice. Thus, working-class Nigerian women become so manipulated by their racist environment in London that they do not even realize how oppressed they are: "As soon as a Nigerian housewife in England realised that she was expecting a child...she would advertise for a foster-mother. No one cared whether a woman was suitable or not, no one wanted to know whether the house was clean or not; all they wanted to be sure of was that the foster mother was white. The concept of whiteness could cover a multitude of sins" (Emecheta 1974:46).

As the ending of the novel makes clear, even elite women fail to make much headway against these internalized and exterior prejudices. On the social level, neither the problems of Nigerian patriarchy nor those of Western capitalism, especially those pertaining to the exploitation of women for sex or money, are resolved; they continue to exist. On the personal level, Adah is not really empowered in any way except by her ability to write; instead she is left alone and without legal and communal support. The man that suddenly appears like "Fate" at the end seems no different from Okpara or Francis and, in any case, fails to even comprehend Adah's situation. Neither Adah nor any other women in the text are able to achieve an "uncolonized mind." Instead, the social and economic bases of exploitation of elite women remain in place. The underlying metaphor of this and other Emecheta novels, then, is that womanhood is "a condition of victimization and servitude" (Frank 1982:479) and freedom or free will is hard to attain. And this concept is further complicated by the fact that Emecheta frequently invokes the West as a haven of freedom for women, while suggesting that Africa is a continuous grind of oppression. Therefore, despite her best efforts, Adah is always defined in terms of the exploitation she experiences, and not on her own terms.

In conclusion, then, it could be said that the postcolonial elite woman in all three novels is an isolated figure who has only a few choices open to her to alter her condition. Hillela chooses a form of sexual politics, Sonali uses a sense of commitment to other people's problems, while Adah resorts to religion and writing. While the ending of Sahgal's novel is hopeful and seems to call for more involvement, yet the closure is unconventional and leaves a lot unsaid. So too, Gordimer's novel is cynical and seems to call for more than just sexual bonding because there is no sense at the end of any kind of empowerment. Finally, Emecheta's outlook for a future without female oppression is bleak and pessimistic. While Adah's fate appears to be unique, exceptional and singular even among the other female elites, all three novels in fact reveal that these fates of their protagonists are typical. In this regard, all three novels present complex and disturbing views of the situation of women in a post/neo-colonial society.

Notes

[1]Cythera derives from a painting by Watteau called "Pilgrimage to Cythera" (1712) in which it seems to be an idealized place, and it retains the same meaning in Charles Baudelaire's poem, *Fleurs du Mal* and in Derek Walcott's poem *Summer* (1984), item xx, "Watteau."

VISIONS OF ALTERNATE WORLDS IN *BURGER'S DAUGHTER, THIS TIME OF MORNING,* AND *DOUBLE YOKE*

In his influential study of the spread of nationalism in modern Europe, Benedict Anderson defined the Western nation as an "imagined political community [which is]...both inherently limited and sovereign" (Anderson 1983:6). It is "imagined" because all its members will never really know each other (6); it is "limited" because it has finite boundaries (7); it is "sovereign" because it replaces the power of the divinely ordained monarch (7); and it is a "community" because it evokes a deep sense of comradeship (7). However, while it is true that many nations are discursive constructs and do not have a pre-existing essence,nevertheless, they often cannot be reduced to products of the imagination. Also, some communities within the nation can experience a simultaneous sense of comradeship and estrangement. Indeed, many postcolonial nations are depicted, in fictional discourse, as either barren wastelands run by corrupt rulers, as in Ousmane Sembene's *Xala* (1974), or constructs that have many different structures, official and unofficial, as in Ngugi wa Thiong'o's *Petals of Blood* (1977). Three novels that take somwhat different approaches are Nadine Gordimer's *Burger's Daughter* (1979), Nayantara Sahgal's *This Time of Morning* (1965), and Buchi Emecheta's *Double Yoke* (1983). Gordimer, Sahgal, and Emecheta seem to endorse, in various ways, the idea that the neo- or postcolonial nation, as constructed by imperialism, is false and unnatural,[1] with imaginary claims to unity and collectivity, and corresponding to no real geographic space.[2] Instead of describing such artificial constructs, Gordimer, Sahgal, and Emecheta concern themselves with the visions and dreams of alternate (or, to use Anderson's phrase, "imagined") communities of characters who believe that the present neo-colonial situation in which they find themselves is intolerable and confusing. As in Doris Lessing's *Four Gated City* (1969), Bessie Head's *A Question of Power* (1974), and Tsitsi Dangarembga's *Nervous Conditions* (1988), characters in *Burger's Daughter, This Time of Morning,* and *Double Yoke* "dream up" alternate or possible worlds characterized by freedom and equality, faith and security. These alternate worlds are made real in the minds of the dreamers by a kind of internalization of concepts of time, space, and action that are at odds with the neocolonial world that surrounds them. Thus, the dreamers create alternative histories and identities for themselves that set them apart from their environment.   More importantly, Gordimer, Sahgal, and Emecheta use these dreams of alternate worlds to present specific themes. The theme of *Burger's Daughter* is that the only way for a white South African to live without guilt under apartheid is to give oneself up totally to an ideology that involves the eradication of suffering, even if that ideology is doomed to repression and failure. The theme of *This Time of Morning* is that to achieve success as a political leader or bureaucrat, you need to have a strong connection to a source of faith, good communication with your people, dedication, honesty, and the patience to move slowly and methodically to achieve your goals. The central theme of *Double Yoke* is that to live honestly in post-independence Nigeria, one has to come to terms with the rival claims of the patriarchal community and individual freedom. All three themes suggest that the alternate worlds are only partially achievable.

On the surface, *Burger's Daughter* describes the biography of the Burger family in urban South Africa of the 1960s and 1970s, and of other South African whites like them. The Burgers seem to be singled out for study primarily because of their lifelong commitment to active resistance to apartheid and their dedication to communist ideology. In describing this Burger brand of resistance, though, family romance becomes displaced into a record of one person's past: that is, how Rosa, Lionel Burger's daughter, finds her own identity by coming to terms with her heritage. In narrating Rosa's search for identity, however, the individual story becomes a narrative of dreams and visions because the actions of all the Burgers seem extreme or excessive to others. For example, their dreams and ideals seem unattainable; and their belief in a future of freedom seems a belief in an imaginary state. This narrative of visions in turn becomes a meta-narrative, that is, a narrative of the controversy generated by the publication of the novel itself, a story which included censorship and a scrutiny of Gordimer's own morals and ideology. In this sense, the novel shows how literature positions itself in relation to other narratives and genres and how individuals create their own modes of resistance and interpretation.

Burger's Daughter is a complex narrative of constantly evolving concepts of revolution, dreams, and literary identity. Part of its complexity lies in the fact that in the text, narrative identity contains a concept of the past which "continues to speak...but [which is] constructed through memory, fantasy, narrative and myth [that makes it]...not an essence but a *positioning"* (Hall 1994:395).   Thus, as Macherey (1978) has pointed out with regard to Jules Verne's novels, "the future projects itself in the form of the-past-definitively-surpassed" (190). In other words, in Gordimer's text, the past and present are shown to be necessary but unimportant "relics" on which to build "the Future," which is what makes everything worthwhile (Gordimer 1979:122). Yet most of the novel describes the past from the viewpoint of the present, and the future is only glimpsed at occasionally. In fact, the past and the present are linked to the search for identity (identity in Gordimer implies a commitment to revolution and defining the roots of one's political ideology) while the future is linked to visions (visions in the novel incorporates dreams of freedom and the movement from an "imagined" to a "real" revolution). It is this kind of family romance, then, that the novel describes.

The novel encompasses events from the 1960s and 1970s and describes events that are both fictional (Rosa's self-questioning, her movement away from her father's ideology, and the creation of her own ideology) and real (the Sharpeville and Soweto massacres, the imprisonments of Mandela and others on Robben Island). Yet some characters and events are a curious mixture of the real and the fictional, such as Lionel Burger himself. Gordimer admitted elsewhere that he was modeled partly on the life of Abram Fischer, a white South African communist (Gordimer 1980:31), and other critics have also noted this connection. M. J. Daymond mentions the article Gordimer wrote on Fischer's trial for treason, arguing that it was her "most direct account of a white South African revolutionary" until she wrote *Burger's Daughter* (Daymond 1984:159). Strangely, though, the novel does not set up a very meticulous time frame, and the only exact indications of the passage of time are through references to Rosa's age and to periods of time she spent at one place or another. For example, we are told she was fourteen at the beginning of the novel and we guess she is about twenty-eight at the end. This gap suggests that the actual story of the fourteen or so years that the novel charts is not linear but circular or fluid, so we go backwards and forwards in time, and sometimes remain in the same time period. This kind of cyclical progression suggests what Julia Kristeva has called "women's time," that is, repetitious and eternal time, which is at once reflective of womens' cycles, gestation periods, and "biological rhythms," as well as of "monumental," all-encompassing, and infinite time (Kristeva 1986:191).

Just as time involves an overlay of several different times, so too, place involves many different spaces. Although the action takes place in specific cities like Johannesburg, Pretoria, Nice, and London, yet the locations themselves are less important than the sense of belonging or identification that the characters have to specific spaces like prisons and townships. Frequently, space is linked to a sense of commitment or ideology, especially when it provides the means for racial separation, for dividing "that" (Lionel's) house and the "'place' of those millions who have been dispossessed" (Gordimer 1979:150). What is significant about this definition of place is that it refuses to define, because in such places "categories and functions lose their ordination and logic" (150) due to the fact that they are created— and remain in place—by the white man's mind.

The most important location that determines action is prison, which is described as a barrier to ordinary forms of communication, being a "fortress" (Gordimer 1979:9), with double doors, stone arches, gargoyle-like lamps, iron studs—all of which prevent much sunlight from coming in (15). However, it is also a place which fosters alternative forms of communication, so that even without meeting her, Rosa knows that her jailed mother would guess that she, Rosa, was waiting outside, to give her some provisions (15). Connections occur because for most whites, prison becomes a state of mind, a choice, or a statement of their ideology. Thus, Rosa, having chosen prison over a carefree existence in Europe at the end of the novel, finds a clear sense of identity because the laws of segregation are not enforced in women's jails, enabling the races to mix   freely (354).   Here, prison seems to have become the ideal place or utopia she has been searching for, a place without segregation, where freedom of movement   may   be   restricted,   but   where   inter-racial communication is possible (354).   Communication between the races extends outside as well, through hand-drawn Christmas cards which show "carol singers" recognizable to the recipients as their friends in prison (356).

Another important location that determines action is the Burger household, which is not really a home but an expression of an ideology, namely, "outrage" against atrocities (Gordimer 1979: 3), commitment to black liberation through communism, and the courage of one's convictions against physical and mental opposition.   It is a place dominated by Lionel Burger, whose expectations of loyalty demand that you "jump in" and "trust" yourself to him (117).   It is also a place where family members have few "exclusive rights" toward each other because the Burgers belong to other people and other people belong to them (84).   Instead, the family tries to live for the ideal future (86). Future time, in fact, determines the atmosphere of the house, and the attempt to achieve the ideal "Future" is part of the "everyday mythology of that house" (111).

If prison and the Burger household represent different aspects of location in South Africa, Nice and London seem to be no place at all, a never-never land or artificial paradise in which people carry on empty lives in non-existing spaces, where the horrors of apartheid or life imprisonment are unknown, and in which time is always in the immediate present (Gordimer 1979:287).   In this space, Rosa lives permanently in the present, which she inhabits "completely" in a kind of "time-space equilibrium" (272) that never changes.   Space is vague because it is filled with individuals who have no secrets (224); and time is static because "continuity never seems to break" (249). Ultimately, though, Rosa opts for commitment to the Future and restricted space, which is full of danger and fury (Smith 1980:164). This final space is a lot like the no-man's land between black townships and the city's landfills that Rosa encounters in the middle of the novel, a place where illicit liquor is manufactured, wrecked cars are dumped, and prostitutes do business, but which is absent from official city maps (Gordimer 1979:206-207). This place—that doesn't exist on paper, that is hard for white people to imagine, and that contains only crime, lust and pain—is the real space of the novel, the space that Rosa is trying to access, the space that contains all the impossibilities and contradictions of a history gone mad, a space without roots.

Since both time and space are fluid in the novel, it is important to analyze how they relate to each other to create this family romance of the Burgers. In this family romance, past and present time and space are associated with the search for self-identity. By contrast, future time and space are associated with visions. The present is dependent on the past, which, in turn, is difficult to unravel because it is narrated by two voices that often contradict one another. The result is that the actual events of the past appear to be subjective and dependent on the narrative viewpoint. Thus, although both voices describe the main events of Parts 2 and 3 of the novel in a roughly chronological order, the events themselves are analyzed differently by each voice. In Part 1, however, both voices are less concerned with chronology than with the degree of impact of certain key events on Rosa.

The first voice we encounter is that of a third-person narrator, who is not omniscient, but who describes all the events in a formal, factual, detached, newspaper-reporter-type mode, and sometimes in a surveillance-detective-type mode. Daymond (1984) calls this voice the unidentified, flat, and cold voice (163), of "disembodied power" (164) and of surveillance being surveyed (164). Sometimes this voice seems to know Rosa's thoughts, while at other times it remains puzzled and mystified. Overall, this voice recounts Lionel's beliefs and actions as well as the rationale behind Rosa's defection from his ideology and her attempt to create her own ideology.

According to the third-person voice, Lionel seems to be different to different people. To his fellow Afrikaners, the narrator tells us, he is a traitor because he enjoys betraying "the white man's power, the heritage of his people" (Gordimer 1979:61). Some Afrikaners see him as a "tragic hero" who uses communism as an "expression of despair" because of his inability to trust his own people (186). On the other hand, to his friends and followers, black and white, he is an inspired, almost perfect revolutionary, who is best remembered for his selflessness and idealism. His Marxist ideology (as is evident from the narrator's quotations from his final great speech) is based on the necessity to solve the contradiction between Afrikaner faith in a just god and in racial discrimination. To him, Marxism is the only solution to a society based on apartheid, because it repudiates racial inequality, encourages the races to work side by side with each other, and advocates a change in both the means of social control and the methods of production. All this, he believes, will result in "national liberation for the African people" (26). The narrator also points out that Lionel has the courage of his convictions because he believes that inaction against apartheid is a crime (27), and he dies in jail rather than desist his activities.

Again, to his children, before they grow up, Lionel's influence is so great that Marxist-Leninist and non-racist concepts were as normal to them as good table manners (Gordimer 1979:50). Although the grown-up Rosa consciously rejects the pain and suffering that results from a total immersion in Marxist ideology, even the narrator concedes that she is unable to ignore the greater suffering that results from inaction: "You can't be afraid to do good in case evil results" (296), she tells a friend. However, to Baasie, a black boy whom Lionel treats like his own son, encouraging him to eat and sleep with them, Lionel becomes a tyrant who monopolizes attention away from heroic blacks by dying gloriously in prison for them (320). Baasie rejects the paternity Lionel had offered him, telling Rosa that when Lionel was forced to send Baasie away it was as if one of Lionel's tame insects had been gotten rid of (320). This anger against what Lionel achieved, the narrator tells us, is partly why Rosa returns to South Africa from Europe.

So the Burger family romance gives us various contradictory views on Lionel's achievements, and leaves a lot of gaps regarding his personal and social relationships. Of Rosa's attempts to define herself against this complex legacy, the third-person narrative voice doesn't tell us much, either. All it tells us are a few facts that seem to corroborate the idea that her past and present involve a search for identity. Some of these facts are: that even as a teenager Rosa was emotionally controlled and even tempered; that she is both knowledgeable and rational about important political events like the Sharpeville Massacre; and that she has never expressed her own feelings about herself honestly because she has "grown up entirely through other people" (Gordimer 1979: 46). However, the narrator never explains why she suddenly isolates herself from her parents' circle after Lionel's death, nor why she disassociates herself from all the activities her father was so involved in. The only clue is Rosa's statement to a government official that "I want to know somewhere else" (185). Nor does the narrator explain the immediate reasons for her sudden departure from Europe, especially as she seems to be enjoying its self-centered, open, and sensual lifestyle so much. Again, the only hint is a statement she makes to a friend that without the desire to create utopia, no constructive action is possible (296). Beyond that, there is just the description of her reaction to Baasie's accusation that she is no different from other whites because of the unconscious power her race gives her. She reacts by crying, vomiting, and feeling guilty and remorseful.

The most significant omission by the third-person narrator occurs in the description of Rosa's political activities in Part 3.   Referring to them as more or less insignificant, the narrator tells us only that she sympathized with the children who participated in the Soweto uprising.   Also, the narrator takes pains to point out that she could not have had any direct experience with the killings and maimings because she did not live in a black township (Gordimer 1979:343).   Finally, the narrator describes the curious way Rosa occupies her time when she is imprisoned, pointing out that, rather than planning another revolt, she draws pictures of castles with forests in front of them and seas behind.   However, "through some failure of perspective they [boats] were sailing straight for the tower.   The light appeared to come from everywhere; all objects were sunny" (355).   What is the significance of this picture?   The narrator doesn't tell us, although the boats and sunlight suggest Europe.   The real significance, though, is explained by the voice of Rosa, speaking in the first person, which provides some insights about her search for her own identity.

Rosa's first-person voice is musing, reflective, and unemotional and often provides some general information about her actions while professing ignorance about why or how things happened.   It addresses its discourse to Conrad (a friend) in Part 1, Katya (Lionel's first wife) in Part 2, and Lionel in Part 3, because each addressee seems to be the best person, at that moment, through whom "she can...best perceive and understand her own reality" (Daymond 1984:163).   However, Rosa's voice makes its own unreliability very clear right at the outset, claiming that all versions of history are "concocted," or a series of reflections in mirrors (Gordimer 1979:14) that are ultimately unrecognizable because it is impossible to know even oneself completely.   So the adult Rosa will not know how to separate her adult perspective from her memories of her childhood (14).   Thus, as Daymond points out, when she is talking to Conrad, she has no knowledge of what will take place during her visit to Katya (Europe); so too, when she talks to Katya, she is ignorant of her showdown with Baasie and her subsequent return to South Africa (Daymond 1984:164).

Despite these limitations, Rosa's first-person voice provides the most clues about Rosa's search for her own identity and roots, and again, the search for identity takes place in the past and present. Rosa's first-person voice critiques concepts and ideas from Marxist discourse and replaces them with less complex but more immediate "metaphors for suffering" (Gordimer 1979:196). The most striking metaphors this voice uses are those related to land and water. It links land (especially prison) to commitment, and water (especially boats and the sea) to non-commitment or escape. Similarly, this voice connects the belief in the revolution and the power of children to bring it about, to commitment, while it connects the self and its pleasures to non-commitment or escape. The idea of rootedness to the soil being a metaphor for one's sense of identity or commitment is one that Gordimer used to describe J. M. Coetzee's *The Life and Times of Michael K.* Gordimer argues that in that novel, "the death of the soil is the end of life," so that the act of "killing, everywhere, by scorching, polluting, neglecting, charging with radioactivity, the dirt beneath our feet" represents the "mutual destruction of whites and blacks in South Africa" (Gordimer 1984:6). Similarly, the fire that scorches Mehring's farm in *The Conservationist* is regarded by Mehring and the narrator as a death-blow which destroys everything. Yet in *Burger's Daughter* most white people feel connected to the land not as loving gardeners but as legal or political possessors: "For the man who had married my father's sister," Rosa muses, "the farm 'Vergenoegd' was God's bounty that was hers [his wife's] by inheritance, mortgage, land bank loan, and the fruitfulness he made of it" (Gordimer, 1979:72). The Burger family, on the other hand, believe that this kind of connection is false and its claimants

are imposters who will eventually be eliminated. Thus, Rosa
reflects one night when she is alone on her uncle's farm that if
some of his black laborers suddenly attacked her with crude or
sophisticated weapons, a sort of justice will have been done (352).
Rather than possessing the land, then, Rosa takes up a more
abstract kind of involvement, learned from her father: sympathy
with the suffering people who have been dispossessed. Even
though she rejects Marxism as a way of doing that, she admits
that "that was the real definition of loneliness: to live without
social responsibility" (77). Thus, although she is drawn to the sea
and boats as means to escape that responsibility, she knows that
"when you take passage...it's to flee...[to] the bourgeois fate,
alternate to Lionel's: to eat without hunger, mate without desire"
(117). Finally, she is able to articulate her own metaphor to
describe her own brand of commitment to suffering, saying that
all that she is concerned with is "how to end suffering" (332).
Rowland Smith calls this kind of commitment "neither a failure
nor a triumph. It is inevitable. Rosa has a new sense of sorority"
(Smith 1980:172). More importantly, she connects the pain
within and outside her to get "outside" herself.

    And how does Rosa learn to articulate such metaphors?
First, she frees herself from her father's lifestyle, sense of
commitment, ideology, and discourse. She tells Conrad that she
was always grappling with the resentment she feels at being
Lionel's and Cathy's daughter (Gordimer 1979: 62). She frees
herself from this inheritance by carrying on, in her mind,
arguments and accusations against her parents. She tells them
how she hated being used as a convenience, whether as a female
object to be used to glean political secrets or as an "object of
inquiry" used to "assess my strength" (159). Yet, she admits, she
didn't really know her parents at all, because Lionel, for one, was
part father, part political activist, and part intelligent and sensitive
mind—all of which created, for her, a mysterious essence that
official biographies examining his politics cannot reveal (171-2).

Second, she looks for options other than those created for her by her father's belief in the future. She gives up his idea that the present is a failure until the future is achieved, or that resisting failure achieves revolution (Gordimer 1979:125). She rejects these ideas partly because, as Daymond suggests, in the immediate political context that she finds herself (Black Consciousness, international terrorism), the old ideas do not work because they are unacceptable to the new generation of blacks, and partly because the death of a tramp on a park bench makes her realize that her parents' visions cannot prepare her for all aspects of life (Daymond 1984:166). What she takes up instead is the idea of responsibility and involvement, so that she begins to accept that all white South Africans must accept responsibility for all black suffering, and realize that their responsibility derives from the economic or class-based power they have over blacks (161). Even as she escapes to Europe she seems aware of the accountability she faces just by being white and her father's daughter, and she eventually accepts that no matter how happy and uncommitted she is in Europe, "no one can defect" (332).

The final significance of Rosa's new sense of identity and the power of her discouse is not described, though, even by the first-person voice. As Daymond suggests, by ending the narrative with Rosa in prison, the text leaves her "on the sidelines of her world...and whatever personal development may have occurred in her is denied expression in action" (Daymond 1984:166). More importantly, her removal from active politics at the end could mean that she does not have the same "possibilities of action" that her father did, so she cannot participate in politics the same way he did (162). It could also mean that her new kind of commitment is one that can develop in any space: jail, house, or hospital.

Thus, taken separately, the two narrative voices provide us with two kinds of family romances: the story of the Burger family ideology and the narrative of Rosa's search for her own metaphors for commitment. Yet, taken together, the two voices also weave a third kind of story: that of visions by people who believe in a future that doesn't exist, an imaginary space where freedom exists and an imaginary time when the black revolution is successful. This time and space (conceptualized differently by Lionel and Rosa) is the core of all the Burger's ideology and is based on their individual dreams and visions of the future. Indeed, dreams and visions are linked only to future time.

According to both voices, the Burgers dream about an alternate world because they possess a quality that makes them appear abnormal to others, namely, an inability to accept the economic privileges that accrue to people of their race (Gordimer 1979:73). The third-person voice, in dispassionately chronicling the various arrests and imprisonments, abuses and betrayals that characterize life for the Burgers, shows that this is a life "outside the self" from which, as Rosa's voice tells us, you cannot even defect if the going gets too tough, because it is a part of you. What makes the going particularly tough is the intense sensitivity to suffering that all the Burgers have, and, as Rosa's voice tells us, being unable to cope with that suffering is what drove her to defect in the first place. Recalling her feelings when she saw a donkey being beaten by an old, oppressed black man, she states that rather than seeing an isolated animal in pain she saw "the infliction of pain broken away from the will that creates it; broken loose, a force existing of itself...pure cruelty gone beyond control" (208). Even as she describes it, Rosa tells us that others can't see the agony the way she does, that is, connected to all the other evils of society (209). These connections that she finds between different kinds of violence suggest that she has achieved some kind of insight and vision into South African history.

Only a visionary and idealist, both narrators imply, could live a lifestyle that leaves him/her open to accusations from both ends of the political spectrum: accused of betrayal by white racists and culpability by black extremists. The third-person narrator describes a scene in which Baasie tells Rosa that her father's sacrifices should in no way separate her from other whites who are racist (Gordimer 1979:322). Rosa knows no answer to that except feeling guilty and returning to the suffering that prompted Baasie's anger.

Finally, it takes a different kind of visionary to believe, as Rosa does at the end, that freedom and justice will be achieved not by black extremists but by poorly educated children. As the third-person voice asks, "Who could believe children could revolt of their own volition?" (Gordimer 1979:356). Yet Rosa's voice clearly suggests that children are, in fact, the revolutionary force of the future and that it takes a particular kind of blindness to ignore that fact.

Both voices seem to suggest, then, that it takes a special kind of imagination to be able to live with one's conscience as a white South African, an imagination that makes, in Macherey's words, the imaginary into the real and the future into the present (1966:171). This imaginary time and space is most often described as an alternate world, similar to the "a-topia" described by Kristeva which is the dream of "radical feminists": "a counter-society...a sort of alter ego of the official society, in which all real or fantasized possibilities for *jouissance* take refuge...harmonious, without prohibitions, free and fulfilling...the only refuge for fulfillment since it is precisely an a-topia, a place outside the law, utopia's floodgate" (Kristeva 1986:202). In this alternate world, the future becomes the present, or the world contains what Kristeva would describe as "a strange temporality...a kind of future perfect, where the most deeply repressed past gives a distinctive character to a logical and sociological distribution of the most modern type" (188-189). This "future perfect," as described by Rosa's voice, always connotes achievement of success, or a time when the communist revolution will occur (Gordimer 1979:109-111). The predicted future for which they are waiting shapes their identity in the present and is the reason why they do "without the pleasures and precautions of other white people" (110) and prefer prison.

And what is the predicted future? It is, for Lionel and his followers, Marxist revolution which will liberate black workers and peasants (Gordimer 1979:112). All this is to be initiated by those people, black and white, who have already, in their minds, achieved a "social revolution" (126). Rosa realizes, though, that when this revolution of the future is made present, it could take various forms: a place of freedom where race is irrelevant in the distribution of civil rights and economic privileges; or a new class of free black capitalists, exploiting the lower classes equally, regardless of race; or the arrival of a "messiah" in the form of a new generation of children who have "the real revolutionary initiative" and who can "teach" their fathers how to be "radical" (348). Rosa regards these children as the most concrete manifestation of the future because she believes they know what they want: civil rights, self-determination, and economic power (349). Ultimately, then, the future as Rosa sees it lies not within the Marxist ideology of Lionel and his generation, but in the visions and strong will of a younger generation who have a greater sense of identity and determination. More importantly, Rosa's view of the future suggests that the time period represented by Lionel's politics is over, and a new period in which blacks conceptualize the future for themselves is about to begin (Daymond 1984:160). As Daymond suggests, the force of Black Consciousness has "erupted" into the novel as it did into South African history, and Gordimer uses this fact to "historicize" Lionel's generation (161). That is, for Lionel's impact to be really appreciated, he has to be "released by history" (161) and that is also why Rosa must formulate a new sense of South Africa's future.

There is one final narrative level that *Burger's Daughter* chronicles, and that is the narration of its own story, and, by implication, all other such romances about the revolutionary future. As Rosa admits near the middle of her narrative, the real impact of her search for identity lies not just in great events or the skills of the storyteller, but in the interpretation of the readers who will interpret it in many different ways (Gordimer 1979:171). The truth of that statement is most clearly seen in the contents of the tract, *What Happened to "Burger's Daughter" or How South African Censorship Works.* Written by Gordimer and others, and published by a private, non-profit press, it is a brief description of the life of *Burger's Daughter* after its initial publication on June 8, 1979 and shows how all political literature like it can become subject to misinterpretation and suppression. The tract's six sections describe the impact of the publication of *Burger's Daughter.* Three sections deal with interpretations of *Burger's Daughter* by various groups. For example, the committee of censors appointed by the South African government label it "undesirable," a promoter of "black consciousness" (Gordimer et al 1980:6), indecent, offensive (7), harmful (8), "prejudicial to the security of the state" (8), and, ultimately, "counter-productive" rather than "subversive" (39). Certain "experts" hired by the censors to read the novel label it a "responsible" (40) and tragic (46) novel about a "personal dilemma rather than a general political issue" (48); while scholars outside South Africa praise the novel's power (61), religious intensity, richness (62), technical mastery, political honesty (63), authenticity (64), moral vision (65) and realism (66). Overall, the foreign critics are very positive, but few discuss its narrative function.

So Gordimer herself, in another section, does that. As she points out, during the time period of the novel, the communist party was the only existing political organization run by whites (besides the ANC and the PAC, which were illegal) that regarded blacks as equals. Thus, most liberation-minded whites chose it despite the repressionist politics of Stalinist Russia (Gordimer et al 1980: 18). However, Rosa rejects it because she realizes that she must find other means to fight against suffering (20).

More importantly, this tract documents how censorship

works in South Africa, with regard to creative writing in general and political novels in particular. In an early section, Gordimer herself tells us how the novel was first banned by the government, then reconsidered by the censorship committee, and finally released from the ban because its impact was considered too trivial to warrant the continuance of the ban (Gordimer et al 1980:1-2). Gordimer claims that she was at once indifferent to the ban (the censors misread the novel and she is opposed to censorship in principle) and wary of it (the censors tried to buy her off by lifting the ban) (2). Like the white revolutionaries in the novel, she declares she "cannot be bought off" and will continue to struggle against censorship because as long as it exists "the release of a single book, mine or anyone else's, is not yet a victory for the freedom to write....I publish here the facts of what happened to *Burger's Daughter* in order to place on open record the totally arbitrary powers of censorship in South Africa, and exactly how they work" (3). This idea of how censorship works is taken up in another section by a critic, John Dugard, who argues that in South Africa under apartheid, censorship attempts to "preserve political orthodoxy and moral conformism by isolating the public from radical political thought and contemporary literary trends" (Gordimer et al 1980:67). Dugard also suggests that if censorship works in such an arbitrary fashion to silence an established and talented writer like Gordimer, "how much more arbitrary is it likely to be when it is dealing with the work of a relatively unknown writer, in particular a black one?" (73). The implication is that there are lots of other potential histories of South Africa and the search for identity than are presented to us in *Burger's Daughter,* but these are silent histories. These other histories cannot be heard partly because they have been displaced by the lifting of the ban on *Burger's Daughter.*

From this synopsis of the story of the banning of *Burger's Daughter* it is evident that the concept of the family romance itself has been radically transformed by the novel. Characters like Lionel create their own heroic stories of resistance, while others like Rosa write idealistic versions of how to connect oneself to suffering and death. The various narrative modes create their own alternate worlds by misinterpreting and reinterpreting each other, while political organizations which surround the novel alternatively repress and control its impact. In the final analysis, narrative itself seems amorphous, shifting, fluid, and constantly displacing while being displaced. Therefore, time and place are subjective, while causality, determination, and the possibilities for free will and choice become a matter of perspective.

Time and place are also subjective in Nayantara Sahgal's *This Time of Morning,* but the alternate or imagined world that is visualized by the characters is very different from that in *Burger's Daughter.* In *This Time of Morning,* characters visualize an alternate world based on freedom and equality, faith and security because their own concepts of time, space and action are at odds with the neo-colonial ideology that surrounds them. However, unlike the characters in *Burger's Daughter,* those in Sahgal's novel tend to valorize the Gandhian ideals of faith in the individual and the importance of each person's contribution, while denigrating personal ambition and ruthlessness in achieving results. These ideas create not a complex family romance, as in *Burger's Daughter,* but a narrative of the victory of good over evil, or of faith over faithlessness. Moreover, the source of political power is not, as in the other novel, problematized or critiqued.

Nevertheless, like *Burger's Daughter,* there are several layers in this family romance set in the time-frame of Indian politics during and after the securing of independence. On the surface, the novel describes the involvement of the Vrind family in the Indian freedom movement and its aftermath (1930s to 1960s). The Vrind family and their associates seem singled out for study primarily because of their commitment to the maintenance of freedom and democracy.   In describing the Vrinds, family romance shifts and displaces itself into a record of one person's struggle to find her sense of identity.   The novel describes how Rashmi, Kailas Vrind's daughter, tries to achieve a sense of self-esteem despite personal and political upheavals all around her.   In describing Rashmi's attempts to find her roots, her story becomes a narrative of corruption and aberration, or a record of how ruthlessness and greed temporarily become powerful while freedom of expression and rule by consensus become weakened. This chronicle of corruption, however, ultimately becomes replaced by the presence of ancient wisdom and faith, that contains all contradictions and achieves a kind of synthesis.   This ancient faith is part Gandhian ideology and part a humanist moral standard.   Ultimately, the alternate world that is visualized is based on a synthesis between Gandhian faith and humanist morals. However, this synthesis is shown to be almost impossible to achieve completely.

The world that first appears in the narrative, however, is the present-day world of neocolonial India of the 1960s, in which social and political freedoms seem to be in imminent jeopardy. Although Indian society and politics are described as being in a state of flux, the solutions to these problems (or the creation of the alternate world) are presented in a clear and unambiguous way. Overall, the present suggests a condition of transience while the future implies the achievement of success. But it is the past that provides the solutions and puts everything into the correct perspective, because it contains wholeness and truth and knowledge. Thus, although most of the novel is set in the present, and the future is referred to only occasionally, the past is what gives the story a sense of balance or completion. In fact, as in other political fiction, in this novel too the past is a legacy that is reflected in the present and helps to change the central political tenets of Indian society (Kaushik 1988:44-45). The past, then, is what helps visualize the alternate world.

The novel encompasses the 1920s to the 1960s and describes events in terms of how they relate to the achievement of political independence in 1947. Some of the characters and events are real (for example, the salt *satyagraha,* the Quit India Movement), while others are fictional (Kailas Vrind, Rashmi Vrind's affair with Neil Berensen, the construction of the Peace Institute). There are also some characters who are fictionalized versions of historical figures (for example, "P.M." is Jawaharlal Nehru and Abdur Raman is Maulana Azad). However, as in *Burger's Daughter,* time moves strangely in the novel, so that we go back to the 1920s through Kailas' memories, but the events in the present span less than a year. The past is juxtaposed with the present in alternate scenes, so that flashbacks can be used to analyze a particular character's history or different characters can be linked (Jussawalla 1977:43). Overall, the progress of time is dependent on one's viewpoint, so that time is static to those who want to progress in a hurry and dynamic to those who value historical insight more than the actual progression of events. In fact, the contrast between speed or revolution and slowness or deliberation is an important conflict in the novel, because it marks the difference in the method chosen to achieve success. The wrong way to succeed in the future is clearly haste, while the right way seems to be careful deliberation. This basic difference in outlook towards time and history is what propels the novel forward, a difference that is symbolized by the two rival politicians, Kalyan and Kailas. Kalyan Sinha, the working-class demagogue turned diplomat, believes in speed, his argument being that starving people need quick results. Kailas Vrind, the upper-class freedom fighter, valorizes slow deliberation, his point being that freedom of expression, consent, and diplomacy must accompany progress. It is on the tension between these conflicting views that the narrative is balanced. However, as the ending of the novel suggests, the resolution of tensions lies not in a synthesis but in the victory of deliberation over revolution, or of upper-class values over working-class ones. This is because in the ideal world of the future, slow deliberation is the key to progress.

If time is subjective in the novel, place carries with it certain ideological associations. The action takes place in urban north India (Delhi, Allahabad, Lucknow) and, for a short while, America (Boston). Although Delhi as a well-defined space clearly dominates the action,[3] location is less important than the sense of identity (that is, both belonging and power) the place transmits. While belonging means a sense of rootedness or feeling at home, power connotes access to the means of political control.

In the novel, home is a place associated with safety and security as well as a sense of community. Most of the younger characters who are politicians or bureaucrats, like Rakesh, live for short periods of time all over the world and consequently don't have any place to call home. The narrator tells us that they were trans-national (Sahgal 1965:8). Delhi becomes their temporary home, nothing more. Rashmi, Kailas' daughter, doesn't feel very much at home in Delhi, either, despite having lived there a while, and tells Neil Berensen, a friend, that Delhi is just a place where politicians, bureaucrats, and military personnel live temporarily (21). Neil, despite being a foreigner, also seems to suffer from a sense of homelessness, admitting to Rashmi that there is "no one place" or person that matters more to him than any other (138). At best, home is an emotional attachment developed in childhood toward a place, that disappears in adulthood, leaving only a sense of nostalgia. So Rashmi thinks of her home in Allahabad as the place she grew up in, with an "atmosphere of safety and sanity" (122).

To the older generation of politicians and bureaucrats, however, home is a definite place with long-lasting associations. Thus, Abdul, Kailas' colleague, gets an almost physical delight in going to his home-town, Lucknow, after a period of absence: he notices the trees and bushes and longs to be near them (Sahgal 1965:212). Thus, home seems to be a concept or a connection to the soil that is absent in the post-independence generation.

Since place, for most characters, does not suggest a sense of belonging, it connotes instead a notion of isolation and loneliness, of quick fortunes and political ambitions that don't last. In fact, place in the novel suggests, more than anything else, power and influence, uncertainty and anxiety (Rao 1976:32). Depending on where you were located and what space you occupied in that location, you have access to different degrees of power over other people. Certain buildings, like *Rashtrapati Bhavan*[4] and the Ministry of External Affairs (the civil service office), symbolize power. Thus, Kalyan, when he stands inside *Rashtrapati Bhavan* senses the presence of "great vanished empires" and the power of the new "young republic" (Sahgal 1965:131). Being at the center of power is a very satisfying experience for him. To Nita Narang, a young, upper-class debutante who works in a newspaper patronized by Kalyan, this association between place and power is confusing, because she has never been placed near its center before and is thus bewildered by all the political gossip (130). However, to Saleem and other bureaucrats like him, the power that Delhi symbolizes is neither gratifying nor mystifying, but miraculous. Pointing out that because it is home to no one, it is not like the rest of India, Saleem suggests that its isolation from people and its connection to power makes it strangely appropriate as the link between the government and the governed. Thus, to him the Houses of Parliament symbolize "faith" or the "public conscience, the assurance that certain rules would be observed, the guarantee that no man could arise and say, 'I am India'" (103). There is a strong suggestion here of politicians being able to connect to the ordinary people, to talk to them, and to understand their needs. It suggests that the notion of place in the novel as a whole means not just isolation and power, but also, paradoxically, communication.

The narrator also reinforces this idea by suggesting, at several places in the narrative, that India, the real space of the novel, is a mixture of chaos and communication, of disorder checked by dialogue. The dialogue, though "bitter and noisy," fostered peace and harmony (104).

The necessity to connect to the common man is a recurrent theme in the novel. However, this theme is elaborated through characters rather than through institutions and means of control. The narrative makes frequent contrasts between those politicians who prefer not to take the consent of the governed in implementing change and those who do. In doing so, the narrative degenerates into a simplistic depiction of the victory of good characters over evil ones, and there is no analysis of power structures and instruments of control. Moreover, the governed, whose consent seems so important, don't appear at all in the narrative, not even as silent presences. Hence, the ambivalence and contradictions that characterize place in the novel remain undeveloped.

Since time and space are subjective in the novel, it is important to analyze how they relate to each other to create this romance of the Vrind family. The family romance begins, in a sense, around the time and place *Burger's Daughter* breaks off, with the success of the revolution and the achievement of independence. Yet, unlike *Burger's Daughter,* in this family history present time and space are connected to the search for identity and the causes of aberration (here, identity means defining one's ideological roots, and aberration means misusing power and strength to achieve material success), while past time and space are linked to visions and ideals (here visions mean the conceptualization of freedom and justice for all). The alternate world of the future, based on freedom, is almost absent from this narrative because it seems to be impossible to realize completely. Freedom is shown to be incomplete, constantly under attack, and achievable only occasionally.

The narrative is linear, with some lengthy flashbacks or digressions into the past, and there is only one omniscient, third-person, narrative voice. As Ruth Van Horn Zuckerman (1970) suggests, the voice seems to be that of Rakesh, a young bureaucrat who acts as the "seeing-eye, the unifying character in the novel," while at the same time remaining a minor character in the narrative (84). Feroza Jussawalla echoes this idea in claiming that Rakesh is the character who is present in all the different situations, although he remains an observer, looking in from the outside, and not really participating much (44). Whether the voice belongs to Rakesh's consciousness or not, it does seem to suggest that the history of the time and place that the Vrinds inhabit is confused and divided (Sahgal 1965:92), and its significance lies in its ability to revive the sense of completeness that was achieved in the past. The narrative voice uses little irony and introduces flashbacks with the object of showing that when the wholeness of the past can meet with the transience and confusions of the present, future security and happiness can be achieved.

In the Vrind family romance, the narrator presents Kailas as an intelligent, noble, selfless, and dedicated politician whose achievements include fighting for freedom both before and after independence. Regardless of their personal differences, most of his acquaintances would agree with this description of him. There seem to be no ambivalences or contradictions within him, so that A. V. Krishna Rao (1976) calls him a "Gandhian-type of Freedom fighter and social worker," who is deeply concerned with the individual person (27). Kailas' wife, Mira, regards him as courageous and selfless, because he doesn't mind being imprisoned for his attempts to secure India's independence from Britain. She also notices that he believes in the basic integrity of the ordinary Indian and that this belief sustains him in his actions. He feels compelled to champion the cause of liberty, and she is obliged to abide by that (Sahgal 1965:42). Like Lionel Burger,

Kailas, when charged with treason by the British colonial government, tells the court that he has only done his duty as a citizen of India and that his crime is loving his country (41). However, unlike Lionel Burger, Kailas' faith lies not in a political ideology, but in affection for the average Indian and his leaders. In fact, he consciously rejects political ideology, so that the narrator tells us, "He had doubts about non-violence...but he accepted it as the finest way for India at that moment in her history to win her freedom...it was a rescue from the spirit's stagnation" (46). Unfortunately, though, he tends to speak for the people rather than letting them speak for themselves, and their voices are completely absent from his consciousness.

One of the few average Indians in the novel who does speak is Hari Mohan, formerly a sweet vendor and later Minister for Industries in Uttar Pradesh. To Hari, Kailas is an ideal person, a noble leader who provokes instant loyalty and self-sacrifice. Yet he also sees him as a rival and obstacle in the way of getting rich and powerful quickly. In Hari's narrow and rigidly stratified world view, Kailas is, at first, a born leader with divinely appointed graces (Sahgal 1965:81). Groping for a way to deal with his feelings for Kailas, he resorts to religious mythology, resolving, when Kailas is arrested by the British colonial government, that "he would wait for his return, guard his kingdom, save his own homage till then. He would be Bharat to Kailas' Rama" (82).[5] Yet when Kailas ignores his homage and criticizes his bigotry and corruption, Hari thinks of him as a "back number, finished, forgotten" (82) and does everything he can to discredit him.

Finally, unlike the Burger family romance, the Vrind family romance gives us a view of Kailas' inner thoughts about himself and his culture. From his monologues with himself, we realize that he thinks of the present as a time in which he is confused and powerless to initiate change; while the past was, for him, a time of completeness and true knowledge. Thus, he constantly makes comparisons between Gandhi's steadfastness (Sahgal 1965:14) and the showmanship and unstable temperament of the politicians who came later; or between the "revolution of value" and "truth" started by Gandhi and the direct dealing with ends and not means started by Kalyan. He also contrasts his own preference for caution and vigilance with Kalyan's desire for haste and flourish, and is puzzled by "P.M.'s" appreciation of Kalyan's penchant for getting things done fast. Finally, he frequently differentiates between his own faith in evolution in the present and communist ideology's faith in total revolution and a new future. He tells Rakesh on one occasion that a person's integrity is the most important thing to consider, but it is often ignored in violent revolutions, like Communist revolutions, in which society is entirely reshaped (127). Kailas believes that his faith in slow evolution and the individual's consent is the best creed because ultimately politics has to do with making individuals fit the new social order and that requires freedom. Clearly, he equates freedom with individualism, rationalism, and evolution; servitude with ruthless material change, communism, and revolution.

Kailas' notion of the differences between freedom and servitude is elaborated in various ways in the narrative and, in the process, the concepts change problematically. For example, freedom means many different things to Kailas and his colleagues, the least of which is economic independence or the reduction of poverty and the achievment of self-sufficiency (Sahgal 1965:128). More often, freedom means political independence or dedicating oneself to the achievement of that independence. This suggests the ability to endure troubles and insecurities, to do one's best under all circumstances, and to work slowly and patiently towards one's goal. As he tells his daughter, "Freedom must resemble the majestic banyan with its roots deep in the soil, the Program [Gandhi's] was their watering and care and together these made Politics" (37). Ultimately, though, freedom becomes a kind of visionary insight, or the ability to put things in the right perspective, or a humanistic moral view of the world that includes hard work, tolerance, understanding, balanced judgment, reason, and faith in each person's abilities. Therefore, it becomes the ability to interpret ancient religion positively as a living faith (Jain 1978b:35). As Kailas says in a speech to his fellow politicians, "we have made the human being the unit and measure of progress so we can never at any stage abandon our concern with him" (Sahgal 1965:198). Overall, then, freedom for Kailas means primarily intellectual and moral righteousness.

Although Kailas' story is based on an elaboration of all these contradictions and concepts, the concepts ultimately seem somewhat over-simplified and vague. Unlike Rosa Burger, Rashmi offers no effective counter-argument against her father's ideas and the ordinary people don't argue with him either. Moreover, there is no critique of the source of power in the present that brings all these contradictions to the surface. Instead, the source (the office of Prime Minister) is looked at with wonder and awe, being analogous to Kailas' inner conscience as well as being an honored leader (Sahgal 1965:18). Thus, Kailas' ideology is based on a slow evolution of material conditions through a change of heart, and on a man who, he believes, has "taken upon himself a challenge unique in history: that of raising a people to modern times with their own consent" (20). In conclusion, then, the Vrind family history, which is really Kailas' history, is about the need to make the past ideals of communal harmony, social progressivism, and dedication to the country as elaborated by Gandhi and Nehru (Kaushik 1988:53) fit the needs of the present to make a future of freedom possible.

Of Rashmi Vrind's attempts to define herself against her father's legacy, the narrative voice does not tell us very much. It describes how Rashmi is preoccupied with the past but also tries to find a sense of order out of present chaos. Rashmi's attempts at self-definition suggest that rootedness in past heritage, especially in the idea of being dedicated to a cause, is necessary to secure peace and security in the present and future. However, it also suggests that Rashmi's idea of dedication involves not the creation or revival of a political ideology, but the creation of a connection to a man who has internalized his own set of ideas. She seems unable to gain a sense of self-esteem and create her own history without support from such a man.

The present is clearly not a pleasant time or place for Rashmi. Due to the failure of her relationship with her husband, Dalip, she seems strangely suspended in time, a "dangling woman" (Rao 1976:26) who is numbed and deadened, just as if she had "narrowly survived an ugly accident" (Sahgal 1965:13). She seems listless and lacking in will-power, aloof and remote from most people outside her immediate circle. But she does find temporary solace in a place: the construction site of the proposed building called the Peace Institute. She finds it remote during the day and beautiful at night, and this helps her forget who she is so that she can empty herself of emotions and feelings. Zuckerman (1970) suggests that through Rashmi, Sahgal stresses the need for people to communicate effectively with each other (85), but just like Rosa in Europe, Rashmi tries to avoid people connected to day-to-day politics and justifies this on the grounds that she is the product of a culture that prizes reticence above all else. Only Rakesh, her old friend, realizes that her withdrawal is something developed in the present, and not really a part of her, because as a child she was happy and carefree. To him, the Rashmi of the present seems like a "moth trapped in cement" (Sahgal 1965:35).

The future is an equally unpleasant place for Rashmi because she cannot cut herself loose from her present misery, even though she knows a clean break is best. The narrator describes her as a woman who believes she is destined to silently endure all hardships (Sahgal 1965:13). She takes a positive interest in understanding the past through her father's heritage. From her father she takes the idea that faith in people and politics must grow slowly because "there's no quick way to grow trees, is there? They just grow in their own time, and if the roots aren't strong, they can't grow at all, Papa says" (37). She learns from him how to enjoy each moment of happiness as it happens because it is better to "live in pain and misery than not at all" (39). She is very sensitive to people (Rao 1976:31), and admits to a friend that the past actually shapes her identity (Sahgal 1965:137).

Although the narrator describes Rashmi's passion with the past in quite a bit of detail, it doesn't really explain how her search for an identity based on the past links her to Neil Berensen, the Danish architect, especially since he is described as a man who lived only in the present. Zuckerman argues, unconvincingly, that her affair is both believable and predictable (1970:85), while Rao suggests that Neil is "too impermeable" for Rashmi to make much of an impression on him (1976:31). I would argue that Rashmi sleeps with him because she wants a way to recreate the sensuous joy in living for each moment that she had experienced as a child. Thus, she comes out of the affair with the courage to cut off her ties to present sources of pain and create a better future. However, joy and courage are not the only aspects of her relationship with Neil, because she remains dissatisfied. His rootlessness unsettles her, and she tells herself at one point that she wanted to know more about his past and present life, but he had no desire to reveal it (Sahgal 1965:157). She ends the affair on the argument that being with Neil and without the past is like experiencing emotions cut off from their roots (157).

Rashmi's method for connecting to people and institutions is not sufficiently developed by the narrator. Rather than showing us how she uses her knowledge of the past to develop her own sense of rootedness and identity, the narrator tells us only that after she breaks off abruptly with Neil, she realizes that Rakesh, her old friend, is the only one who can sustain her desire for wholeness. However, she also admits that by tying herself temporarily to Neil, "she had lost the special contact she had had with him [Rakesh,] the warm strong invisible bond that she now knew had nurtured and sustained her. She would have to recover it consciously" (Sahgal 1965:216). Her future, one assumes, will consist of recovering this lost bond with Rakesh. And on this note of anticipation, the narrative of Rashmi's search for her identity ends. Unlike Rosa's search, there is no sense here that she has developed any way of dealing with political and personal barriers. Instead, she seems to conclude that barriers are created mainly because of the undue stress that people place on haste. At the end, she argues that because people are unwilling to spend enough time with each other, they are unable to love each other fully. However, she seems unable to realize a concept of identity independent from male power, defining herself always against a man. Hence, her story becomes a narrative of displacement, that is, of constantly making her presence felt through the ideas and emotions of others.

Thus, *This Time of Morning* provides us with two kinds of narratives: that of Kailas' involvement in politics and that of Rashmi's undeveloped search for a sense of identity. There is also a third kind of narrative in the novel, namely, that of aberration or corruption, of people who believe in a quick and relentless path to success and who deviate from the humanistic moral standards of the past. This third narrative is set up in opposition to the first.

According to the narrator, there is a group of politicians in Delhi who believe that a newly-independent government must be strong and firm and not weak and vacillating, and that strength requires ruthlessness in implementing change (Sahgal 1965:218). Kalyan, as this group's chief exponent, disregards "inessentials" like tact, consensus, and freedom of expression in favor of getting things done. While Kailas is presented as idealistic and self-sacrificing, Kalyan is selfish and cruel, capable of sacrificing anybody, "from his government superior to the women who love him" in order to find his own sense of identity (Zuckerman

1970:84). Instead of arguing his points diplomatically, he is blunt and dictatorial and threatens the very spirit of the newly-won freedom because he is inhumane. As Kailas muses, the size and complexity of Indian society prevent quick fixes to problems, and that slow and steady solutions were best (Sahgal 1965:18). The idea, reiterated in many different parts of the narrative, is that the temptation to produce results quickly is a trap because it costs dearly in individual freedom and free will. Jasbir Jain points out, Sahgal believed that any change in society brought about through a sudden break with the past would be disastrous, and a revolution that tries to do that would not have the consent of the people (Jain 1978b:29). In fact, Sahgal herself believed that those "rulers who do not understand our history go terribly wrong and even grotesque in judgment and action" (Sahgal 1976:n.p.). And Kalyan seems to be the embodiment of that grotesque judgment. Unfortunately, the narrator makes him so grotesque as to be a caricature, a man who is wholly destructive, who ruins others before he ruins himself. Also, the difference between him and Kailas always seems to be a matter of temperament and morals rather than ideology. That is, it is a difference between a man who prefers present success versus a man who prefers future glory.

Kalyan appears in the narrative as a restless and brooding figure with "unstable judgment" (Sahgal 1965:20), tremendous energy, latent violence, and a nagging sense of urgency. Despite his working-class roots, he seems to have difficulty connecting to people, mainly because he doesn't give them enough time to build a relationship. He regards time as his enemy, so that when he becomes the most powerful minister in India after the Prime Minister, he sees time as his enemy because there's never enough of it to do a thorough job of getting rid of poverty and ignorance (32). Kalyan lives for a future marked by economic progress, and the main reason for his sense of urgency seems to be his sense of rootlessness.

The narrator describes Kalyan's rootlessness in a long digression or flashback which depicts his working-class childhood and adolescence. In the flashback, Kalyan describes his past to his American lover, Celia, as one in which he was orphaned by famine, raised by foster parents whom he despised, and grew up having (not communist leanings, but) a "consuming belief in himself" (Sahgal 1965:75). This belief led to his being sponsored for studies in America, after which he spent many years in self-imposed exile there because he did not believe in either non-violence or terrorism as the means to achieving Indian independence. Even when he does go back after independence is achieved, he seems to seek only money and power as well as a band of devoted followers who love his personality rather than his ideas. From this life history, Kalyan appears to be isolated, ruthless, insecure, power-hungry, and self-destructive. And his followers, corrupt politicians like Hari Mohan and Somnath, seem to be his coarser and less energetic clones, linked to him by the "seeds of destruction" (184) they carry within them.

And what are these seeds of destruction? They seem to be a complete disregard for justice and humaneness so that, despite the speed and efficiency with which they make their regions rich and powerful, their accomplishments are woefully inadequate and lacking in compassion (Sahgal 1965:212). That is, the accomplishments ultimately fail because they were built on mistrust and cruelty.

So what is the significance of this narrative of corruption in the narrative as a whole? Its purpose seems to be to show that if Kalyan and Hari Mohan (evil caricatures of corrupt politicians) self-destruct, it is because theirs is not a "revolution of value" as Gandhi's and Kailas's is. At one point, the narrator digresses into a long flashback on Gandhi's activities in the 1920s and 30s to show how much Kalyan has deviated from the spirit of Indian freedom. In doing so, the narrator makes Gandhi synonymous with truth and humanism, which is problematic.

According to the narrator, Kalyan's aberrance stems from his inability to understand the significance of Gandhi's belief in non-violence and his faith in the average Indian. Sahgal referred to non-violence as the "most fearlessly active force" in pre-independence politics because it required the individual to be free from fear and hatred and aware of the value of human effort (Sahgal 1968:25). Moreover, Sahgal seems to have considered it an effective force in post-independence politics as well (Jain 1978b:23).   However, in the novel, Kalyan denigrates non-violence, calling it a "belief in the power of suffering" which is a "lie" because "suffering is evil" (Sahgal 1965:71). Kailas, on the other hand, believes non-violence is a philosophy that enables one to protest against unjust laws while at the same time not desiring revenge (174).   Here Kailas' beliefs seem to match Sahgal's own.   The same correspondence is true of Gandhi's emphasis on the worth of each individual Indian.   That is, Kalyan believes that the individual is subordinate to political exegencies and economic necessities.   However, Kailas believes in bringing the average man to the center of politics because no power on earth could conquer people who really want to be free (176).   This difference between the two men is very important, yet the narrator marginalizes Kailas' view even while endorsing it because, although Kalyan suddenly falls from grace, neither Kailas nor the narrator do anything to empower the average Indian worker or peasant or give him a voice.

Since Kalyan falls and Kailas' method prevails, we should examine the results that the latter is supposed to achieve. According to the narrator, Kailas' method will achieve a future world which is not like the one Lionel Burger waited for. That is, it will not result in power in the hands of black workers and peasants, but in an evolution of people's minds toward peaceful co-existence, shared wealth, and tolerance. It is a future in which people's morals will be radically changed because it will be brought about by a "crusade for justice and equality" (Jain

1978b:25) rather than by "a class war [or]...a religious crusade" (24). In fact, Kailas' view of the future seems to be already contained in the past (Gandhian *satyagraha*)[6] rather than being a radical change from the past.

Rashmi also has a view of an alternate world in the future. On a personal level, she sees the future as a break from present misery through a renewal of relationships molded in the past. On a political level, she regards it as the achievement of a kind of welfare state in which the needs of the younger generation of Indians are taken care of. Thus, when she hears from Neil that the state of Denmark takes care of all the materials needs of his children, she tells him enviously that it must be wonderful to have one's future economic needs all taken care of (Saghal 1965:145). Neil, on the other hand, denigrates a future that secures only economic needs, claiming that it leaves a person with "a deep dissatisfaction" because "we have every material thing we want. And sometimes it has dire effects. Like internal haemorrhage, when you don't know what has hit you but you're dying" (145). Here Neil seems to echo Kailas, because Kailas hopes to secure for the average Indian primarily political freedoms and civil liberties, and only after that the opportunity to break free of the cycle of poverty. Overall, the future seems to be a happy marriage of past wholeness and present opportunities, or what Rao would call a blending of the past with the present to project "the image of the future in the mirror of individual consciousness" (Rao 1976:38).

Ultimately, then, it is the past—or rather, the really ancient past, prior even to Gandhi—that determines the kind of world that will be achieved in the future. India's ancient past was a time, Kailas believes, that was based on faith and wisdom, and this created Gandhi's philosophy of humanism and non-violence. It was a time and space which contained contradictions also, that is, a dual philosophy of goodness and evil linked together (Sahgal 1965:40). Out of these contradictions, Sahgal seems to suggest through the character of Kailas, comes timelessness, or a faith beyond space and time that is the real determinant behind Kailas' actions. It is a faith, Kailas learns from a mentor, that "has held this land together, faith that will carry us to our goal...we must resolve to cast out fear and to unite under God to serve this land" (178). The history of this faith—call it Hinduism, humanism, or Gandhism—is the real history of this novel, and (in Kailas' view) of India. It is the story, he tells us, of Hindu, Christian, Jew, and Muslim because India encourages all religions to flourish (40). For Sahgal, then, Kailas and Gandhi adhere to this spirit of religion, because they rely on tradition, emphasize the role of the individual, and stress moral values (Jain 1978b:19). And this spirit of religion, in turn, is based on the concept of *Karma,* which encourages both passivity about man's present state of existence (which is merely a result of his past actions) as well as activity in the power it gives him to create a better future for himself (34). Through Kailas, then, Sahgal seems to be suggesting that traditional religion can "coexist with a liberal, enlightened attitude and that it need not be an inhibiting factor in the development of life" (34). The novel's point, then, is that only a combination of "ancient wisdom/religion" and "faith in the individual" can make the world of the future a reality.

Thus, the alternate world/identity that is conceptualized in this novel is really Sahgal's notion of the importance of religion in society. Characters like Kailas participate heroically in past and present events; others, like Rashmi, search for ways to connect with people and to appreciate past traditions. Some, like Kalyan, try to deviate from their designated time and place to make themselves powerful, but fail. The really significant presence in the narrative is a timeless faith, rooted in space (undivided India), but which is actually a creation of Sahgal's own notion of Hindu *Karma.* This notion is woven into all these characters and ideas so intricately that it doesn't even consider some of the very real problems that resulted from putting

Gandhi's ideas into practice in post-independence India, such as the government's inability to deal firmly with complex communal issues because of the stress on ethics (Kaushik 1988:47). At best, then, Sahgal is offering us an alternate world based on a religion in which faith grows out of superstition, and tolerance out of intolerance. The idea we take away from the novel most forcefully is that out of past contradictions and conflicts comes the renewal that is necessary to conceive of an alternate world of freedom and equality.

The alternate world of freedom and equality that is visualized in Emecheta's *Double Yoke* is based on a form of sexual equality that is achievable through a delicate balance between the rival claims of tradition and modernism. In order to achieve this balance, the narrative suggests, both men and women must have the strength to support social change and to fight abuse. More specifically, it means that men must change their attitudes towards women and regard them with respect and understanding and as individuals in their own right, even if this change requires opposing traditional practices. The alternate world therefore involves notions of time, space, and action that are at odds with the traditional practices that the novel describes. However, as in *This Time of Morning,* the alternate world in this novel is not really achievable.

There are several layers in this gender-based romance set in post-independence Nigeria. On the surface, the novel describes the struggles of an educated Ibibio male (in this case, Ete Kamba) to understand his role as an individual in postcolonial Nigerian society. The narrative describes how he tries to come to terms with his responsibilities towards his community and towards individual women. In describing Ete Kamba's struggles, male narrative displaces itself into a record of one female's struggle to find her sense of identity. The novel also describes how Nko, Ete Kamba's girlfriend, tries to maintain her sense of dignity and purpose despite being trapped and abused by the power structures of patriarchy and capitalism. In describing Nko's attempts to find her own identity, personal narrative becomes a record of the process of social transformation. The transformation involves envisioning an ideal society in which obsolete taboos and damaging prejudices are discarded, and the individual person finds fulfillment both within and apart from his/her community. Thus, the novel valorizes an alternate or ideal Nigeria based on sexual equality which is achievable through the defeat of patriarchy by the forces of individualism. However, how individualism may actually gather enough strength to destroy the patriarchal bases of Nigerian society is not really made clear.

Double Yoke describes Nigerian society in the 1980s as one in which the conflicting demands of communalism and capitalism meet head-on. It is therefore primarily a narrative of loss. The immediate past is a time when both the individual and the community experience a loss of innocence and an exposure to the corruptions of commercialization and economic power. As Anthony Barthelemy (1989) suggests, Emecheta herself seems torn between the loyalties of "race, culture, and sex" and therefore writes about "a world lost and a world becoming, a world destroyed and a world indestructible" (559). In *Double Yoke,* the present is a time of individual crisis and change, of flux and confusion, which seems resolvable only by individual will and creative thinking. Finally, the future is a period of individual and communal delusion, that is, an imaginary time and space which seems to hold the promise of individual and communal synthesis, but which ultimately fails to resolve anything. The alternate world in which the individual and the community achieve a harmonious synthesis, therefore, does not seem clearly articulated.

The novel encompasses the early 1980s in eastern Nigeria and describes events in terms of how they impact the male and the female differently. Unlike *Burger's Daughter* and *This Time of Morning,* government and politics do not play a dominant role in the novel; instead, the politics of gender becomes all-important.

Thus, the characters and events in the novel are not historical or fictionalized versions of history, but are oppositional, important only in terms of how they empower men and oppress women. Rather than using a narrative that uses synchronic time, Emecheta utilizes the devise of time as memory, with Ete Kamba in the present remembering the past and reflecting on the future. To make this effective, Emecheta adds the device of the frame. She constructs the entire narrative as Ete Kamba's memory of the past, and frames it with the present, that is, having him sit in a library and write about the past with the help of a few mentors. Thus, the narrative really becomes a reflection of Ete Kamba's ideology, and Nko doesn't really provide an effective challenge to it.

There are few exact indications of the passage of time in the novel. Only once, at the beginning, are we told that we are encountering the era of the eighties; otherwise, the only other references to time are through indications of Ete Kamba's age. We are told that he is 18 when the memory begins and we guess that he is about 24 when he returns to the present at the end. The real time of the novel is a kind of mixed temporality, which at first seems a combination of "Western diachronicity and traditional African synchronicity...the personal dilemma of the African confronted and lured by Western time and Western culture" (Barthelemy 1989:559). Clearly, time is not just synchronic because that would involve a sense of recurrence and repetition which embodies continuity (560). According to Barthelemy, in this kind of temporality, every incident in the present is actually a repetition of a past incident and an implication of a future one and involves the whole community (560). Yet time is not really diachronic either, because the narrative progresses through an alternation, in successive chapters, between Ete Kamba's reactions to incidents and Nko's. This suggests that what we are dealing with is not a combination of synchronic with diachronic time, but of "men's time" with "women's time." Barthelemy explains that what this means is a combination of African synchronic time (the idea of return) with gendered time (biological rhythms). Emecheta's perception of time is therefore cyclical in both the African and Kristevan sense and is characterized by conflict (560). The conflict arises because time is neither synchronic nor diachronic, so that, in the narrative, "women still remain apart, and female biology and patriarchal imperatives focus the woman's attention on 'liberating' aspects of Western [capitalist] culture even as the women seek to find ways to adhere to indigenous culture that Emecheta believes oppresses them" (560- 561). Overall, then, in the world described by the narrative, time is ambivalent.

If time is ambivalent in the novel, so is place. The action takes place in specific villages and cities like Mankong and Calabar, yet the locations themselves are less important than the degree of hierarchy or division that they convey. The city (Calabar) and the university (the University of Calabar at Malabor) at first seem to embody individualism and freedom (through capitalism and education); while the village (Mankong, Nbamkpa) seem to suggest tradition and bondage (through poverty and ignorance). However, the freedom that the city offers is illusory because it combines the powers of patriarchy and capitalism to oppress the students/inhabitants. Related to this is the idea that a person's rank within a location (in other words, his/her class and gender) is more important than where he/she is situated physically. Therefore, an upper-class male can use his rank and gender to oppress-lower class males or women of all classes. Thus, place in the novel suggests that poor people and women are usually more oppressed when they try to relocate themselves in terms of rank and learning than when they remain in their traditional roles. Overall, there seems little hope for change in the future.

Villages, in the novel, represent tradition, the community, and sameness. They are places in which farming is more important than a university education or economic privileges, although there is plenty of competition and rivalry between different families. The fact that Ete Kamba, a village boy, can actually work his way up towards a university education in the city seems to be unusual, and is regarded as a momentous change for him. It is therefore an occasion for celebration by the whole community. Immediately, Ete Kamba becomes an elite (Emecheta 1983:21). Thus, the idea of the sameness of village life is challenged by the fact that education can change a person's rank and class. The idea of the unchanging village is further problematized by the issue of gender.

As the narrative indicates, when a village woman has the same good fortune as an intelligent village man and gets admission to a university in the city, she experiences not an elevation in status, but difficulties and problems. She is the potential "new woman" who is educated (Emecheta 1983: 94). In other words, a woman's transition from ignorance/illiteracy to knowledge/education is also a transition from happiness to misery because, as the narrator implies, an ignorant woman usually remains happy with village life, a husband and children.

In contrast to the village, the university fosters a kind of individualism that seems, on the surface, to be a great benefit to both men and women because it involves a reformist way of thinking and insists on a rejection of customs that have become obsolete. Thus, a woman at the university can reject traditional taboos against female education and get a "new self" (Emecheta 1983:92). She can question everything, even at the risk of male disapproval, and can develop her own defenses against male exploitation. In one scene, Nko asks herself whether she did the right thing by coming to the university. And she answers herself with a yes, especially sine she can use her looks to influence male professors to give her good grades (110). This statement suggests that the university offers individualism and competition at a cost, namely, the risk of becoming commodified and objectified. The university begins to look, therefore, like a structure based on hierarchies imposed by class and gender, which can oppress women even more powerfully than village patriarchy. In fact, it becomes an institution of capitalist male oppression.

The university is actually a microcosm of society because it is clearly dominated by affluent males like the Reverend Professor Elder Ikot. Ikot is described as a religious hypocrite who uses religious rhetoric and economic status to enslave male students and sexually exploit female ones. Deriving most of his power from patriarchal tradition, he seems able to commodify his students into objects of mental and physical control. According to the narrator, he treats them much the way the Rev. Jim Jones treated his followers in Jonestown just before the mass suicide, because "people did not want to think. These Elders and prophets did the thinking for them" (Emecheta 1983:79). The implied irony in "did not want" cannot be overlooked. To add to this mind-control, he treats female students like Nko as sex objects, using his words and body language to suggest to them that "if you don't let me sleep with you at any time I feel like it, you don't get your degree. Period!" (139). Overall, he seems completely unscrupulous and depraved.

As an institution, the university operates on the assumption that if you have a good degree and an elevated status in postcolonial Nigerian society, as well as the economic means to display your power, you can control the lives of all those below you. If you are a man, you have immeasureably more control. So Ete Kamba decides that he will use his memory of the past to protest the fact that students are forced into cramped quarters, while junior professors live in luxurious apartments and can even get away with seducing their female students (Emecheta 1983:12). Overall, the notion of place in the novel involves hierarchized institutions that stress divisions in class and gender, and create confusions and contradictions by mixing up traditional and Western forms of oppression. This notion immediately suggests that suffering will not be eradicated when one form of oppression is removed, since various forms combine to oppress individuals. The implications of this multiple oppression are described through the interactions between Ete Kamba and Nko in the past, present, and future.

In the narrative, past and present time and space are linked to the search for social acceptance and individual identity (here search for acceptance means defining one's social attitudes and responsibilites while search for individual identity means redefining one's personal values and goals); while future time and place are linked to the ability to create visions (here visions mean the conceptualization of an alternate world based on sexual equality and social justice).

The omniscient third-person narrative voice frequently tells us Ete Kamba's inner thoughts, but hardly ever reveals what Nko or other women are thinking. Overall, the narrative seems to suggest that gender relations in postcolonial Nigeria are based on one-sided exploitation, in that women are continually abused by patriarchal and Western social systems. Like the narrative voice of *This Time of Morning,* this voice uses little irony and reiterates rather obviously the idea that only when the individual has the strength to discard the taboos and superstitions enforced by tradition can the alternate world of the future be possible.

In the narrative of the educated Ibibio male, Ete Kamba is presented as a tradition-bound, intelligent, and sensitive man with decided likes and dislikes. However, unlike Lionel Burger or Kailas Vrind, he is not a political activist. Nor is he completely unconscious of political issues. Instead, he is an activist, more or less against his will, in social reform and the politics of gender. He is also a curious mixture of tradition and modernity, which seem to pull him in opposite directions.

To his family and immediate community he seems thoroughly modern because he wants a university degree and a university-related career rather than a livelihood in farming. He works hard to achieve these goals and his community is also very supportive of him. Therefore he seems anxious to prove himself to his community. Because he is an educated person at age eighteen, despite his peasant roots (his father is a poor farmer), he is, the narrator tells us, the "pride and joy of the whole community. He could do no wrong" (Emecheta 1983:16). He is therefore given the respect usually reserved for adults by his community, such as the fact that he ate with his father while his mother served them (18). He frequently falls back on his community when he needs help; thus, when he is unsure as to what to make of his feelings for Nko, he consults an older male— not from his village, but from his university community. He chooses Elder Ikot for the man's experience, understanding, and neutrality. Unfortunately, Ikot degrades him and gives him advice that is totally inappropriate. He tells him he doesn't need an educated wife and should settle for an average girl (90). Yet besides Ikot, all the other members of Ete's community approve of his choice of Nko as mate.

And what about Nko herself? She clearly idealizes Ete Kamba too. Even when he accuses her of being a whore and beats her, she forgets her pain and goes on loving him. The narrator tells us she is surprised by the intensity of Ete's feelings for her, thinking, how nice it was that he was agonized about her (Emecheta 1983:62). Until the end of the narrative, when she accuses him of forcing her to prostitute herself, she is loving and patient towards him, and feels secure in his love for her. At the end, though, she thinks of him as an unscrupulous male, just like all the others, and decides she doesn't really care about any of them. She is really hurt that Ete had discussed her with Ikot and muses, "So this was life's duplicity" (139). Thus, she moves from idealizing to despising him, and finally she seems not to care for him at all.

Ete is also somewhat of an anomaly to his university friends, though for very different reasons. Akpan, for example, finds it strange that Ete wants a girlfriend and wife in the same woman, and advises him to give up Nko because her independent ways give him too many "emotional headaches" (Emecheta 1983:130). Yet he is very loyal to Ete and assures him that Ete's problems are his own, too. So he helps Ete beat up Ikot as revenge for corrupting Nko, even at the risk of being expelled from the university. However, Nko's friends feel no such loyalty to Ete, thinking him nice and serious at first, but brutal and stupid later. One friend, Mrs. Nwaizu, ridicules Ete's traditional attitudes thus: "You mean Ete Kamba had to tell a confessor so that he could pray to God to make Nko a virgin again? Honestly, our men are so childish. When will they wake up?" (155).

Finally, this narrative gives us a view of Ete's inner thoughts about himself and about women. In fact, his attitude towards women distinguishes him the most from his community and friends. On many occasions, the narrator describes how he seems to be caught in a double-bind over Nko, so that he is sometimes domineering and brutal and sometimes understanding and respectful. Although he does lean more towards understanding at the end, through most of the narrative he is patronizing and demeaning in his behavior towards her. He seems unable to reject the idea that his wife should be exactly like his mother, only more educated; and the qualities he prizes in a woman are silence and submission, along with education and overall domestic excellence. His list of female virtues is as follows: "a good cook, a good listener, a good worker, a good mother with a good education to match" (Emecheta 1983:26). When Nko is not like that, he begins to polarize all women into "mothers" and "prostitutes." The mother-type of woman, he believes, is one who obeys her husband's orders without ever questioning them (37). The prostitute-type, he believes, is one who lets her sweetheart sleep with her yet puts on an "innocent air," who is actually an expert love-maker and is secretly unashamed of that fact. Most importantly, she is not a virgin, and must be beaten into shame. He seems completely unable to accept that Nko is neither like his mother nor a shameless prostitute, but a unique individual. What is very disturbing about his categorizations of her, though, is that they correspond exactly to the stereotyped images of African women that appear in the works of some misogynist writers (Wachtel n.p.)—that is, they are completely distorted.

Ete reacts to Nko's uniqueness by loving and hating her at once, realizing that "she had brought [him] added happiness ... and somehow taken it all away, leaving him with confusion and baffled resentments. It [sex with Nko] was an anti-climax.... He wished it had not happened ...Yet somehow he was happy as well" (Emecheta 1983:53). In fact, he seems unable to relate to Nko at any level other than as maternal/sex object. Even when he has sex with her repeatedly, he views her as both receptacle and womb. In one scene, scared by the thought that she might not be a virgin, he penetrates her brutally, trying to find " virginal blood" and feels lost when he doesn't find it (60).

Thus far, the narrator seems to be anxious to present the stereotypical African patriarchal male in the charactercter of Ete Kamba. Yet alongside this depiction, there are subtle hints that in many ways Ete's feelings do not quite match the ideals of traditional patriarchy. For example, he has no desire, unlike his friend Akpan, to marry an illiterate teenager capable only of breeding, cleaning, cooking, and obeying orders. Instead, he is happy when Nko starts a university education just like his and tells us that "his cup of happiness was apparently full" (Emecheta 1983:120). But the word "apparently" immediately suggests that in fact Ete isn't quite happy with an educated girlfriend, because he fears that men will take advantage of her on campus, and he is apprehensive that she might overtake him.

The same ambivalence is true of the way in which he allows Nko some amount of personal freedom on campus, but also wants her to obey his commands implicitly. For example, he decides not to stop her from going to listen to Ikot preach so that she can find out by herself how corrupt he is, and he has the sensitivity to realize she doesn't want his protection or advice. Yet he also wishes she was a "simple village girl" who would not ask questions (Emecheta 1983:124). This conflict is summarized in a scene in which he debates with himself about the opposing claims of tradition and modernity on his love life. He thinks how strange it is that Nko's desires for him are rather Westernized, while he is a typical Nigerian male when it came to sexual matters (126). Hence, he reacts in the stereotypical male way when he finds out that Nko has been sleeping with Ikot in order to make a good grade, namely, by beating Ikot up and calling Nko a "whore" (150). He justifies his action on the grounds that his manhood has been challenged, but later his feelings are ambivalent. He feels fulfilled as well as guilty, because Nko lays the blame on him as well as Ikot for making her do what she did. Later, he feels completely lost when she cuts herself off from him completely.

So the narrator presents Ete as both the stereotypical African male and as a multi-faceted person in his own right. To encapsulate his several contradictory selves, the narrator describes a scene near the end of the novel in which his creative writing instructor rather bluntly tells him that two aspects of his personality are in urgent need of improvement, namely, empathy and acceptance. That is, she believes he needs to empathize with Nko's dilemma by putting himself in her shoes and to accept Nko's sexual escapades and appreciate her as she is, without trying to change her. Later, the narrator hints that Ete might have heeded her advice by telling us, through Akpan, that he went with Nko to her village to attend her father's funeral. However, whether he went to support her in her sorrow or whether he wanted her community to believe that all was well between them is never really made clear. Strangely, the narrative itself becomes ambiguous at this point because Ete is absent, and Miss Bulewao, the creative writing instructor, speaks for him. Categorizing Ete as a heroic bearer of a double burden, she tells the class that he is juggling "the community burden of going home with the person we care for to bury her dead, and yet the burden of individualism—that of knowing that we are happier in somebody's company, however tainted we may think he or she is" (Emecheta 1983:163). Here Ete, for once, is being labeled and categorized as both a worthy member of his community and a radical individualist. However, this comment by Miss Bulewao also makes it clear that nobody, not even the narrator, seems able to visualize a position for Ete between the two oppositional social systems, nor are they able to see the two systems as anything but oppositional.

At the beginning and end of Ete's narrative, Bulewao's voice (which, the narrator tells us, signifies modernity) dominates. In between his linear narrative, too, there are interruptions from Nko, speaking not in the first person, but through the narrator. While Bulewao's interpolations empower her discourse, Nko has no narrative power, nor is her discourse very effective as a counter-discourse to Ete's. Moreover, neither the narrator nor Ete make any critique of the source of male power in the past and the present. Although Ikot, the main embodiment of male corruption, is physically incapacitated at the end, yet that fact doesn't really alter the power structure at all. Instead, it makes Ikot even more powerful, because he becomes (the narrator tells us) a sort of heroic battler against juvenile miscreants. As a result, Ete's dilemma is made to look like a sort of personal quirk rather than a pervasive social problem, and his friends reinforce this idea when they all indicate that silent, submissive, hardworking women make the best spouses. Although Bulewao counters this by suggesting that men who want those kinds of women are actually living in a dream world, yet the narrative concludes without reconciling past traditions with present needs, or male domination with the need for female emancipation. Thus, the ideal world based on sexual equality is not really achievable.

Nko's attempts to define herself against the restrictions imposed on her by Ete Kamba and the narrator are confined to a few interruptions to Ete's narrative. These interruptions describe how she is a product of the past (traditional patriarchy), but tries to adapt to the present (educational and social equality for women). Her attempts at self-definition suggest that women cannot remain rooted in the past if they want to achieve economic independence in the future; yet, their efforts to secure that independence lead only to abuse, exploitation, and pain in the present. For women like Nko, life in the present seems "mired in the past [and in]...tradition; African culture provides no comfort, no haven. For women, patriarchal customs encourage antipathy to culture and tradition and intensify oppression" (Barthelemy 1989:572). The overriding impression we get from her narrative is that despite individual courage and perseverance, women are really powerless to initiate change, and that only when men change their attitudes will real social change occur.

Like Rashmi's narrative, the present is not a pleasant time or place for Nko. Due to the exploitation she suffers under Ikot, and the subsequent break-up of her relationship with Ete, she remains deserted and suspended in the present. Saddled with an unwanted pregnancy and an unfinished degree, she realizes that she will have to work very hard to survive. As her friends tell her, she has now matured from a girl "whose only dream was to be a good wife and a mother" into a "sure academician and a mother" who has a "double yoke to carry" (Emecheta 1983:159). Despite her misery, though, she does seem to acquire a modicum of independence, in that she no longer needs a man to help her. However, her independence is short-lived. The narrator abruptly informs us, through one of her friends, that her father has suddenly died and, equally brusquely tells us that she has tried to commit suicide. Later, we figure out that Ete must have stopped her from killing herself. All this suggests that feelings of guilt and self-loathing seem to dominate her existence in the present.

The past is at first a happy time for her, but is later touched by sadness and frustration. Like Ete's past, hers too is full of ambivalence. In one scene, when she realizes that Ete likes her, she lets him have sex with her without enjoying it at all, just to make him happy. Unfortunately, her acquiescence enrages him, because he thinks she is not a virgin and therefore a prostitute. Confronted by his rage, she tells him that her compliance was her way of making him happy (Emecheta 1983:58). Although she seems self-effacing at this point, she does have the courage to claim that men are to blame for women's sexual exploitation because "it takes two people at least to make any woman a prostitute" (58). Strangely, too, she knows that Ete doesn't trust her, yet she continues to go on loving and respecting him. This constant alternation between passivity and self-assertion dominates her existence in the past.

As a sex partner to Ete Kamba and Ikot, she is both passive and assertive, but, overall, passivity dominates. The first time she has sex with Ete, she allows him to do what he wants, but also responds to his passion: "she allowed him, she gave in, and she gave him all, her body yielding, responding to his demands, his thirst, his hunger...she was exhilarating, she was a bundle of soft, tender, warm flesh, very young, very moist, not very difficult" (Emecheta 1983:52). The second time round, though, she has just been beaten by Ete for supposedly not being a virgin, so she remains withdrawn and cynical, fitting the stereotype of receptacle that Ete views her as. So she seems not to care what he does to her body (60).

Her behavior is very similar when Ikot rapes her. Kowing she is in his power, she turns herself into a "wooden doll" and lets him "have what he wanted" (Emecheta 1983:140). Yet afterwards, she asserts herself enough to threaten him with scandal if he doesn't make sure she gets a "first class honours degree" (140). Finally, when she has sex with Ikot again just before Ete beats him up, she walks into his room with her head held high like a "proud criminal," but walks out "like somebody who had completely rejected herself" (149). Even then, she has the strength to assert herself to respond to Ete's taunts by accusing him of hypocrisy. Telling herself that she has nothing more to lose, she refuses to let Ete make her feel guilty.

Nko's constant shuttling between passivity and self-assertion marks all her other activities in the past, too. However, just like in Rashmi's narrative, Nko's story never quite provides all the answers to her motivation, and we are frequently left guessing. As she tells Ete at the beginning of her narrative, secrets help women survive (Emecheta 1983:63). And her sudden transition from quiet and loving village girl to a worldly-wise woman who believes in "bottom power" is just such a secret. She confesses to her mother in one scene that she wants "both worlds" that is, being both "academician" and "quiet nice and obedient wife" (94), but when she is presented with both, she feels obliged to choose only one. The only reason the narrator gives for her determination to get her degree even if it means prostituting herself is her conviction that she cannot go back to her family and admit that she dropped out because she wanted to be a faithful wife. That is, she seems bound by the need to help her family rise out of poverty by getting a degree, but she also wants to prove to the world that a woman could do whatever a man could (107).

Nko's narrative involves a search for identity strung between the opposing poles of a career and domesticity, or, to use the narrator's words, tradition and modernity. As a result, she seems unable to conceive of an existence as anything other than a choice between oppositional binaries. The most she can do is to try to be both at once, that is, making the men give her the means to do both (Emecheta 1983:135). In fact, what being both really means in the context of her narrative, is being doubly victimized, that is, being shunned by her fiancé and made pregnant by her oppressor. Rather belatedly, one of her friends advises her that a woman's identity need not always involve a choice between oppositional binaries, but could also include finding an existence that is independent of both. She tells her to use her brain, not her body, no matter how tempting the latter may be (155). Nko's temporary sense of independence at the end suggests that she is beginning to realize that she doesn't have to see her identity in terms of binaries, even if she does have a heavy yoke to carry. Just a recognition of the factors that limit her self-awareness is a change in itself.

Thus, Nko's past is a period of degradation, abuse, and humiliation resulting from a persistent inability to see herself and be seen as anything other than a series of conflicting, oppositional selves. Perhaps Nko's inability to do so stems from Emecheta's own ambivalent attitude towards tradition. For example, in an interview she stated that tradition is valuable and that "what is good in the old values—let us keep it. I wish not to look down on everything we have as bad or backward just because it is not modern" (Solberg 1983:260). Yet in some of her novels, such as *The Slave Girl* and *The Joys of Motherhood,* she suggests that some traditional customs like slavery and polygyny are exploitative and should be discarded. In Nko's narrative, Emecheta seems to be suggesting that tradition traps the person who seeks the lure of Western individualism, so that she is oppressed by both. What, then, does she suggest about the future? Clearly, Nko's future is bleak, because it is likely to involve a painful process of overcoming the disadvantages of being a poor single mother in an oppressive patriarchal environment. Faced with personal disgrace and family loss, and without either a husband or a degree to back her up, she can only rely on a strong will to survive. However, whether that survival depends on Ete's support or not is left unresolved. As Barthelemy (1989) suggests, traditional culture does not "synchronize itself harmoniously to women; instead it returns to promote hardship and discord and to control female lives" (569). Thus, Nko's search for an identity separate from that tradition, makes her oppressive situation even worse, and the only glimmer of hope is Ete's supposed change of heart. Whether that will provide Nko with a stronger sense of self-esteem is unclear.

Thus far, *Double Yoke* has provided us with two kinds of narratives: that of Ete's attempts to balance his need for traditional male dominance against his awareness of Nko's need for freedom; and that of Nko's unfinished search of a sense of identity that will counter male exploitation and provide her with a degree of self-determination. There is also a third narrative in the novel, namely, a vision of a society in the process of transforming itself by replacing traditional male dominance with an individualism that fosters female assertiveness. This vision is never articulated clearly beyond a few vague suggestions, but it seems to be anticipated in the character of Miss Bulewao. Bulewao is presented as something of an anomaly in the university community because she conceptualizes a time and place in which the problem of conflicting, oppositional selves within each person is solved. The solution she provides seems to be a simple replacement of patriarchal taboos by freedom for women to be socially independent. The positing of such a solution at the end of the narrative is problematic, and it is made more so because it over-simplifies the social problems facing postcolonial Nigerian women.

The vision of an ideal time and place conceptualized by Bulewao is actually an imaginary world. The narrative suggests that it can be created by actually writing changes into the individual's psyche, therefore, Bulewao has her students write a creative description of "how you would like your ideal Nigeria to be" (Emecheta 1983:5). Her students are all male and one of them, Ete, decides to respond by writing about his history, which becomes interwoven with Nko's. The implication of this sequence of events is that even the articulation of the complicated politics of gender is a step towards solving the problem.

Moreover, both Ete's and Nko's narratives actually suggest what the alternate world is like by depicting what it is not. In both stories, the narrator makes various intrusive comments about general social evils which need to be discarded. For example, the narrator disparages the prevalent male desire to be the ravisher of the virginal female body by making it seem ludicrous. When Ete has sex with Nko, he imagines himself to be a proud conquerer of a virgin, an "ancient lamp bearer lighting her way from innocence into maturity" (Emecheta 1983:61). The ironies is this description are obvious, especially since the real lamp bearers seem to be Bulewao, and perhaps Nko. Unfortunately, though, most of the women who are in a position to be lamp bearers are degraded and mocked. Mrs. Edet, a female professor who masculinizes her appearance and her personality in order to be accepted as an academic, is derided by her students for insisting on being addressed with three titles, and they suggest it is to reassure her husband that she is chaste (70-71). And even the potential lamp bearers are brainwashed into believing that they need a man who makes love to them to be considered "sane" (105). Thus Nko dreams of an ideal life with Ete that is wonderful and rosy because she has a degree and a good job besides being happily married to Ete and giving him six children. She imagines a time of material prosperity when she is rich enough to support her parents and siblings without experiencing any hardships. Like Ete's vision of himself as a lamplighter, this picture of Nko as a woman able to balance domesticity with a career seems ludicrous.

Finally, after several of these intrusive comments by the narrator describing the dystopia that is present-day Nigeria, we are given a hint of what can be done to change it. Bulewao, as mentor of the new generation of Nigerians, tells them that "only men with large hearts can love and understand. That does not make them weak. It makes them great" (Emecheta 1983:162). The implication is that when men change their attitudes and learn to respect women as individuals, both they and the nation will achieve greatness. It also suggests that women don't need to change in this way because they have already internalized this greatness. Or it could mean that the only social power that women have is to influence men to follow their own way of thinking and that only when men change will the politics of gender also change.

On this note of muted optimism the narrative ends, and we are left with the impression that it takes a special kind of person to be able to visualize and internalize social change in the Nigeria of the future. In fact, however, all this suggestion of change is no change at all, because it does not imply any alteration to the power structure that causes oppression (the patriarchy). Women are not empowered to carve their own identities and the power to dictate change remains firmly in male hands. At its best, female power in the narrative is the power of survival, that is, the power to keep on struggling. As Emecheta once said in an interview, "our problem is beyond feminism...men...are not free themselves, even in the so-called independent states. They cannot see that they are being used. So until they are free you cannot really...claim to be a feminist" (Solberg 1983:260).

However, in consistently reducing the politics of gender to a struggle between traditional patriarchy and modern individualism, the narrative over-simplifies the true nature of female oppression in postcolonial Nigeria. The fact that individualism (and, by implication, capitalism) can doubly oppress the postcolonial Nigerian woman is not sufficiently elaborated. That is, although the narrative establishes that patriarchy and individualism act together to form a double oppression, it does not follow that this can be resolved or altered by a simple reversal, as the narrative would have it. Change, according to the narrative, means replacing patriarchy with the power of individuals in competition with one another, whereas in fact both situations are often equally repressive. As Ketu Katrak has shown, capitalist-style individualism often reinforced patriarchal forms of oppression (Katrak 1987:159), and therefore both joined together to control women (160). That is, despite gaining access to education and modern ideas of individualism, women remain on the margins of political and economic power (160). In such a context, replacing traditional taboos with modern individualism will not do away with oppression. Instead, a valorization of worthwhile customs from both patriarchal and capitalist traditions might provide some kind of hope for a future of freedom.

By focussing on gender relations, this novel creates a new kind of romance of postcolonial Nigeria. Yet Emecheta's narrative methods and her ideology seem fairly traditional. Although she alternates between male and female perspectives, she doesn't really give female narrative a voice or power, and she doesn't allow for any relationship between them other than an oppositional one. The new African woman who emerges at the end is more conservative than radical because she cannot define the terms of her own existence (Solberg 1983:261). Although the social problems articulated by these narratives are pressing and real, they are made to seem over-simplified. Thus, Emecheta gives us a romance that effectively describes a society in crisis, but provides ineffective causes and solutions.

In conclusion, all three novels present glimpses of alternate worlds that are inspiring, but largely unachievable. In the Burger family romance, the alternate world is one in which white South Africans can connect themselves to and take responsibility for racial and economic inequality; however, it is not a realm of radical social and economic change. In the Vrind family romance, Hindu *Karma* provides a source of selflessness, faith, and tolerance for upper class/caste Indians, but is not really a basis for altering the social and economic hierarchy. In the Ete Kamba-Nko romance of gender, the basis of sexual oppression in

Nigeria is critiqued, but the alternate world provides no means for female empowerment in society. At best, the three romances provide fascinating glimpses of individual and communal ways of coping with social and economic injustice, without revealing any groundwork for change.

Notes

[1] They are false because the actual territorial space of most postcolonial nations were products of imperialism so that they were either drawn at random or to enclose an administrative unit (Hobsbawm 1983:137). Often, nations were created out of existing areas of colonial administration without any knowledge of the cultures within them (171).

[2] One critic who endorses this view is Timothy Brennan (1995) who points out that literary creations are "not only a part of the nation-forming process, but are its realization; that nations are mental projections" (137-138). See also Eric Hobsbawm and Terence Ranger's *The Invention of Tradition* (1983) and Peter Worsely's *The Three Worlds: Culture and World Development* (1984) for further elaboration on this topic.

[3] Note that Delhi has been a city of central importance in Indian politics from the sixteenth century onwards, and was, of course, the capital of British India.

[4] This is the name of the building that houses the President and his office.

[5] Rama is the mythical Hindu king of Ayodhya, an incarnation of the God Vishnu, associated with the golden era or "era of truth" of Hindu cosmology. When he was banished from his kingdom for many years, his younger brother Bharat ruled in his name, always yearning for the day when Rama would return to rule his kingdom again.

[6] Basically, *satyagraha* means a form of resistance based on moral righteousness and ethics, and which uses non-violence as its principal method.

DIVIDED LANDS AND STAGNANT MINDS: WORLDS IN CONFLICT IN *JULY'S PEOPLE*, *STORM IN CHANDIGARH*, AND *DESTINATION BIAFRA*

In writing about revolution and independence, many postcolonial novelists are passionate and articulate. They have visualized the post-revolutionary world in many different ways, but all of them suggest that it is a world in the middle of various kinds of crises. Like *A Sport of Nature* (1987), Nadine Gordimer's *July's People* (1981) also depicts a South Africa in the middle of a bloody revolution, the difference being that, in the latter novel, the collapse of the white apartheid government seems to bring only stagnation and chaos. Another novel that describes revolution and conflict is Nayantara Sahgal's *Storm in Chandigarh* (1988), which deals with the crippling crisis that grips Indian society and politics when two rich northern states, Punjab and Haryana, engage in economic warfare. Similarly,

Buchi Emecheta's *Destination Biafra* (1982), describes Nigerian society and politics in the middle of a bloody civil war caused and fueled by Western economic imperialism and resulting in genocide and economic disaster.   Some of these crises are created by intrigue and corruption, others by the consequence of civil war and destruction, and still others by stagnation and inertia. Whatever the causes may be, the three novelists focus on different aspects of the conflicts.   For Gordimer, the emphasis is on a process that brings to the surface various present but submerged inequalities.   Sahgal, however, depicts the ways in which the mistakes of the immediate past repeat themselves in the present. By contrast, Emecheta focuses on the unprecedented horror that one particular political crisis can bring.   Besides these points of view, all three novelists seem to suggest that the position of women within these societies is very ambivalent.   Sometimes they seem victims of social stagnation and decay, at other times, symbolic of the nation's move toward modernism and independence; then again, at times they seem to be the "privileged repositor[ies] of uncontaminated national values" (Kandiyoti 1994:388).   Overall, though, women in newly independent nations seem to become, in various ways, "boundary markers" of their communities/nations (388).

In *July's People*, politics and society are in a state of chaos and "the fears of the whites in all Gordimer's books have become a reality--the revolution has occurred, the whites are dispossessed and have no means of escape from the riots and burnings of their cities" (Bailey 1984:215).   The bloody power struggle is played out in the background of the novel, while in the foreground we watch the plight of the Smales family, "liberal" whites who flee in panic when the blacks take over.   As the events unfold in the narrative, we slowly get the impression that very little has changed in the way of black-white relations, despite the defeat of the white government;   and that socially and economically, the revolution has brought, for rural blacks, only failure and retreat. The narrative conveys this theme through a creative use of time, space, and action.

Time, in the narrative, is shown to be unchanging, static, and without a sense of renewal. Space seems frozen into jagged images of strangeness and artificiality; while action is circular, despairing, and voyeuristic. Gordimer's point seems to be that although whites and blacks are no longer at opposite ends of the political spectrum, yet economically and socially even the most bourgeois, liberal whites remain hypocrites and exploiters, while upwardly mobile educated blacks remain ignorant and exploited. As Gordimer once stated, "racial problems, both material and spiritual, can hope to be solved only in circumstances of equal opportunity" (Gordimer 1981a:ii). Therefore, in depicting a revolution that fails to bring about that circumstance of equal opportunity, Gordimer is indirectly defending the status quo. Although her narrative may point out the need for radical social and economic change, it may also be read as an indictment of the inability of "black power" to control or effectively govern its people.

The novel is set (and published) in the 1980s, a time in which Gordimer imagines the revolution suddenly and unexpectedly takes place. The narrative depicts a futuristic or apocalyptic time frame, in which all temporal references reflect different ways of looking at the future. Therefore, there is no sense of linearity; instead, time is cyclical, but not really synchronic because there is no sense of renewal, only a return to sameness and despair. This concept of time is illustrated by the strange ways in which time is organized in the narrative. First, there is what I call the "future-past" time frame, or the description of the initial phase of the revolution. This includes both a brief history of the revolution as well as a few memories of life before the revolution, both of which are subjective and unclear. The subjectivity seems to arise from the fact that the future-past can be rearranged and recreated at will. Second, there is the "future-present" time frame, or the detailed account of the revolution in the present. This includes descriptions of the violent struggle as well as the Smales's attempts to survive their sudden immersion into the lifestyle of July's village. Finally, there is what I call the "future-perfect" time frame, or the imagined impact of the revolution. Depending on who is doing the imagining, this is a very diverse time. Overall, there seems to be no difference between time in the past and time in the future. Moreover, the Smales, in a sense, travel backwards in time when they arrive at July's village because they enter the timeless communalism of the remote black village (Bailey 1984:215).

The revolution, as described in the "future-past," seems to have no clear goals, achievements, or progress. It begins, according to the third-person narrator, "weirdly" because it is heralded by strikes and riots, which normally just fizzle out, but in this case turn insidiously into a "chronic state of uprising" (Gordimer 1981b:7). Knowable only through government-controlled radio broadcasts, this uprising seems centered in Soweto and Johannesburg and is temporarily contained by foreign white mercenaries. Inexplicably, however, instead of dying down, these riots are suddenly "transformed" into razed shopping centers and houses as well as wounded civilians (9). Like the situation it describes, the narration of the revolution is chaotic, dominated by the narrator's amazement and ignorance at the way events are unfolding. No phases or leaders are mentioned, and no lists of casualties or victories are provided. Nor are there any clues as to why the Smales family suddenly decided to escape to July's village. They seem to have eagerly awaited the revolution, because they didn't want to be white outcastes in a black continent (8). So before the revolution starts, they make a token show of political activism by joining some political groups, but don't actually put themselves at risk. Nor do they try to leave the country in time because they realize they "couldn't get their money out" (8). At one point they actually withdraw some of their savings with a view to emigrating to Canada, but become trapped in the city when the revolution unexpectedly comes upon them. They escape to July's village and all that we are told about their reason for doing so is that they had delayed their escape too long (11). We are left to conclude that a combination of fear (for money and lives) and indecisiveness led them to put off any contingency plans until it is too late.

Later in the narrative, Bam Smales gives a slightly more detailed account of the revolution when he describes it to the chief of July's village. From Bam's version we learn that the military successes of the black freedom fighters were mainly a result of the defection of the urban black police to the cause of liberation, their access to sophisticated weapons, and the involvement of African, Cuban, and Russian mercenaries from Botswana and other countries. Fear is the real reason why he and his family ran away, but Bam admits this only indirectly. When July's chief questions him, he remains silent and lets the chief answer his own question: "And they want to kill you" (Gordimer 1981b:117). Neither Bam nor the narrator make it clear whether Bam or the freedom fighters have actually disrupted an ideology that has been in place for "three-hundred-and-fifty years" (116). Later, the events in the other time frames suggest that in fact no ideology has been disrupted.

Besides this vague description of the revolution and the Smales's participation in it, the future-past mentions a few incidents from the time before the revolution, which are all half-remembered glimpses from the Smales family history. The impression we get from these glimpses is that the Smales, as prototypes of all white South Africans, no longer have a legitimate past in South Africa. The revolution has made their past vanish, or has mixed it up and rearranged it. Thus, Maureen Smales realizes that her life is now out of her control (Gordimer 1981b:139). Since, the narrator argues, the present time belongs to July, he can rearrange the past (96). The real past, that the narrative does not even describe, is the black South African's past, before the advent of the white man. It is only from the perspective of this absent past, or the "long, long time" (30) of the black man's presence in South Africa, that the revolution can really be said to have a valid significance. In this regard, it is significant because it has finally brought to the surface 350 years of blatant and submerged inequalities.

The second time frame, the "future-present," provides some details about the progress of the revolution, but the information is all second or third hand. This suggests that the narrative focus is really on the Smales family's day-to-day efforts at survival in the village. The progress of the revolution is made known primarily through the radio news broadcasts that the Smales listen to every day. The broadcasts inform them that urban South Africa is ablaze in the violence and fires that result from the struggles to control sea ports, air ports, and city centers. In fact, the radio is the Smales's only link to the outside world at this time (Gordon 1987:103). The only other source of news is July's friends who tell him that there is constant fighting and burning in the mines close to his village. Besides these facts, the narrative makes no attempts to map the progress of the revolution.

Thus, the narrative focus in the future-present is on the impact of the revolution on both the Smales family as well as July's family. For example, it describes how neither family seems prepared for the presence of the other, and both are shocked by the reality of the others' appearance (Bailey 1984:215). More importantly, the narrative chronicles the ways in which the revolution creates a series of presences and absences in both families' lifestyles, especially the areas of economic privileges and personal biases. Overall, the Smales seem to have become "culturally shipwrecked" by the absence of any clear identities and values (Newman 1988:85). Instead of a big house and expensive possessions at the center of their existence, they have only a truck; instead of good food to cheer them up on rainy days they have a small fire and a leaky roof; instead of clear cut duties involving work and leisure, they have vaguely defined hunting, fishing, and farming activities; and instead of friends and family that are familiar and communicative, they have silent women and poverty unimaginable until then. As a result, Maureen, around whom the narrative revolves, becomes totally disoriented in time, "not knowing where she was, in time, in the order of a day, as she had always known it" (Gordimer 1981b:17). Bam is also disoriented because he realizes that he has to live permanently in the present, or for the moment (76). In fact, the true absence in Maureen's lifestyle is her sudden realization that she has no real sense of self and no means to recreate herself in the future (Bailey 1984:215). That is, both she and Bam become slowly stripped of their delusions and realize the true economic realities of their existence (Newman 1988:86), but don't seem to gain any other insight. Instead, they resent the new power and prestige that the revolution has given July (even though it is very limited) especially his control over their present existence. July's becomes the voice of authority in the present, and, as he boasts to his own family, "If I say go, they [the Smaleses] must go. If I say they can stay...so they stay" (Gordimer 1981b:82). However, the irony of this statement is that July has no real material power or authority in the present. Having been employed in the city for so long, he has become isolated from the culture of his own village, and the only real authority he has in it is his ability to bring in money (Temple-Thurston 1988:56). Once that is gone, he doesn't really have much left.

The third time frame, the "future-perfect," depicts the imagined impact of the revolution and the ways in which it will change existence in the future. Just as in the other time frames, however, there is a lot of confusion and ambiguity about just what these effects will be. To the Smaleses, the revolution means nothingness, that is, they believe that they will have nothing and belong nowhere. This nothingness includes a kind of "moral and cultural bankruptcy" (Newman 1988:88) because all their biases and limitations will have been exposed. Moreover, they fear that the future black government will make society even more bloody because it will use tribal passions in such a way that blacks will kill each other continually.   Nevertheless, the future as they would like it to be also features in the narrative, thus, they dream of being mistaken for stranded Europeans and picked up by rescuing American aircraft.   These are hardly liberal visions of the future.

To July and his family, the future promises small tokens of freedom, such as the absence of taxes, passes, and licenses for work and the presence of more possessions like trucks and radios (now possessed only by the whites).   It also promises the possibility of either working in the city with the family alongside; or farming more land in the country, with better equipment and backed up by the profits from a little shop.   These dreams are shown to be naive, however, because the future-perfect also holds the prospect of death and destruction.   Thus, July's chief, who expects to be invaded by foreign mercenaries, wants guns from the white man, to protect himself (Gordimer 1981b:119).   So, whether it is a little more land or a few more guns, the future-perfect for black South Africans seems to be unstable and uncertain.   Overall, for both blacks and whites, the future-perfect is a frightening and unknown time that is inevitable and can only be escaped in fantasy.   Thus, Maureen, who tries to escape at the end, fantasizes about an indefinite time and space in which she has no responsibilities.   It is located "between two continents, where crossed date-lines eliminate time and there are no horizons" (99).   This time and space is actually an accurate description of her time and space in the future because it   represents nothingness.

What all three time frames suggest is that the revolution means not radical change but sameness.   That is, all the physical destruction and political upheavals have and will lead to very little social or economic change at the basic, personal level. Thus, the ideology behind black-white relations will always be based on social and economic inequality. For example, July always plays the role of dutiful servant to the Smaleses even in his own village, and persists in bringing them food and supplies because he had always done that for them (Gordimer 1981b:1). He seems stamped indelibly by service, behaving as if he was serving them at home (10). He continues to call Bam "master" and Maureen continues to use her polite but authoritative manner towards him because she was still his white mistress (66). Frequently, Maureen orders July to stop using the word "master," because she seems to think that a different name will make the relationship look different, yet the words cannot quite enact the change that is needed within their own minds (Gordon 1987:106). Barbara Temple-Thurston (1988) calls this obsession with ingrained roles and positions a "song and dance routine" that is "the proverbial vicious circle, for its polite evasions ensure that whites do not have to face the ugly reality of the system they consciously or unconsciously support, and blacks are trapped into participation" (52-53). Thus, the use of time in the narrative suggests that the old cyclical pattern of exploitation and suffering that characterizes life for blacks in the past and present will stay the same in the future, no matter how many governments are destroyed. As long as blacks are denied access to equal participation in the economy and whites refuse to change their ways of interacting with blacks, there can be no sense of progress. In fact, even the possibility of progress seems remote.

If time suggests sameness and regression in the narrative, space seems frozen and immobile. Moreover, the descriptions seem to suggest that both time and space have been rendered static because of the alien presence of white people in the black village. As July tells Maureen in one scene, the village is the real place for black women, a place where a white woman's labor isn't

needed (Gordimer 1981b:96-97).   If the village is the black
women's place, then Maureen has "no claim to the earth" (97).
This sense of displacement and chaos is conveyed in the narrative
by descriptions of a bush that seems immense and panoptic;
natural objects that seem mechanical; and humans that seem
immobilized or animalistic. In other words, place in the narrative
is a concept that "continually outrages the senses" (Newman
1981:86).

The bush is described primarily from Maureen's
viewpoint, as an ominous and frightening presence. She is
repelled primarily by its vast size and by what she believes is its
ability to see everything at once. Frequently, she feels dwarfed by
its immensity and thinks of it as having "no other side" (Gordimer
1981b:125). It becomes a presence that engulfs her so that her
old life of the past, like the bush's other side, is lost. She believes
she has "fallen" from the fabric of that other life into the "silent
bush, just like "loose buttons drop and are lost" (120). At other
times, she imagines that the bush has become all-absorbing, all-
concealing, and homogenous. Yet even its homogeneity is illusory
because it looks different at different times of day. Sometimes it
seems to move, at others, it appears to contain people and
animals, all of whom remain invisible, and at still other times, it
becomes a huge but contained space (26). Some of the qualities
that Maureen attributes to the bush are actually part of her own
personality; thus she views the bush as secretive and deceptive.
At the end, when she runs away from the village, she seems to be
trying to escape from the eye of surveillance that she thinks the
bush represents; an eye that sees all her biases and limitations and
presents them to her. Yet, even as she runs away from this eye,
the narrator tells us that the "real fantasies of the bush" (160)
delude her, suggesting that the qualities she has imputed to the
bush are really within her. Rather than being the understanding,
liberal woman she claimed to be at the beginning, she is really
prejudiced, hypocritical, and selfish.

Besides the bush, nature itself seems mechanical and mirror-like. For example, circular ruts that are formed by rain underneath house supports seem "hard and smooth as and the colour of toothless gums" (Gordimer 1981b:113); fruit hanging from trees resemble "hat pins" and the soil itself seems to taste "sour" (148). Light and shade seem strange, too, so that light falls in "diagonals" (84), and "tin-bright angles" (123) across "slide-rule" like doorways (123), and on "painted eyes" (29). The sunlight also bounces off incongruous, non-reflecting mirrors that "snap" but don't reflect anything (29). Moonlight has strange effects because the moon itself sometimes looks like a piece of cloth pasted on the sky (145), and is capable of suddenly making itself look shimmering like a mirror (150). Here again the mirror seems to reflect nothing, because below it Maureen and July stand arguing about power and social roles that eventually change neither of them. Even instruments of death have an eye-like quality, so that Bam's gun, which is an object of wonder to July's friend, Daniel, has barrels that look directly at him with a perfect sort of vision (76). Like the bush, nature and man-made objects also seem to gaze at people and immobilize them.

Part of the immobility in the people arises from their inability to communicate with each other. Blacks and whites don't understand each others' languages and so they cannot convey their desires to each other. Jennifer Gordon (1987) suggests that as the Smales's old ideas and concepts break down, they find it harder and harder to communicate with anyone (103). So they resort to "a train of formulas, said with feeling but without deep thought, satisfactory and useful between servant and master, but completely inadequate for any deeper relationship" (107). Even black people have difficulty talking to each other: Martha doesn't talk much to anyone and doesn't show her emotions much; even when she talks to her husband, July, she thinks she's talking to herself because she's so used to being without him that she answers her own questions to him by brooding on them (Gordimer

1981b:82). Only when she is with other black women does she talk more, and the community of women seems to form a close-knit, more-or-less harmonious group. However, they seem to be the only group able to achieve a kind of mutual understanding, so that Gordimer's point might be that proper communication between people in South Africa hardly ever happens; instead, people use "rigid formulas, inaccurate translations, intentional misunderstandings, and useless word games" (Gordon 1987:108).

One example of the use of rigid formulas is Maureen's inability to move out of a self-righteous mode of criticizing others' actions without examining the basis of her own. The narrator explains in one scene how Maureen takes a long time to realize that a person's morals are determined much more by his/her economic necessities than by abstract ethical impulses. Thinking of July's relationship with his city mistress, Ellen, Maureen suddenly realizes that moral judgments about people's sexual/marital fidelity should take into account their economic status, so that absolute moral judgments are avoided (Gordimer 1981b:65). What this comment suggests is that Maureen's moral values are valid only in one context and that, depending on the economic means available to her, they may be very different in another context (Newman 1981:86).   Yet despite such a long narrative aside on the role of economics in ethics, the narrator fails to point out the irony that Maureen makes this connection only after she herself has been forced to the bottom of the economic scale, with neither possessions nor lovers. There is also no elaboration of the further irony that, despite her awareness of ethics, Maureen refuses to remain frozen at the bottom of the pile, with no power or possessions, and constantly tries to exert her will over July. And finally, the narrator does not point out the ultimate irony that July, like Maureen, is equally powerless because he has no source of income (Temple-Thurston 1988:56).

Maureen's aggressive desire to assert some control over her situation dominates the action of the narrative. According to

Temple-Thurston (1988), the narrative centers around Maureen's search for self-knowledge (51); but, like time and space in the narrative, her search is circular and moves in grooves of despair and madness. Two types of action that exemplify this circularity of her search are her "rape"-like encounters with July and her attempts to escape from responsibility. Both types of action signify what the operation of time and space have already suggested, namely, that political upheaval does not always produce changes in society and economics. In fact, Maureen actually regresses in her search for control because she moves from being active to being idle, from using black labor to living off it (Newman 1988:87). She also regresses from a congenial understanding with July to a relationship based on mutual contempt and humiliation. These ambivalent feelings of shame and scorn seem, according to the narrator, to travel from the Smaleses blood to July's, as if it were a shot of some sort of narcotic (Gordimer 1981b:62).

There are three rape-like confrontations between Maureen and July. In each of these, Maureen makes a concerted effort to humiliate July, but the narrator describes the incident as if Maureen was experiencing the white woman's stereotypical sexual fantasy for the black man. In fact, gender is as important as race in their relationship as a whole (Temple-Thurston 1988:51) and Maureen begins to realize that the qualities she had liked in July were not actually a part of him, but were a mask he assumed in order to fit the idea she had of him (Newman 1988:86). That is, the three encounters reveal Maureen's long-time "desire to translate July into her own cultural terms, to interpret their relationship in ways flattering to her own self-image" (90).

In the first encounter, Maureen insults July while returning the keys of Bam's truck to him, because she seems unable to accept the fact that he owns the vehicle in practice if not in theory. The narrator emphasizes the fact that she and July are alone because Bam has gone hunting, and that although Maureen could have gone to July's hut to give him the keys, she forces him to meet her in a somewhat secluded space between their respective huts. In doing so, she shows, according to the narrator, "the meanness of something hidden under a stone" (Gordimer 1981b:68). Yet, simultaneously, Maureen seems to feel a pang of guilt that "changed her from persecutor to victim" (68). These contradictory feelings of meanness and persecution/victimization are not explained further by the narrator and we are left wondering if Maureen is really a victim of helpless rage or whether she tries to convince herself that she is one in order not to feel guilty. Almost immediately, though, July accuses Maureen of mistrust, and complains that although she had always been kind and understanding in the past, she had never trusted him completely: (70). As Temple-Thurston suggests, this accusation hurts her because it shows up her hypocritical liberal sentiments (1988:54). At this stage, too, July deliberately uses the jargon of servitude in talking to Maureen (for example, he refers to Bam as "master" and demands his wages from her) as a way of degrading her into meeting him only on "the lowest category of understanding" (Gordimer 1981b:71). He refuses to answer her as an equal and carefully maintains the role of a servant (Gordon 1987:104-105). He assumes the role of a servant when he wants to and not out of need, and this makes Maureen realize that his status does not depend on her good will (105).

Maureen's next action seems a kind of retribution for his insulting use of the jargon of servitude, because she suddenly asks him what Martha thinks of Ellen, his city mistress. Immediately, her words produce pain and humiliation in July because he at once stops the sarcasm, and puts on a submissive face which is open to visions for both of them to see (Gordimer 1981b:72). Again, the narrator fails to explain how July suddenly moves from derision to submission and what kind of vision Maureen or he sees.

In fact, the narrator complicates this whole conversation

by describing it as if it were a lover's quarrel. There is a stress on body language (she puts a fist on his arm, he avoids touching her hand when he takes the keys) and on the concept of fencing: they are presented as combatants who "will never escape what each knows of the other" (Gordimer 1981b:72). Thus, when July answers Maureen's question about Ellen by claiming that Maureen should be satisfied with his work as servant (72), the word "satisfy" has a sexual double-entendre. It associates Maureen, his economic mistress, with Ellen, his sexual mistress (Newman 1988:90), and that has a grotesque effect. Yet, in a strange way, the association is accurate, because July and Maureen are like lovers in the knowledge they have of each others' weaknesses, and they also know how to use that knowledge to hurt each other (Temple-Thurston 1988:54). Overall, though, the encounter seems meaningless and no one seems to gain anything. Since neither of them has what Temple-Thurston would call "the makings of a martyr or a revolutionary hero. Maureen is not a Rosa Burger nor a Helen Joseph, and July is not a Baasie nor a Steve Biko" (52); all they are able to achieve is a revelation of the others' limitations.

In the second encounter, Maureen and July confront each other over Maureen's participation in the farming and harvesting work that Martha and the other black women do daily. Although Maureen actively seeks out July, this time it is July who ensures that they are alone. He tells her brusquely that farming is not her sort of work, presumably because he thinks that her act of farming will degrade him. He views farming as inferior work, and since his prestigious status in the village derives from her superior status as a white woman, he does not want her to do inferior work (Temple-Thurston 1988:55). However, Maureen makes no attempt to explain to him her need to help the black women in their work. Instead, she thinks only of the fact that her family is being fed and clothed by his family (Gordimer 1981b:96). She remembers not only that she is dependent on them, but also that she has been unable to communicate very effectively with them, despite having been a good communicator in the past (Bailey 1984:223). All these thoughts seem to goad her into meanness against July, and she accuses him of fear (that she will tell Martha about Ellen). At the same time, she looks at July with tears in her eyes (Gordimer 1981b:97-98). And just as in the first encounter, July experiences an intense and violent anger which prompts him to beat his own chest (98). Again, Maureen shows that she is unable to trust July or relate to him as an individual. Moreover, the sudden fear she feels seems similar to the stereotypical fear of a white woman for black male sexuality (98). The fact that the narrator chooses to explicate this fear at such length is significant. It suggests that for the first time in her life, Maureen is facing up to her own hidden fears and biases. Unfortunately, this facing-up does not prompt her to change her attitudes; instead she becomes determined not to tolerate being inferior to or dependent on July (101). Thus, in this second encounter, we get a clear understanding of Maureen's motivations and beliefs.

In the third encounter, Maureen orders July to find Bam's missing shot-gun and July refuses. It is significant that all Maureen's clashes with July are over technological objects which function as "symbols of the transference of power" (Temple-Thurston 1988:53). Maureen's command, "You've got to get it [the gun] back" (Gordimer 1981b:149), becomes almost a refrain, and when July is indifferent to this refrain, Maureen suddenly decides that his friend Daniel must have stolen the gun, simply because he has suddenly left the village. In exasperation, July tries to shake off any responsibility for the gun or its thief, accusing Maureen of making too much trouble for him (151). Unlike in the other two episodes, here July is in control of the discourse, and he uses Maureen's own sarcasm against her. After that, he suddenly switches from English to his own language, and his face "flickers." Yet, despite the language barrier, Maureen understands how he is presenting a self to her that corresponds to her own notion of what he should be like (152). She realizes that she had been assigning him roles based on what she wanted to see, but that she won't be able to do that anymore. Yet she still cannot resist telling him to take on the role of "gangster" because this will make him think he is "a big man, important" (153). Here Maureen seems to recognize the fallacy of his belief that he will be able to achieve success and fulfillment in the future (Bailey 1984:217). By tempting him with the glory of material possessions, Maureen seems able to make July into a potential victim of the lures of capitalism, just as she had earlier made him a victim of the cruelties of apartheid (218). As in the other two episodes, in this third one too the narrator describes the encounter as if it were an abrasive contact between two lovers. When Maureen at first looks for July, she feels as if nature were caressing her intimately (Gordimer 1981b:147). Later, when she meets him in the secluded place near the truck, a "gauzy" (145) moon shines on the truck and throws them into the shadows (150). In these shadows, they talk and when she accuses him of petty theft, the narrator tells us she had a wild desire to destroy their relationship (152). This wild need seems very much like the wild jealousy of a distraught lover, and this impression is strengthened by the later description of her feelings when she challenges him to steal the truck: "The skin of her body was creeping with an ecstatic fever of relief, splendid and despicable to her" (153). This fever of relief seems very much like a sexual release, and what makes it seem more so is the fact that the cool breeze seems to mistake them "for lovers" (153). As if to play up her part, Maureen suddenly poses like a gangster's moll against the vehicle and then slaps it "vulgarly" (153). She seems to want to make July into another caricature: that of the libidinous black male, but the pose and the gesture get no response. At the end of this third encounter, then, July is left alienated from whites as well as blacks, while Maureen is unable to connect to anyone.

Overall, the three encounters between July and Maureen describe moods and actions at odds with each other. Maureen debases and stereotypes July in intimate and sensual settings, and frequently seems motivated by frustration and bitterness. July humiliates her and dissociates himself from her, thereby severing all means of a livelihood. The implication is that the revolution has succeeded only in bringing each person's limitations to the surface, but is unable to change social intolerance and economic inequalities. The three encounters also suggest that Maureen's limitations are, in some ways, typical "boundary markers" of her community as a whole.

The descriptions of the Smales's attempts to escape also reveal these intolerances and inequalities. There are two main escape scenes in the narrative: the first is the initial journey the Smales family makes from the city to July's village, and the second is Maureen's flight toward the mysterious helicopter that lands in July's village at the end. The first is described as a miraculous escape from death and horror, while the second is more an instinctive drive toward freedom and survival. Both are connected in some way to madness or delirium and possess a dream-like quality (Bailey 1984:215-216).

In the first escape, the journey itself is described as an "impossibility" (Gordimer 1981b:11) because it takes place by means of a truck meant primarily for recreation, driven along fields and ditches and stony roads at night, without headlights, and with insufficient gas. The details of the escape are precisely stated: it was a distance of 600 kilometers, covered in three days and nights, that began in the Smales's house in Johannesburg and ended in July's village somewhere in the country. However, despite the realistic details, it seems like a nightmarish, delirious adventure because it ends with their complete transformation into "another time, place and life" (29). This new life is obviously very different from the Smales's expectations and involves imagining the unimaginable (whites dependent on blacks and reduced to complete powerlessness). It is, in fact, the opposite of what Maureen imagined. In one scene, she tells Bam how she had once imagined visiting July at his village, during one of Bam's shooting trips, and acting like lady bountiful with presents for his family, who would all fall in line, showing appropriate degrees of delight at receiving the gifts (38). Most importantly, the Smaleses consistently refuse to see this escape as an inevitable result of 350 years of injustice and apartheid and keep referring to it as the result of a mistake/miscalculation on their part. Both Bam and Maureen believe they were caught unprepared and on the wrong foot, and Bam even blames Maureen for staying on too long because she didn't want to look like she was running away. Later, Maureen tells Bam they were "mad" to run like they did (46). Clearly, both see their predicament as a result of a bad calculation, or of waiting too long, and not as a necessary or inevitable result of centuries of economic exploitation.

The second escape is much more ambiguous. Narrated in the present tense, it is described in strange symbolic terms and seems almost like a dream. There are no precise details provided beyond the fact that Maureen, sewing alone in her hut one afternoon, hears a helicopter in the sky and, knowing it is about to land, runs toward it. What the narrator tells us, though, is that Maureen first senses the presence of the helicopter through a change in sound (Gordimer 1981b:157). It is almost as if she hears a sensation within herself. When she goes outdoors to look and listen, she experiences what seems to be an orgasm induced by the helicopter: "A high ringing is produced in her ears, her body in its rib-cage is thudded with deafening vibration, invaded by a force pumping, jigging in its monstrous orgasm" (158). Clearly, the helicopter has become a phallic symbol that penetrates Maureen's body and mind and induces her to move toward it. It seems to hold out the promise of excitement and release into a new life. However, it is equally possible that the helicopter, whose deafening sounds shuts out natural sounds, is not a herald of a new life at all (Bailey 1984:216) and might, in fact, bring death and destruction. The fact that it is identifiable by its sound is significant because Gordimer once said that the force of revolutionary change in South Africa will be a "demonic dance" with lots of sound (Gordimer 1983:21). Whether it brings life or death, Maureen seems eager to meet it and follows its progress "with a sense made up of all senses" (Gordimer 1981b:159) and knows instinctively where it lands.

At this point, Maureen begins her run—slowly at first and then later, picking up speed, ignoring the sounds of her family, experiencing a "baptismal" in a river (Gordimer 1981b:159) and becoming increasingly like a lone animal whose instincts are only for survival (160). Temple-Thurston believes that running is "Maureen's first authentic action" and that she achieves a sense of "rebirth" and "balance" in crossing the river (1988:57). However, I would argue that she is running away from social and political responsibilities and guilt towards what she thinks is selfish pleasure and survival. As Nancy Bailey (1984) points out, she runs to a "return to the illusion of identity created by a world of privilege and possession. What she runs from is her failure to find any creative source of re-birth" (222). However, regardless of what she thinks she is running toward, she actually runs out of the narrative, and we are left to conclude that she is willing to give up any contact with her family just so that she may be released from social pressures and responsibilities. We may also conclude that she disappears because Gordimer wants us to see that in post-revolutionary South Africa there is no place for a woman like Maureen.

So what kind of post-revolutionary South Africa and what kind of white woman does the novel seem to valorize? Perhaps it is an invisible white woman, that is, a woman who "isn't there" (Gordimer 1981b:148) in the text because she doesn't yet exist. As Gordimer once said in an interview, white South Africans must "undergo a long process of shedding illusions in order fully to understand the basis for staying in South Africa. Unfortunately, there aren't enough people who have the will to attempt this. It's hard to peel yourself like an onion, without producing a lot of tears in the process" (Boyers 1984:13). This kind of "peeled" woman would be one who is born white but lives with and like black people, and who tries to "give up" both the pleasures and privileges of being white as well as the ideology and unconscious biases of being part of the ruling race. This idea of the peeled/invisible woman would explain the emphasis on voyeurism and seeing in the narrative; the fact that everyone is conscious of being seen by others without wanting to look within themselves very closely. Until such a peeled woman exists, the narrative seems to imply, the revolution and the society will remain static, changeless, voyeuristic, and unproductive. This in turn suggests that the failure of the white world to enlighten itself is equivalent to a failure of the black revolution, which is problematic. Thus, just before Maureen begins her final run, the narrator describes this voyeuristic South Africa, or a South Africa seen through the stereotyping and distant eye of a European tourist or commercial photographer (Gordimer 1981b:156). This, in fact, is another version of South Africa's future: commodification and exploitation by Western capitalism. In conclusion, the novel as a whole provides a grim and pessimistic view of a South Africa in the middle of a revolution that fails to dislodge hypocritical white escapists and powerless black domestics.

The characters in Sahgal's *Storm in Chandigarh* are also in the middle of a revolution, and the narrative viewpoint is also grim and pessimistic. The focus, however, is on the disastrous consequences of repeating the mistakes of the recent past in the present. There is also the suggestion that women in such a society are, in some ways, "boundary markers" of the fragmentation and exploitation prevalent in the society. In the narrative, Indian politicians try to face the challenge of preventing two states from destroying each other's economies, and the political stability of the whole nation hangs in the balance. Based on the actual events that led to the linguistic bifurcation of Punjab in the 1960s, this novel looks not at an imaginary revolution (like *July's People* does), but at the way in which a contemporary event had an impact on the future.   In Sahgal's narrative, political maneuvers and struggles for power dominate the action, but these frequently influence—and are displaced by—the social and marital problems that plague the Mehra and Sahni families. These two families are caught up in a vicious circle of misunderstanding and betrayal that partly reflects the political hypocrisies and conflicts that unfold around them. Both plots are connected through the figure of Vishal Dubey, a bureaucrat who participates in the action of both plots and whose point of view dominates.   As the events unfold in the narrative, we begin to realize that independence has heralded not stability and peace in India, but fragmentation and failure, because government and society have fallen victim to the "Partition mentality" as well as to greed and hypocrisy.   Sahgal's point seems to be that independence in India has led, as in *July's People*, not to radical change in society and economics, but to a continuation of exploitation based on caste, class, and gender. Sahgal does present some solutions to these problems, but these are vague and problematic. Both the problems and their solutions are conveyed through a creative representation of time, space, and action.

Time in the narrative is synchronic, but without a sense of renewal. It is actually regressive, because it constantly looks into the past in order to explain and solve problems in the present and future. Space seems fragmented into units of volatility and paralysis. Action is both confrontational and circular because the two main forms of resistance to oppression are abrasive confrontations and passive acceptance. Moreover, there is no real resolution at the end. Sahgal's main concern seems to be to convey the sense that, in the present, people and institutions are so paralyzed by the fragmentation of ideology and ethics that their impulse for change is completely dormant. Only a return to a Gandhian sense of fearlessness and openmindedness, Sahgal suggests, can offer hope for the future.

The novel is set in the late 1960s, about 20 years after the achievement of independence, when political and economic conditions in the Punjab suddenly take on the appearance of a crisis. Unlike the narrative of *July's People*, this narrative utilizes a strangely backward-looking time frame, in which all temporal references to the present are made through a comparison with the past. The recent past is described as a time of fragmentation in politics and miscommunication in social relations; the present is a period of deeper divisions in politics and a pervasive sense of paralysis in society. The paralysis is defined through emotional outbursts and violent attitudes (Rao 1976:4). The future, however, is never referred to and is therefore an ominous absence on the margins of temporality, in which we are left to imagine that the violence and exploitation will continue unchanged. Thus, the past and the present are so mixed up and confused that there often seems to be no distinction between the two. Overall, mistakes made in the recent past recur in the present and seem to block off the possibility of future harmony; however, the harmonious ancient past seems to hold a clue for future hope. In all this, the women in the past and the present reflect the divisions and barriers in the society.

Independence, as described in the time frame of the recent past, seems to have given India a legacy of violence, petty ambitions, and a ruthless and greedy notion of material progress. The genesis of such a legacy seems to lie, according to the third-person narrator, in the bloody partition of the country in 1947. Described by the narrator from the viewpoint of an adolescent Sikh boy, Harpal Singh (later Chief Minister of Haryana), this Partition brings death, devastation, and chaos to a whole generation of Indians. Leaders inflame people's minds by using religion as a means of mind control, so that mob violence becomes the order of the day. Gangs loot and kill, houses go up in flames, and in general the country seems to be in a state of chaos (Sahgal 1989:32). Whole towns become "death traps" full of "clamouring, bedraggled crowds" (33), whose ability to survive depends more on the money they can pay to touts and middlemen than on their innocence or intelligence. Moreover, refugees fill up the streets of the big cities like "pockmarks," (34) until they either die or are nurtured by the kindness of strangers (35).

More importantly, this Partition also creates what Harpal describes as the "Partition mentality," which is an ability to stick only to selfish ambitions and gains at the expense of social justice. Gyan Singh (later Chief Minister of Punjab) seems to exhibit this mindset best, because even as a young man, he makes a quick profit from the miseries of the Partition by briskly selecting the richer refugees as passengers for his bus, with as much enthusiasm as if he were conducting a "sightseeing excursion" (Sahgal 1989:33). He seems completely at ease amid all the suffering, and seems to Harpal (who has just lost his parents), to have the equanimity of the devil. After the Partition, he seems equally at ease organizing boycotts and strikes by industrial workers, and by savagely smashing the head of a political rival (43).

In political terms, however, the most serious consequence of independence and the Partition is geo-political fragmentation. As the clash of temperaments between Gyan and Harpal is explained by the narrator, it becomes clear that Gyan's breed of politician prefers unchallenged power in small divisions of territory rather than political competition in large regions. They are willing to use any arguments necessary (such as the claims of language, religion, or ethnicity) in order to procure those bits of territory. As the narrator's comments make clear, the same principle that partitioned Punjab the first time drove Gyan to demand its bifurcation again, namely, linguistic self-determination, which enables him to get a separate state (Sahgal 1989:142). Clearly, a government that is so eager to divide up its own territory seems to be based on indecision and wrongheadedness, and Harpal seems to recognize this when he argues against the second partition. His reasoning is based on economics and logic, but these are not accepted by Delhi because they are boring: "Economy, and the strength and security of a border region, could not hold out against the colourful and emotional appeal of the mother tongue" (144). Thus, despite the fact that to men like Harpal a divided Punjab is grotesque and revolting, it quickly becomes a reality within the immediate past of the narrative.

One other important circumstance that the Partition has fostered in the recent past is the exploitation of women. In the narrative, the time frame of the immediate past suggests that Indian women, no matter what class or ethnic background they come from, are fragmented and exploited. They are fragmented because in post-independence Indian society "a woman was not entitled to a past, not entitled to human hunger, human passion, or even human error" (Sahgal 1989:192). Therefore, if there is anything outside the acceptable norm associated with a woman's past, she is denied a full participation in the present. Such is the case with Saroj Mehra, whose adolescent love affair means forfeiture of the "right to radiance" and branding with the name of "sinner" (97) by her husband, Inder. To Inder, Saroj's past is the source of his humiliation and madness in the present, because it perpetually "rises" in his consciousness "in dreadful images to taunt his manhood" (98). For Mara Sahni, the wife of a prosperous industrialist, the past is a time of misunderstandings and mistakes, when one made bad decisions in selecting a husband (102). Even for Vishal, the past is a time when he married the wrong woman, a woman whose secrecies, lies, and silences form a "growing gulf between them" (72). Even this woman's death is a mystery to him because he can't find the answers to his questions. He wonders why she had decided on an abortion, and why it had killed her. He concludes that it was his own fault for not loving her enough (219). Overall, for educated upper-class women, the past is a time of misery and miscommunication which seems irreconcileable to a happy existence in the present. Thus, as Vishal suggests, one of the main impulses in the narrative is the necessity for men and women to "accept comradeship" with each other's pasts, that is, with "all of it, and with all of [the other]....That is the meaning of living together" (226). The actual events in the present, however, suggest that all such attempts at comradeship fail.

The present depicts a society that is fragmented and immobilized due to the political and social mistakes of the past. Although most of the narrative attention is directed toward the disintegration of Saroj's relationship with Inder and the growth of her friendship with Vishal, yet the clashes between Gyan and Harpal actually dominate the narrative. In the present, therefore, political divisions seem to have created a sense of fragmentation, isolation, selfishness and paralysis in society as a whole. Feroza Jussawalla (1977) claims that, in the present, India is "strike-ridden" (46); and Vishal realizes the impact this has on people when he visits a factory in a suburb of Chandigarh in the middle of the narrative. The factory exudes, he believes, a kind of listlessness or paralysis (Sahgal 1989:37). Harpal believes this immobility in people to be a result of the Partition mentality which obliterates "twenty years of effort at unity and integrity" (29) in the Punjab. Harpal argues that this is a "sinister" kind of mindset because "mankind's journey was towards integration, not the breaking up of what already existed" (30). More importantly, he suggests that the divisions themselves aren't so harmful as the "little loyalties" they create (30), such as Gyan's refusal to share land, water, and electric power with him. A shrewd political opportunist, Gyan translates his demands into the threat of a strike by electric and water plant workers, which would effectively leave Haryana without any power. This threat hangs over all the events in the present like a cloud, ominous in the fact that it can happen unexpectedly and cause irredemable damage to both states.

The act of waiting passively for disaster to strike is the dominant condition of life in the present. The point Sahgal seems to be making is that the means and will for decisive action are absent in the present. So all people can do is watch and wait. Jasbir Jain (1978b) calls this tendency to wait the result of India's bewilderment at its own retreat from Gandhian values (25), and Vishal too seems to think that people are unable to even rationalize their fears anymore. Instead of protesting against the crisis, he finds that they take the crisis for granted (Sahgal 1989:70-71). The real crisis, then, is not so much the fact that the strike will cause power outages for extended periods of time, but that the political leadership in Haryana and at the Center are unable to devise an effective means to counter it. As Jain (1978b) suggests, the problem is no longer a question of the appropriateness of violence or non-violence, but of taking or not taking a stand (25). The reason for this inertia seems to be the indecisiveness and wrongheadedness of politics in general. As Vishal realizes after individual talks with Gyan and Harpal, the political stability of India in the present rests on the outcome of a conflict between men who "sit paralyzed waiting for heaven to send us a sign," and men who "charge like bulls into the ring and call it action" (Sahgal 1989:75). Either form of action seems likely to push India toward disorder and decay.

The same conflict between indecisiveness and wrongheadedness (or bullheadedness) prevails in the relations between the Mehra and Sahni families. Personal relations between and among these two families are dominated by hypocrisy, disharmony, pretence, and snobbery (Rao 1976:43). For example, Mara decides that she wants more than one man in her life because her husband, Jit, is soft and docile while her lover, Inder, is hard and aggressive The naivete of her desires is proven by events that show Jit's softness to be part weakness and part confidence and Inder's hardness to be part brutality and part insecurity. Saroj, on the other hand, realizes that because of her past, happiness in the present can only be temporary. Although she tries to stop mutely submitting to Inder's rage, she knows that there will always be a "kink" in her present existence (Sahgal 1989:202). Thus, when her moment of crisis arrives and she is faced with a choice between submission and independence, she lets Vishal do the choosing for her.

As for the future, there is no narrative attention directed towards it. At the end, when Gyan's strike is deflated without any major setbacks and Saroj leaves Inder without too much heartbreak, we are left with the impression that the future will be a happier time for all. Yet, like the invisible ideal white woman in *July's People*, the absence of any vision for the future in the narrative as a whole suggests that actually nothing has been resolved. Saroj seems to realize that fact when she visualizes a future with Inder as a completely bleak but very possible fate. In this imagined future she sees Inder fighting with her, and then reconciling with her, and repeating this pattern of hostility and friendship endlessly so that no real bonds could exist between them anymore (Sahgal 1989:224). Thus, when Vishal returns to Delhi at the end of the narrative and faces hostile questions from a colleague, he realizes that what he thought was change is really a matter of altered alliances and renewed rivalries.   The real solutions are put off for the future that never comes. The phrase "something must be worked out" (245) becomes the watchword of a government that continually abrogates responsibility.

What the time frames in the narrative suggest, therefore, is that indecisiveness is the dominant condition of the political and social scene. In reviewing the violent legacy of India's recent past, Vishal realizes that "waiting" is not good policy and is, in fact, a "disease" (Sahgal 1989:10). Even Harpal admits that his overly cautious approach to political action is the main reason why he has been put in charge of a new state (146). As for Saroj, she seems unable to do anything except wait in the anticipation of wasting her life in submission to Inder's will. Overall, Sahgal seems to be suggesting that the worst kind of ideology for post-independence India/Indian woman to profess is none at all, that is, avoiding doing "anything at all for as long as possible" (152) when faced with a crisis.

If time is unchanging and non-regenerative in the narrative, so is space. Time seems to unfold in a divided landscape, in which the land or the countryside is volatile and fragmented, the city space is congested and violent, while the inhabitants of both reflect a bit of each. The country, the city, and the ordinary people are connected to and influenced by each other in a strange way: they share the same Indian soil which was rich with history (Sahgal 1989:150). Although this comment by the narrator refers specifically to the pecularities of the laws of land ownership, it also suggests a relationship between space and human personality that is maintained throughout the narrative. The truncation of the land by politicians is actually a metaphor for human and spiritual decay. Thus, the land is described as a jumping jigsaw puzzle or a "welter of separate, sensitive identities," each with its own psychology, history, geography, and economy (15). Most of the pieces or identities seem dominated by a violence that is imposed by men's bodies as well as their minds, and this gives each piece the atmosphere of an active volcano about to erupt. One of the newest pieces, Haryana, seems dominated also by strangeness or unreality, because it did not exist in the past, and even though it seems non-existent in the present, it actually contains 44,000 square miles and over seven million people. What makes its unreality most apparent, according to Harpal, is that it has been stamped, not with the identity of those seven million people, but with the names, ideologies, and egos of selfish men who are not interested in it for its own sake. Therefore, it evokes only petty loyalties.

The truncation of the land is also reflected in the congestion and violence of the city. Unlike the atmosphere of decay and aimlessness in the country, in Delhi violence is organized, pervasive, brutal, and calculated. Chandigarh, being the very new capital of both Punjab and Haryana, as well as being a younger city than Delhi, seems at first to exude a kind of reborn optimism. To its first inhabitants, it symbolizes healing and peace (Sahgal 1989:29). Therefore, it seems to suddenly symbolize some kind of alien order (Jussawalla 1977:46), and becomes a site of contention and chaos, pulled in two directions at once. It signifies the truncation and division within the politicians' minds.

City space is also very confined. Delhi, for example, seems full of the "small talk and small ideas of a confined society" (Sahgal 1989:11), a society that thinks only in terms of rivalries and promotions. The locus for people who want material comforts without exerting their minds, Delhi is also the point of convergence for talented people who squander their intelligence at parties and functions rather than at places that need it. Chandigarh, being newer, seems at first a kind of "adventure" (161) for people who like an atmosphere "untainted" by politics, a "second chance" for people divided by the Partition to forgive and start over again (51). But later it becomes confined to the rhetoric of political "cant" (51).

Yet, despite the suffocation and violence of the city, it does have some utopian qualities. Saroj, for example, imagines a space for herself in Chandigarh in which there will be none of the pain associated with Inder's cruelty. She visualizes this as an "immensity of space and light, the dazzling dimensions of a world without pain" (Sahgal 1989:92). She dreams that a life based on truth and honesty would look like a room that is really familiar but temporarily forgotten. As she reminds herself, she's never really experienced happiness (92). At other times, she draws inspiration from the beauties of the countryside, and she enjoys the violet and purple shades of the hills and the lake because they seem to her to be friendly and comforting. On some occasions, though, the beauty of nature is strange and changeable. The water of the lake outside Chandigarh, for example, is sometimes rough and gray like granite, at other times copper colored and ridgy, and later, alive with a satiny glow. Overall, it seems to have a secret personality. The point of all these references to shades of natural beauty seems to be that the land is pure and regenerative despite being politically dismembered and that, if one can involve oneself in it closely enough, one can be revived too. Thus, at the end of the narrative, when Vishal has decided on a course of action to resolve the crisis, he feels bound to the landscape in an "active embracing" way (223). Although this active participation with nature seems to suggest that his final actions are decisive and conclusive, that is not really true. Thus, these temporary phases of active interaction with nature do not bring about a renewal.

The ordinary people that live in these city and country spaces are passive and stagnant. Part of their immobility seems to arise from hundreds of years of confinement to the margins of political, social, and economic power. According to Vishal, the decay of Hindu philosophy into a "sheeplike adherence to ritual" or a "worship of subtleties and abstractions" (Sahgal 1989:78) has already made the average Indian apathetic to change. All the vitality of society seems trapped beneath a big rocks of obsolete traditions (88). Added to that heritage, the political situation in Punjab leaves the average Indian with only two options to achieve social justice: to wait like pawns for the conflict between Gyan and Harpal to play itself out; or to get temporary redress and titilation through the power of mob violence. Overall, passivity dominates, so that Vishal at one point marvels at the ability of the people to put up with the inefficiencies of government and politic. Even when the strike is about to happen, the government shows no desire to decide how to get things working again z (213). However, he also seems to believe that if the Haryana government does not take decisive action to maintain the essential services threatened by the strike, then the people's patience might suddenly end. But he quickly reassures himself with the thought that the average Indian wouldn't resort to violence (213). All these statements make middle/working class Indians seem like one large, undifferentiated, mindless mass, polarized between these two types of action. In fact, the narrator rarely gives us glimpses of the ordinary working-class Indian's reactions to the political drama, and the only time they speak or act they do so through the mediation of Vishal or Jit or Inder. All these mediations suggest that the working-class Indian just mutely submits to political and social injustice.

However, there are a few instances that contradict this suggestion of mute submission. Twice in the narrative there are descriptions of mob violence, which seem to erupt at random. By way of explanation, the narrator suggests that Gyan's strike threat seems to instigate industrial workers in Chandigarh to throw stones and burn their factories at the slightest provocation (Jussawalla 1977:46). For example, Inder's workers suddenly confront him aggressively about the quality of the wheat used to make their food. They face Inder as a "solid wall of hostile faces" which remind him of an angry but clever animal (Sahgal 1989:65). Their complaint seems spurious and politically motivated, and they seem to be intent on destruction for its own sake. Thus, in another incident, they swarm into Inder's office, smash his furniture and upholstery, burn his textile factory, and beat him up till he is unconscious. Both these acts of violence are not really explained, but seem linked to Gyan's aggressive personality.

The conflict between Gyan's type of personality and Harpal's is actually the root cause of the strike threat. There are two important encounters between these personalities in the present, which are paralleled by two important encounters between Inder and Saroj. In both sets of encounters, the urge to control and dominate people and events seems to motivate Gyan and Inder, as well as a tendency to misunderstand or miscommunicate with others. Jasbir Jain (1978b) suggests that Gyan and Inder both have a disdain for other people yet still manage to attract some followers/friends (25); however, A. V. Krishna Rao (1976) suggests that they are the "result of cultural alienation and emotional rootlessness in modern India" (48). Vishal refers to this disdain and alienation as the "seed of violence" (Sahgal 1989:184) within some men that makes them want to dominate others. At other times, he refers to it as the "cave" mentality (133) or the fear some people have of revealing their true natures to each other. Overall, such people seem unaware of past mistakes and thereby are able to combine a sense of ruthlessness with a spirit of dedication (Jain (1978b:26).

The two confrontations between Gyan's and Harpal's personalities that take place in the present do so through the mediation of Vishal, and not directly or face to face. The only time they meet each other one-on-one is in the past (during and just after the Partition). The fact that they never face each other in the present suggests that in some way the recent past really influences and shapes their personalities. In the first encounter, Vishal meets Gyan at the latter's cable-wire factory just outside Chandigarh, with the intention of persuading him to call off his strike. However, rather than arguing about the pros and cons of the strike, they take a tour of the plant. Gyan explains with pride how it is a "model" plant because it is automated and efficient. He boasts that he is solely responsible for Punjab's "industrial revival" (Sahgal 1989:73). To Vishal, these claims show Gyan's ability to work hard as well as his huge pride and desire for recognition. In fact, Rao describes Gyan as a "megalomaniac" who has visions of grandeur and glory and supreme strength (Rao 1976:43). Later, the two men again avoid direct discussion of the strike and instead trade jokes. Carried along by Gyan's sudden mood swings, Vishal silently labels Gyan unreliable, uncomplicated, and a smooth manipulator. Strangely, though, here, as in the rest of the novel, we are told only what Vishal thinks about Gyan and not vice versa. The result is that we understand Gyan's impact on other people but have a poor idea of his beliefs and motivations.

Finally, when Vishal comes to the subject of the strike, he argues that it will be an economic disaster to both Punjab and Haryana. Gyan, however, sticks to legalities, arguing that the strike is not an illegal act. He concludes by pointing out that the present is a time for action, not talk. So the conversation ends where it began, with Gyan determined to prove his political power through the strike, but with no narrative power to justify his actions. Vishal ends with the power to label and criticize Gyan, but with no power to stop the strike. Moreover, Vishal never critiques the leadership that allowed Gyan to accumulate all this power, and looked the other way when he began to organize the strike. Only once, earlier in the narrative, are we told that the Prime Minster and his colleagues gave in to Gyan's demands for a separate state in a hurry because they wanted to resolve the problem as quickly as possible.

The second encounter takes place between Vishal and Harpal, during which Vishal makes his support to Harpal clear. This encounter is remarkable mainly for the comment it makes on the nature of the leadership that made the quick decision about the creation of Haryana. Vishal, listening to the proposed solutions to the strike suggested at a special session of Harpal's cabinet, realizes that no one had seemed very concerned about solving the problem and instead hoped it would disappear by itself (Sahgal 1989:207). In a mood of frustration, the narrator tells us, Vishal urges Harpal to "take a stand" (207) against the strike despite the complicated strategy and planning that that would require and despite the possibility of failure. At this point, the narrator makes a strong comment on the failure of leadership, suggesting that Harpal's "fear of failing in this situation seemed an echo of some deeper failure with which Harpal still grappled" (208). This deeper failure seems to be the inability of individual politicians to learn from the past and stop Gyan's ego from becoming too inflated. However, no one ever reproaches the political system. Thus, when Vishal formulates a strategy to counteract the strike, he thinks of his mentor, the Home Minister (the last surviving politician in the Gandhian mode), who, he believes, has the right attitude toward duty and discipline. Clearly, Vishal's faith lies in using individuals to cleanse a system.

The two main encounters between Inder and Saroj also reflect the damaging impact of one person's ego and power over the other, in a relationship based on violence and miscommunication. Saroj and Inder find it hard to talk to each other because there are very few "safe and unguarded topics between them" (Sahgal 1989:93). The only thing that seems to bind them is sexual attraction. While Saroj wishes she could "tear away the blinds" between their minds and tell Inder her innermost thoughts (94), Inder seems unable and unwilling to tell her anything at all because of his jealous rages. Blinded by his recollections of Saroj's first lover, he frequently reacts towards her with stereotypical male outrage. He derives his idea of male superiority from a narrow conception of female chastity (Jain 1978b:37), while Saroj, who has been brought up in an environment of freedom and trust, expects him to treat her as an equal (51). Thus, Inder refers to his marriage to her as a "mockery and a betrayal" (Sahgal 1989:95), and he dreams of the satisfaction he will get from slowly killing her lover. He seems to take a positive delight in torturing Saroj with questions about how shocking sex with her first lover must have been and how ashamed she must feel about it. Unable to accept the incident as finished, he recoils from her with revulsion every time the mood of rage and jealousy attacks him. In fact, he is obsessed with the incident and uses it to humiliate her and destroy her sense of innocence (Jain 1978b:1-52). His mood of rage is described as a fragmented and bleak landscape from which she is excluded (Sahgal 1989:99). It is only when he shakes off his mood and allows her to come close to him that they can carry on a normal existence again, rather like the way Gyan "calls the tune" on when and how to cripple Harpal with his strike. Inder believes he has been "cheated" by an "abomination" (98), while Gyan believes he is being cheated of his power and prestige. Basically, both are examples of the wrong kind of individual to lead the way, and they are two versions of the wrongheadedness that is plaguing India.

As Jain suggests, Saroj's premarital affair is only an external manifestation of a difference in Inder's and Saroj's attitudes. Saroj wants to be recognized as a person in her own right, while Inder treats her as a possession (Jain 1978b:52). In another incident, therefore, Inder hits Saroj for being out on a walk with Vishal instead of being at home in time for lunch with him. Again, Inder seems to be a person fragmented by jealousy and rage, while Saroj tries ineffectively to appeal to his compassion. This time, though, the landscape is not just bleak, it's flooded. Thus, when he beats her he feels as if his ears, head, and chest are bursting with water (Sahgal 1989:195). Here Inder seems dominated by emotions that dictate his actions like a flood overrunning a landscape. On the other hand, Saroj, who tries to steel herself to resist, becomes in Inder's view a hollow statue. There is an "inbred reaction" in him that "pours" Saroj's "emotional and sexual nature into one rigid mould from which nothing—no mortal thing—would liberate it" (198). Overall, their relationship is like two opposing cultures trying to form a union. Truth is not possible between them and Saroj is condemned to isolation (Jain 1978b:53).

So how are all these problems to be solved? Unlike the openendedness of *July's People*, Sahgal presents a number of ways to resolve these conflicts through hints and suggestions in the narrative. Most of these hints are ideas formulated and proposed by Vishal, that he and others try to put into practice. For example, Vishal repeatedly stresses the need for politicians and bureaucrats to think beyond petty loyalties and rank and profess a "love for the very act of living" (Sahgal 1989:76). He doesn't ever explain whether this means a love for humanity at large or something more specific, but Sahgal's own comments on the Hindu attitude toward evil might shed some light on this. According to Sahgal, Hindus relegate evil to an unknown future and do not deal with it adequately in the present. This causes problems because it is a philosophy that "contains no dynamic of its own, no inner bone structure to constitute what the rest of the world calls character. It cannot inject that iron into the soul which will help it to hold its own against other strong encroaching forces. The Hindu does not hold his own. He succumbs" (Sahgal 1975:n.p.). So perhaps Vishal's love for the living means loving the good in people and resisting the tendency to passively accept the evil. Connected to this idea of love for living is Vishal's self-proclaimed impulse toward a quest for value (Sahgal 1989:82). Later, he tells us that choosing a better value is not enough—one has to become what one values. However, whether this value that we need to choose and become is a Brahmanical code of conduct or a sense of social justice is left for us, the readers, to figure out. The only hint Sahgal provides about the nature of this value is her stress on Vishal's belief in "duty unallied to reward" (81), which is explained as a kind of Hindu humanism. However, the idea of value and duty could be interpreted by readers in various ways as a duty to one's country or caste or even one's self-esteem, and it could be applied to factory workers as well as to politicians. As Jain (1978b) points out, Sahgal once criticized Hindu religious leaders for equating caste with the concept of *Karma*, that is, for claiming that a person's position in society is governed by the fact of birth, ignoring the temporal origins of the caste system and "investing it with a moral significance which it was never supposed to have" (39). This criticism is a valid one, but Sahgal's own concept of value and duty is rather influenced by caste also and is so vaguely defined that it leaves itself open to the same kind of misinterpretation.

Other catchphrases that Vishal uses in the novel as suggested solutions to Saroj and Inder's problems—but never quite explains—are the idea of making freedom not just a political condition but a "habit of mind" (Sahgal 1989:227); basing human relations on love and truth; and cherishing one's individuality. Rao (1976) summarizes these as communication, candor, and freedom of the human spirit (46), that is, being oneself oneself without hypocrisy (49). Jain explains Sahgal's concept of freedom as a defiance of convention, a refusal to accept injustice, and, for women, making a sexual relationship "multi-dimensional" rather than simply physical (66). All of these ideas are presented as options to choose from to counteract the problems created by inertia and petty loyalties.

Ultimately, though, as in Sahgal's other novels, all these suggested solutions really add up to a belief in the distant past, in particular the Gandhian notions of truth and human dignity. Towards the end of the narrative, for example, we are told that politics in Gandhi's day meant fearlessness and pride (Sahgal 1989:241), that is, a belief in the ancient Hindu notions of truth and will power. This kind of will power is, Vishal believes, latent in the Indian psyche, whence it can be "drawn...up like water from a well to banish the thirst of defeat and despair" (241-242). However, how this drawing of the water of truth from the well of the Indian psyche will overcome ingrained barriers imposed by caste and class is not explained. The idea is further problematized by the ending of the narrative, which suggests that truth and will power are ultimately inadequate forces to resist the divisive powers of petty rivalries and political ambitions.

At the end, Vishal averts Gyan's strike by placing loyal officers and chargemen inside the four electric plants, and by deploying large numbers of policemen outside the plants to prevent the striking workers from getting inside. However, he is unable to prevent a disgruntled policeman from making an unsuccessful attempt on Harpal's life, nor a colleague from making unfair accusations against himself for lapses of judgment. Although Rao (1976) claims that Harpal's injuries are actually more symbolic than real because he is a Gandhian type of politician and must purify himself accordingly (47), this does not really sound convincing, especially since the policeman who shot him had legal charges pending against him, which Harpal had avoided pressing despite being urged to do so. Moreover, the accusations that are hurled against Vishal by his colleagues have to do with his inability to prevent a breakdown in law and order in Haryana as well as his confrontational attitude toward Gyan. He is further blamed for a lapse of judgment in granting a liquor licence to an unreliable person. Since none of these charges seem to match up to actual events, it seems that Vishal is in disgrace because of rivalries and hyprocrisies and not for real mistakes.

On the personal front, too, Vishal succeeds only in averting a crisis, not containing it. By putting Saroj and her children in a car bound for Delhi, he saves her from further humiliation from Inder, but he cannot destroy Inder's terrible anger. Thus, when Inder beats him up for interfering with Saroj's life, Vishal thinks of the vital necessity to quell Inder's tendency toward violence before it affected other lives (Sahgal 1989:243). However, at the end, both Inder's kind of violent jealous rage and Gyan's kind of enormous pride are just temporarily contained, but not checked. The mistakes of the recent past do not act as a warning and the wisdom of the ancient past is not "drawn up" from the "well." The only positive achievement Vishal can claim is having displayed a fair degree of courage in trying to implement these changes (Jain 1978:26).

So how, then, does one destroy the Partition mentality and the urge towards violence? More importantly, what relevance does containing these urges have to the concept of India itself? The novel does not provide clear answers. One way to come to terms with India's divisive urges that is not explored in the novel would be to examine the patterns of institutionalized oppression that foster division and violence. For example, one could study the ways in which caste, class and gender act together to oppress working-class males and females. As Deniz Kandiyoti (1994) suggests, "definitions of *who* and *what* constitutes the nation have a crucial bearing on notions of national unity and alternative claims to sovereignty as well as on the sorts of gender relations that should inform the nationalist project" (378). Rather than looking at the whos (like Vishal) and the whats (like Gandhism) for solutions, then, perhaps we, as readers, should use the ending of the novel to examine the caste and class biases that lie behind them and that are embedded in the socio-political problems that plague post-independence India.

Class and ethnic biases are also embedded in the social and political problems that plague post-independence Nigeria. In Emecheta's *Destination Biafra* (1982), Nigerian politicians are so preoccupied with deposing each other and signing away their oilwells for arms that Nigeria becomes a bloodbath that exposes the fragility of the tidy colonial notions of national identity. The novel depicts the political corruption and confusion in Nigeria before and during the Nigerian Civil War of 1967 to 1970, during which the eastern section of the country temporarily seceeded from Nigeria and called itself Biafra. The narrative focuses on the unprecedented horror that this war brought to Nigeria as a whole, a horror that is still fresh in many older Nigerians' memories and which completely changed the present and future of Nigerian society. Political and military maneuvers dominate the action, but these are ultimately displaced by the struggles of the protagonist, Debbie Ogedembge,[1] to find her sense of identity as she tries to make peace between the two warring factions. The novel suggests that independence has brought Nigeria not peace and prosperity, but neo-imperialism, political corruption, and genocide. Emecheta's point seems to be that Nigerian independence is quite meaningless unless it is economic as well as political. She shows how dangerous it is to have rulers who are just puppets serving Western economic interests rather than the needs of the people. Indeed, this is the most anti-imperialist of Emecheta's novels because here she definitely questions Western values and philosophies. She implies that the only hope for Nigeria in the future is the strength and will of upper-class Nigerian women, who emerge as the battered boundary markers of freedom at the end. The novel describes both the war and Debbie's struggles through a creative use of time, space, and action.

Time, in the narrative, is diachronic, because the progress of the war and Debbie's journey from Lagos to Asaba are described in linear progression; and there is a sense of renewal or optimism at the end. However, the optimism is rather muted and doesn't seem to herald any major change. Space is fragmented into images of division and brutal violation. Action is destructive and bestial because cruel and savage rapes and dismemberments dominate. Emecheta seems to be suggesting that the very idea of nationhood becomes questionable in the context of mass rapes and genocide. The only hope for national identity and peace in the future lies with compassionate, enlightened women.

The novel is set in the 1960s, just before and after the achievement of independence, when a crisis in leadership results in a military coup, political assassinations, and full scale civil war. The past is a time of inequality and exploitation; the present a period of betrayal, hypocrisies, and bloodshed; and the future an era of idealism turned to despair. Overall, the three time frames suggest that the average Nigerian peasant and worker will always be betrayed by the bourgeois politicians in league with the economic neo-imperialists.

Incidents that take place in the past explain how the British imperialists viewed Nigerian independence as a means to assert economic control while abrogating political and administrative responsibilities. As the last British governor-general, MacDonald, points out just before the official ceremoney granting independence takes place, "All independence will give them [Nigerians] is the right to govern themselves. That has nothing to do with whom they trade with" (Emecheta 1982:7). Trading partners are important to the British because they fear that indepencence will give Nigerians the confidence to strike deals with the Soviets and others regarding the pumping of Nigeria's vast deposits of crude oil. So even before the first free Nigerian election takes place, MacDonald and his advisers decide to use "proportional representation" as the voting principle. In doing so, they hope to ensure that the Hausa, who are the largest ethnic group in Nigeria and, in their opinion, "ignorant and happy in their ignorance" (6), will "rule forever" (7). Even before the election campaigning begins, the British imperial government secretly backs the Hausa candidates; private British companies fund Yoruba candidates; while the candidates themselves campaign erratically. The only Nigerian politician with any awareness of national issues is Dr. Ozimba, the Ibo party candidate, who, despite his experience as a political activist in the past, is unaware of the political maneuvers taking place around him. He seems to have a definite ideology (Pan-Africanism, one Nigeria), but is no match for the imperial manipulators. Clearly, the British imperial government is motivated by greed, because their credo is that they themselves, rather than the Nigerian government, should reap the benefits of Nigeria's economy, because the Nigerian government would make the country even poorer (26). The hypocrisies in this statement are obvious, besides which it is false. The country does become poorer, not because of the Nigerian government, but because of the British.

Overall, then, this account of the background to the first election suggests that it was a time of economic inequality and political injustice.

Economic and political inequality characterizes gender relations, too. The past is also a time when the position of women in Nigerian society was very different from what it is in the present. The narrator points out that before colonialism Nigerian women were treated as more or less equal to men, but colonialism later took that equality away. This is a reference to the fact that in the African patriarchal system, Ibo women were allowed to form their own political and legal institutions, including associations to protect their rights as farmers and traders (Katrak 1987:162). Evidently, the combination of imperialism and patriarchy was a double oppression to Nigerian women. Thus, most of the older upper-class Nigerian women in the novel appear to be passive and docile, at least in the presence of their husbands.

Most of the narrative attention is focused on the present, which depicts a political system and a society characterized by betrayal and hypocrisy resulting from "indirect rule" and "divide and rule." As regards indirect rule, the narrative shows how proportional representation enables the British puppet, Mallam Nguru Kano, a Hausa politician, to take over as first Prime Minister of independent Nigeria, even though he has no contact with the realities of Nigerian politics. More importantly, this policy causes dissatisfaction and unrest in the country because the average Nigerian believed that Dr. Ozimba would be first Prime Minister. Kano, being a member of the feudal Muslim elite and leader of a people the British have favored with the top positions in the military, allows the British imperial government to maintain economic control over Nigeria. Thus, independence is really valid only "on paper" (24). Also, as Debbie realizes, this control is likely to remain in place for a long time, so that the neo-imperialists may "rule the country indirectly forever" (42). Most of the novel's narrative attention is directed toward showing how the neo-imperialist policies of post-independence Nigeria led to so many tensions that they finally erupt into civil war.

Through these two policies, the British neo-imperialists are able to manipulate political and ethnic rivalries in such a way that the country is engulfed in an atmosphere of fear and uncertainty, which in turn leads to riots and demonstrations. Soon the rioting becomes so endemic that the army has to take control and the coups and counter-coups begin.   Unlike the narrative of *July's People*, the narrator here describes all these incidents in precise detail.   For example, we are told how the army chiefs quickly eliminate many of the corrupt politicians; which prompts disgruntled ethnic groups to assassinate some army chiefs; which causes ethnic rivalries to become so intense that the country is suddenly "plunged into the bloodiest carnage ever seen in the whole of Africa" (Emecheta 1982:79).

One aspect of the war that is described in detail is the response of the government to the systematic massacres of Ibo civilians.   We are told, for instance, that despite the thousands of slain Ibo families in all parts of the nation, the government does nothing to stop it.   Moreover, when the Ibo army officer Chijioke Abosi responds to this inaction by seceding from Nigeria and forming the independent nation of Biafra, the massacres only get worse.   The narrator explains that Saka Momoh, the Nigerian head of state, is so indecisive that he is unable to defeat the Biafrans except by starving and bombing them into surrender. Moreover, British neo-imperialists like Alan Grey take full advantage of Momoh's indecisiveness by manipulating both sides to his own advantage.   At first, Grey agrees with Momoh's decision to let Abosi create Biafra, knowing that Momoh is unaware that he is thereby losing control of the Eastern oil reserves.   And then he works on Momoh till he changes his mind and takes control of the East, prompting Abosi to declare war. As one of Grey's friends, a diplomat, remarks Momoh is giving Abosi his only chance to pay off all his debts: the eastern oilwells, but that doesn't really matter to the British, so long as they get good dividends from the oil revenue (Emecheta 1982:102). Thus, it is really the British policy of divide-and-rule that dominates the progress and outcome of the war. Only an upper-class educated Nigerian woman like Barbara Teteku, Debbie's friend, has the courage to articulate the fact that this neo-imperialism is going to ruin Nigeria. In one scene, she points out to Debbie that white people are really the ones in control of the war: they supply the guns and the weapons while at the same time taking over the production of oil (110). Clearly, both sides are being manipulated by Western economic interests, and the newly achieved independence is just a "sham" (117).

As the war progresses, Grey continues to profess sympathy for the Biafran cause while secretly colluding with the Nigerian government for oil in exchange for arms. He sells both arms and mercenaries to Momoh in exchange for control over the eastern oil reserves, and he brings food and medicines to Abosi to ensure that the neo-imperialists appear impartial and moral. He reasons that a quick victory would be good for Britain, especially since he was now, as the narrator suggests, trading guns and bodies in exchange for oil (Emecheta 1982:156). However, most of the ordinary Nigerian citizens remain unaware of this trade and are stirred by the passions and rhetoric of the politicians. Occasionally, though, they do criticize local leadership for the terrible losses in human life. In one scene, an embittered Ibo man tells Debbie that the quality of the Biafran leadership is faulty because it is ill-prepared for war and greedy for success and money. He tells her sadly that it is suicidal to fight a war without proper weapons (165). Similarly, Debbie sometimes thinks of the role of the politicians (Biafran, Nigerian, British) in the war as so many hawks sitting on the fence, waiting for the war to end (165). While the British neo-imperialists seem motivated by greed for oil money, Abosi and the Biafrans seem compelled by their desire to make their country into a utopia where ethnic and economic harmony will have been achieved (128). As for Momoh and the Nigerians, they seem to be motivated purely by revenge (on the Biafrans for seceding).

Ultimately, the British neo-imperialists are able to play up the passions of the leaders of both sides to such an extent that the suffering and misery of the ordinary people are prolonged. As Juliet I. Okonkwo (1986) suggests, both sides were "manipulated like puppets in a struggle whose ultimate motivations, conduct and outcome depended almost entirely on external powers and their material interests" (162). On the one hand, Abosi refuses to surrender even if millions are killed in the process; on the other hand, Momoh uses ruthless mercenaries to wipe out Ibo civilians. These mercenaries are very effective killers because their actions are based on a shoot to kill policy (Emecheta 1982:204). Despite this, the British "quick kill" theory doesn't work (242) so that Biafra has, literally, to be bombed out of existence. At this point, Abosi escapes like a coward on a private plane and Debbie realizes that the people of Biafra have been betrayed all round, and that Abosi has left the Nigerian people with a shameful heritage (257-259). Emecheta herself seems to answer that question when she tells us in her introduction to the novel that she hopes that Nigerians and other black Africans never again let themselves be manipulated so thoroughly by the West (viii).

Thus, the present is a time of horror and betrayal. As for the future, it seems to be a curiously ambivalent time. The ideal future is that happy time when the utopian aspects of Biafra can be realized without death and destruction. To those who believe in it, Biafra represents the ideal state. Momoh, who later becomes Biafra's destroyer, articulates this idealism when he is still a young army officer. According to him, Biafra will be a country free of strife and corruption and full of economic opportunity (Emecheta 1982:60). Abosi, who at first fights for Biafra and then deserts it, calls it a "destination" to be achieved once the "stooges" of the colonizers are eliminated (60).

Onyemere, the first head of state of Biafra, visualizes it as nation freed of tribal conflicts and where state boundaries will cut across tribal loyalties. To the educated Nigerians who are either Ibo or members of minority ethnic groups, Biafra represents freedom from corrupt and greedy politicians. When Biafra is almost destroyed by Nigerian bombs, it becomes "the right to live in our homeland. The right to be ourselves, the right to live" (240). As all these definitions suggest, Biafra is more an ideal or a symbol than a reality.

In reality, the future of Biafra is full of misery and horror. Momoh, who has systematically played out his country's power of economic self-determination into Grey's hands during the war, is likely to remain head of a reunited Nigeria in the future. Therefore, just as Governor-General MacDonald had predicted, the British neo-imperialists seem poised to rule Nigeria indirectly forever. Moreover, Momoh will probably lose more and more control over Nigeria since other Western powers might react to the war by saying: "See, they can't rule themselves" (Emecheta 1982:42). Overall, the real future is grim and oppressive. The only optimistic note in all this is Emecheta's own directive to her fellow Nigerians in the introduction to her novel, namely, "it is time to forgive, though only a fool will forget" (vii).

What the time frames of the narrative suggest is that although economic interests and selfishness dominated the outcome of the war, the real horror and betrayal can only be gauged by examining its tremendous human cost. Thus Emecheta provides a lot of detail on the tragedy and the catastrophe that it became for all Ibos. Frequently, she suggests that the war was not just a matter of "simple tribal rivalries" (Sample 1991:445), but was actually a national disaster. In many ways, the critics suggest, the war reflected all that was wrong with post-independence Africa, with its coup d'états, military dictatorships, bloodshed, and moral corruption. Yet, in other ways, it was also a unique war, characterized by genocide—about

50,000 Ibos were killed in the riots in the north alone (446), not to mention the ruthless bombing of innocent civilians (447) and destruction of men and resources (Okonkwo 1986:162). In the early riots, for example, the narrator tells us that Ibos living in the North (Hausaland) are "hacked," "clubbed," and "battered" to death; their body parts are cut off (Emecheta 1982:87); they are hunted out of their homes in "witch hunts" (88); and their women are raped and cut into pieces. Moreover, those who survive make it back to their hometowns in the east with terrible wounds, most of the women having lost their breasts or eyes, and the men, their limbs or penises (90).

Later, the narrator describes how peasant and working-class Ibos are systematically massacred by the Nigerian army when the war is at its height. All major sea ports are controlled by them and so they prevent any food or ammunition from reaching the Biafrans. The Biafrans who can fight, therefore, do so with "empty bellies" (Emecheta 1982:184) and without weapons. In one incident, for example, hundreds of hungry, unarmed students are wiped out by well-equipped Nigerian troops (185). Those who cannot fight are dragged off roads and buses and shot so that "the air was again filled with the cries of men dying. The men were bleating like goats and baying like hounds. In no time, it was all over" (177). Emecheta's point in providing us with all these gruesome details seems to be to show how heavily the civilians paid for the mistakes and the greed of the politicians.

Besides describing how Ibo civilians were slaughtered by the Nigerian army, the narrative also describes very effectively how many rural Ibos in border villages became scapegoats, caught in between the two warring factions. In this respect, the narrative, like many other sensitive war novels, gives us a vivid picture of a nation gone completely out of control, in which innocent people are continuously victimized (Sample 1991:447-448). One such group are the Western Ibos near Asaba, who are left exposed to the direct wrath of the Nigerian army when Biafra loses control of Benin state. Abosi decides summarily to abandon them to their fate (Emecheta 1982:182). In fact, he leaves them in a trap, because when Asaba is taken by the Nigerian forces, the people are killed and the few Biafran soldiers hiding among them desert them. As Debbie realizes when she gets there, the people of Asaba had been betrayed and abandoned by the very troops that were supposed to protect them (223). To add to this betrayal, the women are raped and the few men that are left alive are then shot by other Biafran soldiers for giving the Nigerian soldiers information. As a result, the Western Ibos as a whole become "fed up with serving Abosi and being betrayed" (234) and refuse to help either side any longer. All this makes it clear that the politicians initiate and prolong the war but the real suffering and degradation is borne by innocent farmers and workers. As one rural woman asks Debbie sarcastically, "Do you think those at the top will starve? No, they are probably there drinking champagne. And as for the businessmen, they don't want this war to end" (190). The implication is that the war is as much a product of class differences as it is of ethnic or ideological differences.

If time is non-regenerative and depicts inequality and division, so does space. Time seems to unfold in a divided landscape in which the land or countryside is completely fragmented and unnatural, the city space is suffocating, while the women who hide out in both are dispossessed and desperate. In fact, the novel's use of space shows the plight of the African woman (and of women in general) trapped between two sides. The fragmentation of the land by the Nigerian politicians and the Western powers is actually a metaphor for the decay and degeneration of their minds. Thus, there is a lot of narrative focus on the constant formation and reformation of boundaries that enclose different kinds of spaces. For example, the boundaries enclosing and dividing Nigeria seem quite arbitrary, being dictated more by Western economic interests than a sense of identity among the people within it. As Debbie realizes, "Nigeria was only one nation as a result of administrative balkanization by the British and French powers" (Emecheta 1982:175). In fact, national boundaries around Nigeria are drawn to ensure that the British neo-imperialists have control over the mineral deposits of the north and the oil in the east. And within this arbitrarily created space that is Nigeria, ethnic boundaries are used to subdivide regions. Ethnic boundaries are frequently used because for most Nigerians, ethnic or communal loyalties are stronger than a national identity.   To the British, ethnic loyalties are a convenient lever for economic and political manipulation.   The geographic locations of the various ethnic settlements within Nigeria are therefore used effectively in dividing up territory, yet these divisions change constantly, depending on who is doing the dividing. Onyemere, for example, mixes up ethnic groups when he subdivides Nigeria, ostensibly to prevent each group from forming strong and aggressive political units. However, when Momoh comes to power, he also mixes up ethnic groups and forms twelve states, but he claims this is necessary in order to protect the ethnic minorities (124).   However, Momoh's regrouping prompts Abosi to break away from Nigeria because he (Abosi) realizes that Momoh's lines are drawn not to protect minorities but to divide up and weaken the various ethnic groups, especially those in the east, so that they would not revolt (106). Thus Abosi regroups Nigeria to make two separate countries, Nigeria and Biafra.   The folly of this regrouping is noted by Debbie, a somewhat impartial participant in the war, because she points out that both Abosi and Momoh are really trying to keep the oil under their power, and that even if Biafra gives Abosi control over the oil, he cannot hope to win the war. She asks Alan Grey: "How can a quarter of a nation fight the other three-quarters and win? It's sheer common sense" (114). The only person who seems to accept the land as it is, is Barbara Teteku, who argues that regardless of how arbitrarily colonial Nigeria's boundaries were drawn in the past, the Nigeria of the present should stick to those boundaries because Nigerian leaders need to focus on present problems within the nation, no matter how arbitrarily constructed, rather than destabilizing the nation with ethnic conflicts (119). Thus, Nigeria as a geographic space is a site of contention and a locus of contradictory ideologies.

The fragmentation and constant reapportioning of the land are also reflected in the stuffiness and artificiality of the city. In Lagos, in the stillness of a pre-dawn morning, Debbie's father is murdered as part of a coup plan, and Debbie awakes to find the air inside her room is unnaturally quiet and humid (Emecheta 1982:61). Soon after, the Sardauna (religious leader of the Hausas) is murderered, also as part of the coup, in the northern city of Zaria, and as a result, silence "hangs" in the air of that city like a tangible presence (72). Later, just before a group of Ibo officers are murdered in the army barracks at Ikeja, they are stuffed into a small, stifling room which soon begins to make them choke with the smells of sweat and excrement (81). Within five days, those same officers "were agonizing and dying little by little in their airless one-room prison" (83). The suffocation of the city is therefore symbolic of the death and torture that takes place in the country as a whole.

Besides suffocation, the city is also an unnatural place where even natural objects become unreal. Thus, as Debbie looks out of her window in the early morning light of the day her father is murdered, she notices that the bushes in her garden suddenly begin to move toward the house (Emecheta 1982:62). So too when Debbie reports to Momoh after joining the Nigerian army, she meets him in her father's house, which Momoh has taken over and converted into his headquarters. Inside, instead of the quiet atmosphere of her childhood home, she finds cold but efficient furnishings and a frosty atmosphere (123). Overall, then, life in the city is stifling, artificial, and unnatural, and seems just as meaningless as the constantly shifting lines that separate the different states.

The people who suffer most from the fragmentation of the land and the suffocation of the city are the dispossessed peasant and working-class women on both sides of the war. They are the real casualties of the war because they witness the brutal deaths of their husbands and children; see their homes destroyed; and roam about in the forests and remote villages in order to stay alive. Rather than presenting them as rugged individualists, Emecheta presents them as long-suffering survivors, thereby showing that in this war, as in other wars before it, the most vulnerable sections of society suffer the most. Moreover, in this war, the women are defeated not just by the machines of war (guns and bullets), but also by the agents of war (male politicians and soldiers). They suffer starvation, rape, and mutilation by whichever side they happen to fall afoul of. As one Ibo peasant woman tells a Biafran soldier, they will no longer help either side because they are "tired of being in the middle. Your Biafran soldiers killed our men and raped our girls, because you accused us of harbouring enemy soldiers, then Nigerian soldiers would accuse us of the same thing even though we were innocent. There was nobody to protect us so we formed our own militia" (Emecheta 1982:230-231). As Debbie realizes when she travels with them, "the real war is being fought here" (231).

The war that these women fight involves learning how to survive and making a lasting peace. Debbie, for example, because of her father's great wealth and her own exclusive education at Oxford, has the intelligence and the potential to change men's attitudes by joining the Nigerian army as an officer. In the army, she orders arrests and killings when necessary, and is assigned to two peacemaking missions. Yet, despite all these activities, she, like the other women in the narrative, is unable to stop the carnage and her actions become increasingly futile, despairing, and mad.

One reason for this futility is that the men, chiefly the soldiers on both sides, are very aggressive towards any women caught in their path. In fact, the main action of the narrative as far as Debbie is concerned is made up of her encounters with cruel men. Despite her father's money and her own education and sophistication, Debbie is raped and disgraced in the war, not once, but several times. Here, Emecheta's point seems to be that women are always victims in a war, regardless of whether they are rich or poor. Debbie's experiences with rape and disgrace are central to the action of the novel.

Before she is raped the first time, Debbie finds out that women of all ethnic backgrounds are constantly being beaten or raped or abused, usually by soldiers whose commanders refuse to accept responsibility for these actions. Instead, the soldiers claim that "'It is war, and in a war situation men lose their self-control,' as if that were explanation enough" (Emecheta 1982:119). Even the worst atrocities against women go unpunished, and pregnant women are cut open and their beheaded foetuses are left lying on the roads; captured women of all ages are stripped and then squeezed and poked by enemy soldiers at all times of day or night; and murdered women are regarded as war statistics and are rarely accounted for.

In one scene, Debbie is gang-raped by a group of crude Nigerian soldiers when she is on the road to Asaba to try and persuade Abosi to surrender. Having stopped her car outside Ibadan to help a poor Ibo man and his sickly, pregnant wife, she is then faced by their ridicule toward her army uniform and gun. They refuse to believe that she is really an officer, as do the Nigerian soldiers who suddenly pounce on them from nowhere. After shooting the men, stripping Debbie's mother, and cutting up the pregnant woman, they gang-rape Debbie till she becomes unconscious. After this experience, all her will and determination vanishes, and she alternately wants to die or hang her head in shame. Her self-respect completely disappears when she hears the casual attitude of the Ibo soldiers who rescue her: "hundreds of women have been raped—so what? It's war. She's lucky to be even alive. She'll be all right" (Emecheta 1982:135). As she realizes bitterly, she has been made a victim by the very people she had been trying to help, the Nigerian side, and that no self-respecting bourgeois Nigerian or Biafran man would desire her after she has been raped by poor, black Nigerian soldiers. Her final humiliation comes when her mother consoles her with the advice that this is the "fate of all women" (157).

Debbie is severely battered by this attack, both physically and mentally, and realizes that now the male world regards her as spoiled goods (Emecheta 1982:159). Yet she gets her will to survive back when she realizes that the Nigerian army is continuing its genocidal campaign against the Ibos, and that the only way to stop it is to get Abosi to surrender. So she sets off alone towards the east and, after many misadventures, is almost raped again. This time, she is captured by Nigerian soldiers while travelling in a bus full of Ibo refugees, heading toward Asaba. The Nigerian soldiers strip the women and interrogate the men and Debbie is brought in front of the commander, Lawal Salihu, her one-time colleague. Taunting her for proving herself a poor soldier and a weak woman he boasts that, by raping her, he will show her that she is "nothing but a woman" (175). The only reason he spares her is because she confesses that she has already been raped by ordinary soldiers. Seeing his confusion and disgust, she taunts him with ridicule, telling him that rather than "using" a white man's girlfriend for sex, as he had originally throught, he is actually dealing with "a woman who has slept with [black Nigerian] soldiers" (176). The irony is that Lawal, and later Grey, both react with horror at having touched a woman who has been raped by common black men. Debbie realizes bitterly that they would probably have been less disgusted if white men had raped her. Strangely, then, she escapes rape through rape, so that rape itself becomes symbolic of all male aggression and power. Just as men parcel up and destroy the land, so too, they destroy their compassion for women. The point, then, of all these descriptions of violated female bodies is to show that male greed for money and power makes them little better than animals. By treating women and children as subhuman objects to be devoured and destroyed, the men cease to be human.

Ultimately, though, despite all these outrages committed against them, Debbie and the poor women she travels with do find the strength to maintain their self-esteem and conclude that they are actually better off in a world without men. As one homeless woman tells another, men have never been very good at bringing up children and managing a house and their usefulness is therefore limited (Emecheta 1982:213). In other words, despite being brutalized by some men and made sorrowful by the death of other men, they themselves are the most important survivors. Their inner strength can help them to nurture the future generation and teach them the value of peace. Debbie, for example, is chosen as official peacemaker between Momoh and Abosi, because being an Itsekiri, she is able to empathize with both sides. Emecheta seems to have wanted her to portray an ethnically neutral figure because in her introduction she claimed that Debbie was "neither Ibo nor Yoruba nor Hausa but simply a Nigerian" (viii). Debbie accepts the job of peacemaker despite realizing that the men make the mess and then expect women to clean it up. Moreover, she also knows that the men choose her as peacemaker because they want her to use her "feminine charms" (123) to persuade Abosi to surrender, and not because they believe that women are inherently better peacemakers. As if to confirm their cynicism, her peacemaking missions fail. Although she meets Abosi twice and tells him it would be better to surrender than to let the genocide continue, yet both times he claims the right to go on defending his homeland, even if millions died in the process.

Other women, too, begin to voice doubts about their peacemaking abilities, suggesting that it is impossible to change men's war-mongering instincts, and they will always find an excuse to go off and kill each other rather than staying at home and help bring up the children (Emecheta 1982:214). One could argue that Emecheta's point is that men make wars and women suffer them, that men (both black and white) use wars to serve their own interests, which always work against women's needs. Women's needs are, in fact, the boundary markers of the needs of the society as a whole.

Despite this pessimism, at the end, women are the only hope for the future. For example, Debbie goes to London and stirs up public opinion against the British Prime Minister and Momoh to get them to stop the killings. Later, she pledges to bring up some orphaned infants with her father's money. Finally, she resolves to write a book about the war and thereby tell the world the story of "how a few ambitious soldiers from Sandhurst tried to make their dream a reality" (Emecheta 1982:258).

In the final analysis, however, the critique that this novel makes against British neo-imperialism and Nigerian bourgeois compliance with that imperialism is somewhat muted. Although Debbie emerges as the hope for a different future, yet she is clearly implicated in the bourgeois system herself. At the end, she claims that she is not like Abosi because unlike him, she is a true African who will not leave Africa when things get tough (Emecheta 1982:258). Yet she belongs to the same bourgeois class as him and therefore cannot help being subject to its ideology. She even sleeps with a white man despite despising his politics and, before the war, only made half-hearted attempts to protest social injustice. For example, she complains that rich Nigerians show off their wealth too ostentatiously at parties, but herself wears gold-framed shoes herself just to please her father. As Chidi Amuta (1984) points out, most novels written about the Nigerian Civil War reflect the ideology and attitudes of the bourgeoisie, yet often the protagonists of such novels are critical of or opposed to these values (61). He concludes that although the Nigerian war novel was "inspired by the hegemonic ideology of the bourgeoisie," it often became quite critical of and even hostile to "the position, interests and role(s) of that class" (61). In this regard, Emecheta does not seem to be as critical of bourgeois values as the other novelists Amuta mentions, and nowhere does she suggest that one of the chief reasons for the failure of African independence is the failure of elite leadership of the bourgeoisie. The furthest she does go is to suggest that the bourgeois leaders are puppets of the West, and are therefore complicitous in the carnage of the war. In fact, throughout the middle section of the novel Debbie seems to be just "slumming it" for a while with the Ibo peasant women, and she returns at the end to her elite status and escapes from the suffering masses. Nor are the suffering masses, despite their resilience, the central focus of the novel; instead, it is Debbie's realization that she is not one of them. Unlike them she cannot carry babies on her back while at the same time doing all the farming and cooking: (Emecheta 1982:191). In fact, I would agree with Amuta's conclusion that like most other Nigerian war novels, this one too indicts only the "*quality* of bourgeois leadership, not the *basis* of that hegemony" (Amuta 1984:69). This throws into confusion the optimism of the novel's ending, because it suggests that the agency of change— Debbie—is complicitous with the cause of the problem, the corrupt leaders, being of the same class as them. Finally, then, a possible way to get rid of that hegemony that is not explored in the novel would be to empower the strong-willed peasant women whose plight Debbie temporarily shares, since they display the determination to survive; can adapt to a world destroyed by and emptied of men; and are not completely controlled by the bourgeois ideology of the politicians.

In conclusion, all three novels depict post-revolutionary societies gripped by crises that result in stagnation rather than change; inequalities rather than freedom; and horror rather than hope. Both Gordimer and Emecheta stress the need for economic change as a primary condition for the revolution to be successful. Gordimer makes her point by depicting changelessness and a pessimistic view of the possibility for change. Emecheta argues her case by depicting horror and betrayal, thereby underscoring the urgent need for action. Sahgal, however, suggests that the solution is not economics, but religion, and points to ancient Hindu *karma* as the force of change. However, she does not provide any immediate remedies for social and economic inequality. All three, finally, view postcolonial women as reflective of both the social ills as well as the cure. Their novels imply that women must begin the process of change by internalizing their own versions of social and economic equality.

Notes

[1] Debbie's name suggests that she is a cultural hybrid because it is both Western (Debbie) and Nigerian (Ogedembge).

BIBLIOGRAPHY

Ahmad, Aijaz. *In Theory: Classes, Nations, Literatures.* London & New York: Verso, 1992.

Alexander, Peter F. "Political Attitudes in Nadine Gordimer's Fiction." *AUMLA: Journal of the Australasian Universities Modern Language Association* 70 (November 1988): 220-38.

Althusser, Louis. *For Marx.* Trans. Ben Brewster. London and New York: Verso, 1990.

Amuta, Chidi. "History, Society and Heroism in the Nigerian War Novel." *Kunapipi* 6, 3 (1984): 57-70.

Anderson, Benedict. *Imagined Communities: Reflections on the Origin and Spread of Nationalism.* London and New York: Verso, 1983.

Arora, Neena. *Nayantara Sahgal and Doris Lessing: A Feminist Study in Comparison.* New Delhi: Prestige Books, 1991.

---. "*Rich Like Us*: A Note." In R.K. Dhawan, P.V. Dhamija, and A.K. Shrivastava, eds. *Recent Commonwealth Literature.* 2 vols. New Delhi: Prestige Books, 1989. 1: 130-32.

Ashcroft, Bill, Gareth Griffiths and Helen Tiffin. *The Empire Writes Back: Theory and Practice in Post-Colonial Literatures.* [New Accents]. London and New York: Routledge, 1989.

Asnani, Shyam M. "The Novels of Nayantara Sahgal," *Indian Literature* 16, 1 & 2 (January to June, 1973): 36-69.

Bailey, Nancy. "Living Without the Future: Nadine Gordimer's *July's People.*" *World Literature Written in English* 24, 2 (1984): 215-24.

Barrett, Michele. *Women's Oppression Today: Problems in Marxist Feminist Analysis.* London: Verso, 1980.

Barthelemy, Anthony. "Western Time, African Lives: Time in the Novels of Buchi Emecheta." *Callaloo: A Journal of Afro-American and African Arts and Letters* 12, 3 (Summer 1989): 559-74.

Boyers, Robert, Clark Blaise, Terrence Griggory, and Jordan Elgrasly. "A Conversation with Nadine Gordimer."

Salmagundi 2 (1984): 3-31. [Rpt. in: Nancy Topping
   Bazin and Marilyn Dallman Seymour, eds.
   Conversations with Nadine Gordimer. Literary
   Conversation's Series. Jackson and London: University
   Press of Mississippi, 1990: 185-214].

Brennan, Timothy. "The National Longing for Form." In *The
   Post-Colonial Studies Reader,* ed. Bill Ashcroft, Gareth
   Griffiths and Helen Tiffin. London and New York:
   Routledge, 1995: 170-175.

---. "India, Nationalism and Other Failures." *The South Atlantic
   Quarterly* 87, 1 (Winter 1988): 131-146.

Brown, Lloyd W. "Buchi Emecheta." In *Women Writers in
   Black Africa:* Contributions in Womens' Studies #21.
   Westport and London: Greenwood Press, 1981: 35-60.

---. *Women Writers in Black Africa.* Contributions in Womens'
   Studies #21. Westport and London: Greenwood Press,
   1981.

Brydon, Diana. "The Myths that Write Us: Decolonizing the
   Mind." *Commonwealth* 10, 1 (Autumn 1987): 1-14.

Chakravarti, Uma. "Whatever Happened to the Vedic Dasi?
   Orientalism, Nationalism and a Script for the Past." In
   Recasting Women: Essays in Indian Colonial History
   ed. Kumkum Sangari and Sudesh Vaid. New Delhi: Kali
   for Women, 1989; New Brunswick: Rutgers University
   Press, 1990: 27-87.

Chinweizu (ed. and introd.). *Voices from Twentieth-Century
   Africa: Griots and Towncriers.* London and Boston:

Faber and Faber, 1988.

Cixous, Helene. "Castration or Decapitation?" *Signs: Journal of Women in Culture and Society* 7, 1 (Autumn 1981): 41-55.

Daymond, Margaret J. *"Burger's Daughter:* A Novel's Reliance on History." In *Momentum: On Recent South African Writing* ed. M. J. Daymond, J. U. Jacobs, and Margaret Lenta. Pietermaritzburg: University of Natal Press, 1984: 159-70.

de Lauretis, Teresa. "Displacing Hegemonic Discourses: Reflections on Feminist Theory in the 1980's." *Inscriptions* 3-4 (1988): 127-41.

Derrett, Margaret E. "The Day in Shadow," in "Book Reviews." *Journal of Asian Studies* 32, 4 (August 1973): 727-28.

Dhawan, R.K., P.V. Dhamija, and A.K. Shrivastava, eds. *Recent Commonwealth Literature.* 2 vols. New Delhi: Prestige Books, 1989.

Dreifus, Claudia. "Nadine Gordimer." *The Progressive* 56, 1 (January 1992): 30-32.

Driver, Dorothy. "Nadine Gordimer: the Politicisation of Women." *English in Africa* 10, 2 (October 1983): 29-54.

Emecheta, Buchi. *The Bride Price.* London: Allison and Busby; New York: Braziller; 1976.

---. *Destination Biafra.* London and New York: Allison and Busby, 1982.

---. *Double Yoke.* New York: Braziller, 1983. [First published: Umuezeokda and London: Ogwugwu Afor, 1982].

---. *Second Class Citizen.* London: Allison & Busby, 1974; New York: Braziller, 1975.

Emenyonu, Ernest N. "Technique and Language in Buchi Emecheta's *The Bride Price, The Slave Girl,* and *The Joys of Motherhood.*" *The Journal of Commonwealth Literature* 23, 1 (1988): 130-41.

Fanon, Frantz. *Black Skin White Masks,* trans. Charles Lam Markmann. New York: Grove Weidenfeld, 1967. [First published in French: 1952].

Frank, Katherine. "The Death of the Slave Girl: African Womanhood in the Novels of Buchi Emecheta." *World Literature Written in English* 21, 3 (Autumn 1982): 476-97.

Gates, Henry Louis, Jr. "Writing 'Race' and the Difference It Makes." Introduction to "Race, Writing and Difference." *Critical Inquiry* 12, 1 (Fall 1985): 1-19. [Rpt. in: Henry Louis Gates, Jr. ed., *"Race," Writing and Difference* (Chicago and London: University of Chicago Press, 1986): 1-20].

Gordimer, Nadine. "Apprentices of Freedom." *New Society* 24/31 (December 1981a):

---. *Burger's Daughter.* London: Jonathan Cape; New York: Viking, 1979.

---. *The Conservationist.* London: Jonathan Cape, 1974; New York: Viking, 1975.

---. "The Essential Gesture: Writers and Responsibility." *Granta* 15-16 (1985): 137-51. [Rpt. in: Nadine Gordimer, *The Essential Gesture: Writing, Politics and Places,* ed. with intro. by Stephen Clingman (London: Penguin, 1989).] [First published: London: Jonathan Cape, 1988].

---. "The Idea of Gardening." *The New York Review of Books* 31, 1 (February 2, 1984): 3, 6.

---. *July's People.* London: Jonathan Cape; New York: Viking, 1981b.

---. "Letter from South Africa." *The New York Review of Books* 23, 20 (December 9, 1976): 3-4, 6, 8, 10.

---. "Living in the Interregnum." *New York Review of Books* 29, 21 & 22 (January 20, 1983): 21-29.

---. *A Sport of Nature.* New York: Knopf, 1987.

---, John Dugard, Hard Smith, Director of Publication, Committe of Publications, Publications Appeal Board, the Press. *What Happened to "Burger's Daughter" or How South African Censorship Works."* Johannesburg: Taurus, 1980.

Gordon, Jennifer. "Dreams of a Common Language: Nadine Gordimer's *July's People.*" *Women in African Literature Today [=African Literature Today]* 15 (1987): 102-08.

Hall, Stuart. "Cultural Identity and Diaspora," in Patrick

Williams and Laura Chrisman, eds. *Colonial Discourse and Post-Colonial Theory: A Reader.* New York: Columbia University Press, 1994: 392-403.

Hobsbawm, E. J. *Nations and Nationalism Since 1780: Programme, Myth, Reality.* [Second ed]. Cambridge: Cambridge University Press, 1983.

Hobsbawm, Eric and Terence Ranger, eds. *The Invention of Tradition.* Cambridge, London and New York: Cambridge University Press, 1983.

Irigaray, Luce. *Speculum of the Other Woman,* trans. Gillian C. Gill. Ithaca: Cornell University Press, 1985. [First published in French: 1974].

Jain, Jasbir. "The Aesthetics of Morality: Sexual Relations in the Novels of Nayantara Sahgal." *The Journal of Indian Writing in English* 6, 1 (1978a): 41-48.

---. *Nayantara Sahgal.* [Indian Writers Series 16]. New Delhi: Arnold-Heinemann, 1978b.

---. "Sahgal: The Novel as Political Biography." In R.K Dhawan, P.V. Dhamija, and A.K. Shrivastava, eds. *Recent Commonwealth Literature.* 2 vols. New Delhi: Prestige Books, 1989: 1: 142-52.

JanMohamed, Abdul R. *Manichean Aesthetics: The Politics of Literature in Colonial Africa.* Amherst: University of Massachusetts Press, 1983.

James, Adeola. *In Their Own Voices: African Women Writers Talk.* [Studies in African Literature Series]. London and

Portsmouth: Heinemann, 1990.

Jameson, Fredric. *The Political Unconscious: Narrative as a Socially Symbolic Act.* Ithaca: Cornell University Press, 1981.

Jussawalla, Feroza. "'Of Cabbages and Kings': *This Time of Morning* and *Storm in Chandigarh* by Nayantara Sahgal." *The Journal of Indian Writing in English* 5, 1 (1977): 43-50.

Kandiyoti, Deniz. "Identity and its Discontents: Women and the Nation." In Patrick Williams and Laura Chrisman, eds. *Colonial Discourse and Post-Colonial Theory: A Reader.* New York: Columbia University Press, 1994: 376-391.

Katrak, Ketu. "Womanhood/Motherhood: Variations on a Theme in Selected Novels of Buchi Emecheta." *Journal of Commonwealth Literature* 22, 1 (1987): 159-70.

Kaushik, Asha. *Politics, Aesthetics and Culture: A Study of Indo-Anglian Political Novels.* New Delhi: Manohar, 1988.

Kristeva, Julia. *The Kristeva Reader* edited Toril Moi. New York: Columbia University Press, 1986.

Lacan, Jacques. *The Four Fundamental Concepts of Psycho-Analysis,* ed. Jacques-Alain Miller. Trans. Alan Sheridan. London: Hogarth Press, 1977; New York: W. W. Norton & Company, 1978. [First published in French 1973].

Lerner, Gerda. *The Creation of Patriarchy.* [Women and History 1]. New York and Oxford: Oxford University Press, 1986.

Levin, Martin. "The Day in Shadow," in "New and Novel." *The New York Times Book Review* 24 September 1972: 40.

Liu, Marcia P. "Continuity and Development in the Novels of Nayantara Sahgal." *The Journal of Indian Writing in English* 8, 1-2 (January-July 1980): 45-52.

Macaskill, Brian. "Interrupting the Hegemonic: Textual Critique and Mythological Recuperation from the White Margins of South African Writing." *Novel: A Forum on Fiction* 23, 2 (Winter, 1990): 156-81.

Macherey, Pierre. *A Theory of Literary Production,* trans. Geoffrey Wall. London and New York: Routledge, 1978. [First published in French: 1966].

Mannoni, O. *Prospero and Caliban: The Psychology of Colonization,* trans. Pamela Powesland. New Foreword by Maurice Blach. Ann Arbor: University of Michigan Press, 1990. [First published: 1950 (French), 1965 (English)].

Mazrui, Ali A. *Cultural Enginerring and Nation-Building.* Evanston: Northwestern University Press, 1972.

McClintock, Anne. "The Angel of Progress: Pitfalls of the Term 'Post-colonialism.'" In Patrick Williams and Laura Chrisman, eds. *Colonial Discourse and Post-Colonial Theory: A Reader.* New York: Columbia University Press, 1994: 291-304.

Mishra, Vijay and Bob Hodge. "What is Post(-)colonialism?" In Patrick Williams and Laura Chrisman, eds. *Colonial Discourse and Post-Colonial Theory: A Reader.* New York: Columbia University Press, 1994: 276-90.

Mohanty, Chandra Talpade. "Under Western Eyes: Feminist Scholarship and Colonial Discourses." In Patrick Williams and Laura Chrisman, eds. *Colonial Discourse and Post-Colonial Theory: A Reader.* New York: Columbia University Press, 1994: 196-220. [Also in: *Third World Women and the Politics of Feminism,* ed. Chandra Talpade Mohanty, Ann Russo and Lourdes Torres. Bloomington: Indiana University Press, 1991: 51-80].

Mohini, V. "Writer at Work: Nayantara Sahgal." *The Literary Criterion* 25, 1 (1990): 60-70.

Nandy, Ashis. *The Intimate Enemy: Loss and Recovery of Self Under Colonialism.* Delhi: Oxford University Press, 1983.

Newman, Judie. "Gordimer's *The Conservationist:* `That Book of Unknown Signs.'" *Critique: Studies in Modern Fiction* 22, 3 (April 1981): 31-44.

---. *Nadine Gordimer.* Contemporary Writers Series. London and New York: Routledge, 1988.

Ngugi wa Thiong'o. *Decolonising the Mind: The Politics of Language in African Literature.* London: James Currey; Nairobi: Heinemann Kenya; Portsmouth: Heinemann; Harare: Zimbabwe Publishing House, 1986.

---. *Moving the Centre: the Struggle for Cultural Freedoms.* [Studies in African Literature, New Series]. London: James Currey; Nairobi: EAEP; Portsmouth: Heinemann, 1993.

---. *Writers in Politics.* [Studies in African Literature Series]. London, Ibadan and Nairobi: Heinemann, 1981.

Nwankwo, Chimalum. "Emecheta's Social Vision: Fantasy or Reality?" *Ufahamu: Journal of the African Activist Association* 177, 1 (1988): 35-44.

O'Faolain, Julia. "The Day in Shadow," in "Victims." *London Magazine* 15, 5 (December 1975/January 1976): 113-20.

Okonkwo, Juliet I. "Biafran War Novels--A Review." *NSAL: Nsukka Studies in African Literature* 4 (1986): 161-79.

Onimode, Bade. *Imperialism and Underdevelopment in Nigeria: The Dialectics of Mass Poverty.* London: Zed Press; Westport: Lawrence Hill, 1982.

Oxford English Dictionary, The. [Second ed.] Prep. J.A. Simpson and E.S.C. Weiner. Volume 5. Oxford: Clarendon Press, 1989.

Parker, Kenneth. "Imagined Revolution: Nadine Gordimer's *A Sport of Nature.*" In *Women and Writing in South Africa: A Critical Anthology,* ed. Cherry Clayton. Johannesburg: Heinemann Southern Africa, 1989: 209-24. [First published in French in *Nouvelles du Sud* 12 (1989): 15-25.]

238   This Is No Place For A Woman

Parry, Benita. "Problems in Current Theories of Colonial Discourse." *Oxford Literary Review* 9, 1-2 (1978): 27-58.

Pecheux, Michel and C. Fuchs. "Language, ideology and discourse analysis: an overview." *Praxis: A Journal of Cultural Criticism* 6 (1982): 3-20.

Peck, Richard. "What's a Poor White to Do? White South African Options in *A Sport of Nature.*" *Ariel: A Review of International English Literature* 19, 4 (October 1988): 75-93.

Porter, Abioseh Michael. *"Second Class Citizen:* The Point of Departure for Understanding Buchi Emecheta's Major Fiction." *The International Fiction Review* 15, 2 (Summer 1988): 123-29.

Prescott, Peter S. and Marc Peyser. "Two Sides of Nadine Gordimer." *Newsweek* 118, 16 (14 October 1991): 40.

Rao, A. V. Krishna. "The Day in Shadow," in his *Nayantara Sahgal (A Study of Her Fiction and Non-Fiction, 1954-1974).* Madras: M. Seshachalam & Co., 1976: 54-121.

Rich, Paul. "Tradition and Revolt in South African Fiction: the Novels of André Brink, Nadine Gordimer and J.M. Coetzee." *Journal of Southern African Studies* 9, 1 (October 1982): 54-73.

Richards, Thomas. *The Imperial Archive: Knowledge and the Fantasy of Empire.* London and New York: Verso, 1993.

Rodney, Walter. *How Europe Underdeveloped Africa.* Rev. ed.

Washington D.C.: Howard University Press, 1982. [First published 1972.]

Rubin, Gayle. "The Traffic in Women: Notes on the 'Political Economy' of Sex." In *Towards an Anthropology of Women,* ed. Rayna R. Reiter. New York: Monthly Review Press, 1975.

Sahgal, Nayantara. "The Book I Enjoyed Writing Most," *Bhavan's Journal* 20, 12 (January 6, 1974): 41-44.

---. "Conscience and the Hindu." *The Sunday Standard* December 12, 1975: 6.

---. *The Day in Shadow.* New York: Norton, 1972a.

---. *From Fear Set Free.* New York: Norton, 1968.

---. "How I Became a Writer." *Indian Book Industry* 5 (1972b): 81-82.

---. A Letter Written to Jasbir Jain. New Delhi: November 19, 1976.

---. *Rich Like Us.* New York: Norton, 1986.

---. "The Spirit of India and the Abiding Influence of Gandhi." *The Atlantic Monthly* [Perspective of India Supplement] 192, 4 (October 1953): 166- 69.

---. *Storm in Chandigarh.* New York: Norton, 1989.

---. *This Time of Morning.* New York: Norton, 1965.

Said, Edward W. *Orientalism.* New York: Vintage, 1978.

Sample, Maxine. "In Another Life: the Refugee Phenomenon in Two Novels of the Nigerian Civil War." *Modern Fiction Studies* 37, 3 (Autumn 1991): 445-54.

Sangari, Kumkum and Sudesh Vaid, eds. *Recasting Women: Essays in Indian Colonial History.* New Brunswick: Rutgers University Press, 1990.

Schwartz, Pat. "Interview—Nadine Gordimer," in *New South African Writing.* Johannesburg: Lorton, 1977: 81.

Sharpe, Jenny. "The Unspeakable Limits of Rape: Colonial Violence and Counter-Insurgency." In Patrick Williams and Laura Chrisman, eds. *Colonial Discourse and Post-Colonial Theory: A Reader.* New York: Columbia University Press, 1994: 221-43.

Sivanandan, A. *A Different Hunger: Writings on Black Resistance.* London: Pluto Press, 1982.

Slemon, Stephen. "Post-Colonial Allegory and the Transformation of History." *Journal of Commonwealth Literature* 23, 1 (1988): 157-67.

Smith, Rowland. "Living for the Future: Nadine Gordimer's *Burger's Daughter.*" *World Literature Written in English* 19, 2 (Autumn 1980): 163-73.

Smith, Steven B. *Reading Althusser: An Essay on Structural Marxism.* Ithaca and London: Cornell University Press, 1984.

Solberg, Rolf. "The Woman of Black Africa, Buchi Emecheta: The Woman's Voice in the New Nigerian Novel." *English Studies: A Journal of English Language and Literature* 64, 3 (June 1983): 247-61.

Sougou, Omar. "The Experience of an African Woman in Britain: A Reading of Buchi Emecheta's *Second Class Citizen.*" In *Crisis and Creativity in the New Literatures in English,* ed. Geoffrey V. Davis and Hena Maes-Jelinek. Cross/ Cultures: Readings in the Post/Colonial Literatures in English 1. Amsterdam and Atlanta: Rodopi, 1990: 511-22.

Spivak, Gayatri Chakravorty. "Can the Subaltern Speak?" in *Marxism and the Interpretation of Culture.,* ed. Cary Nelson and Lawrence Grossberg. Urbana: University of Illinois Press, 1988a: 271-313.

---. *Outside in the Teaching Machine.* New York and London: Routledge, 1993.

---. "Subaltern Studies: Deconstructing Historiography." In *Selected Subaltern Studies,* ed. Ranajit Guha and Gayatri Chakravorty Spivak. New York and Oxford: Oxford University Press, 1988b: 3-32.

Suleri, Sara. "Woman Skin Deep: Feminism and the Postcolonial Condition." In Patrick Williams and Laura Chrisman, eds. *Colonial Discourse and Post-Colonial Theory: A Reader.* New York: Columbia University Press, 1994: 244-56.

Taiwo, Oladele. "Buchi Emecheta," in her *Female Novelists of Modern Africa.* London: Macmillan, 1984: 100-27.

Temple-Thurston, Barbara. "Madam and Boy: A Relationship of Shame in Gordimer's *July's People*." *World Literature Written in English* 28, 1 (1988): 51-58.

Topouzis, Daphne. "Buchi Emecheta: An African Story-Teller." *Africa Report* 35, 2 (May-June 1990): 67-70.

Uyoh, Susan B. "Second Class Citizen." *The Gong* (May 1981): 34.

Visel, Robin. "Othering the Self: Nadine Gordimer's Colonial Heroines." *Ariel: A Review of International English Literature* 19, 4 (October 1988): 33-42.

Wachtel, Eleanor. "The Mother and the Whore: Image and Stereotype of African Women." Unpublished paper.

Ward, Cynthia. "What They Told Buchi Emecheta: Oral Subjectivity and the Joys of 'Otherhood.'" *Publications of the Modern Language Association of America* 105, 1 (January 1990): 83-97.

Williams, Patrick and Laura Chrisman, eds. *Colonial Discourse and Post-Colonial Theory: A Reader.* New York: Columbia University Press, 1994.

Williams, Raymond. *Marxism and Literature.* Oxford: Oxford University Press, 1977.

Worsley, Peter. *The Three Worlds: Culture and World Development.* Chicago & London: the U of Chicago P, 1984.

Wren, Robert M. *Achebe's World: The Historical and Cultural Context of the Novels.* Washington, D.C.: Three Continents Press, 1980.

Young, Robert. *White Mythologies: Writing History and the West.* London and New York: Routledge, 1990.

Zuckerman, Ruth Van Horn. "Nayantara Sahgal, *This Time of Morning* and Nayantara Sahgal, *Storm in Chandigarh.*" *Mahfil: A Quarterly of South Asian Literature* 6, 4 (Winter 1970): 84-87.

INDEX

A

abuse/exploitation (sexual, physical, mental): 19, 38, 42, 52, 55, 69, 70, 72, 100, 101, 106, 107, 124, 148, 154, 160, 161, 163, 222
Afrikaner: 118
Ahmad, Aijaz: 2, 3, 4
alternate world: 111, 112, 124, 125, 129, 145, 147, 165, 167, 168
Althusser, Louis: 8, 9
Amuta, Chidi: 226, 227
Anderson, Benedict: 7, 25, 27, 78, 112
apartheid: 11, 14, 20, 82, 88, 89, 112, 113, 116, 118, 128, 172, 187, 189
Arora, Neena: 46, 52, 90
Ashcroft, Bill: 4, 27
Asnani, Shyam: 47

B

Bailey, Nancy: 172, 174, 176, 177, 185, 187, 188, 189, 190
Barrett, Michele: 99
Barthelemy, Anthony: 149, 150, 160, 163
Biafra: 210, 214, 216, 218, 220
Biafran: 214, 218, 222, 223
Biko, Steven: 185
border: 195, 218
boundary: 210
Boyers, Robert: 190
brahmin: 52
Brennan, Timothy: 27, 169

R

S